Enter If You Dare...

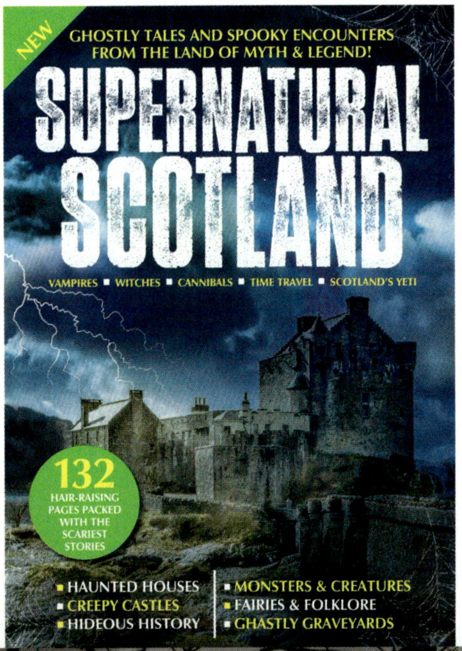
NEW
GHOSTLY TALES AND SPOOKY ENCOUNTERS FROM THE LAND OF MYTH & LEGEND!
SUPERNATURAL SCOTLAND
VAMPIRES ▪ WITCHES ▪ CANNIBALS ▪ TIME TRAVEL ▪ SCOTLAND'S YETI
132 HAIR-RAISING PAGES PACKED WITH THE SCARIEST STORIES
▪ HAUNTED HOUSES
▪ CREEPY CASTLES
▪ HIDEOUS HISTORY
▪ MONSTERS & CREATURES
▪ FAIRIES & FOLKLORE
▪ GHASTLY GRAVEYARDS

Cover Image: SHUTTERSTOCK

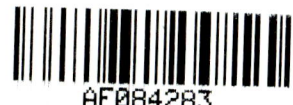

WELCOME to *Supernatural Scotland*, your spine-tingling guide to the country's spookiest encounters and most fascinating phenomena.

Within these pages, find chilling stories to make your hair stand on end, explore haunted locations that will curdle your blood, and encounter monstrous creatures who will have you hiding behind the couch in fear!

Read on to discover the blood-thirsty Gorbals Vampire, a shadowy figure who sparked panic in 1950s Glasgow.

Shiver at Scotland's Cannibal Clan – the horrifying tale of cave-dwelling Sawney Bean and his fearsome family.

Meet the time-travelling wartime pilot who flew into the future in East Lothian, and marvel at the prophecies of Scotland's Nostradamus, the Brahan Seer.

There's more than just Nessie dwelling in the deep with a rundown of the watery beasts to be found in the country's rivers and lochs, while you can get lost in the land of the fairies as we take you through Scottish folklore history.

Some of the country's eeriest places also feature, from a Poltergeist Manor in Fife to a Highlands House of Horror as well as the hotels, castles and graveyards that echo with bumps in the night.

There's a guide to the frightening Scots locations featured in famous novels as well as a countdown of some of the country's scariest horror movies – how many have you seen?

Finally, we look at the Scottish origins and terrifying traditions of Hallowe'en.

Supernatural Scotland is brought to you by the award-winning team behind *The Scots Magazine*, founded in 1739 making it the oldest magazine in the world still in publication. Turn to page 130 for a superb *Scots Magazine* subscription offer to ensure you never miss an issue of your favourite read.

Happy haunting!

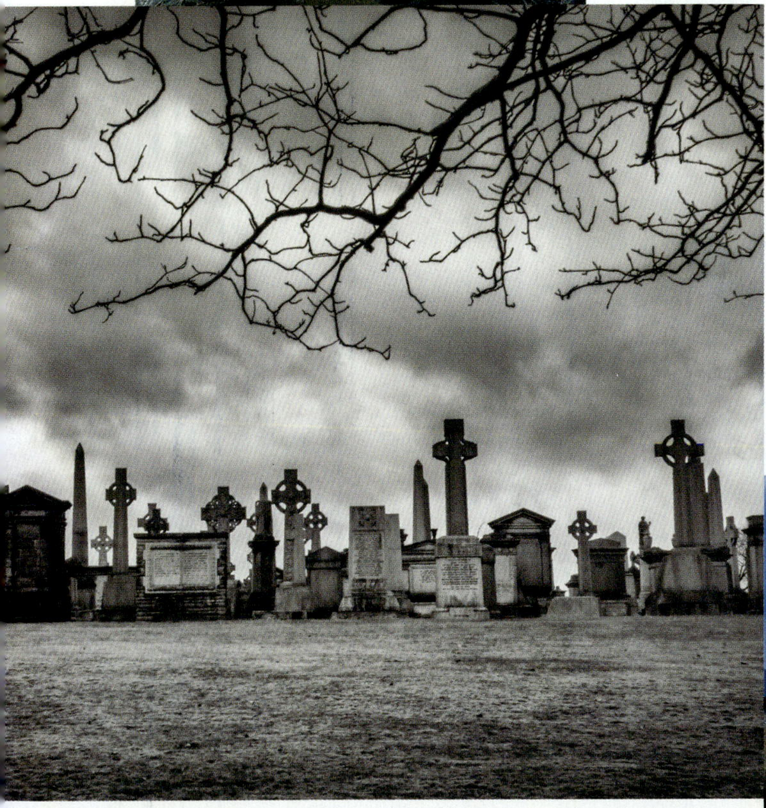

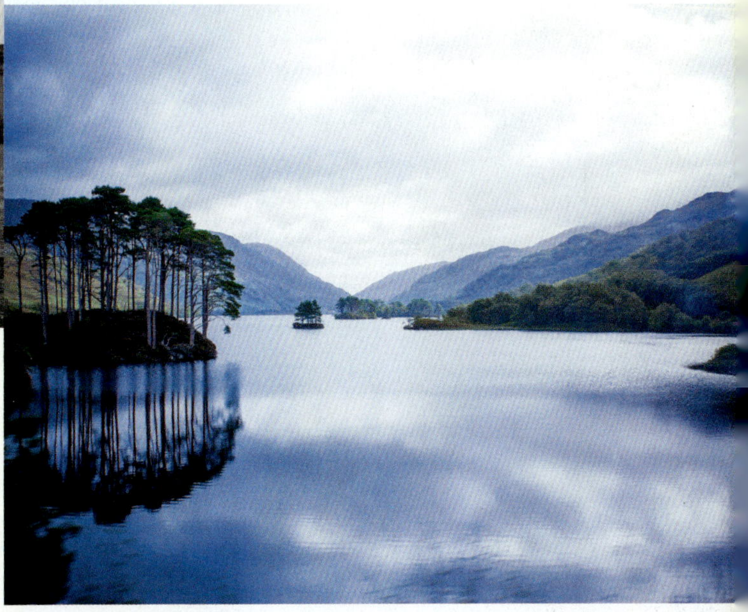

Published by DC Thomson & Co Ltd. © DC Thomson & Co Ltd. 2024 While every reasonable care will be taken, neither DC Thomson & Co Ltd, nor its agents, will accept liability for loss or damage to any material submitted to this publication. We will only use the data provided to contact people in relation to competitions or letters. You can find our privacy policy at www.dcthomson.co.uk/privacy-policy/ We are committed to journalism of the highest standards and abide by the Editors' Code of Practice which is enforced by the Independent Press Standards Organisation (IPSO). If you have a complaint, you can email us at Readerseditor@dcthomson.co.uk or write to the Readers' Editor at The Scots Magazine, DC Thomson & Co Ltd, 2 Albert Square, Dundee DD1 1DD

DC THOMSON

Contents

100 STOKER'S DARK DAYS

7 HAUNTED HOUSES
8 House Of Horror
10 Poltergeist Manor
14 The Haunting Of Ringcroft
18 The Sauchie Poltergeist
20 Room With A Boo!

25 GHASTLY GRAVEYARDS
26 City Of The Dead
30 The Spooky Seven

37 HIDEOUS HISTORY
38 The Cannibal Clan
42 Strange Visions
44 A Quartet Of Curses
48 Royal Revenge
50 Back To The Future
52 Route Of Evil
54 The Pittenweem Trials
56 The Queen Of Witches
58 Scotland's Last Witch
60 Tales From The Vault
62 Spooky Superstitions

63 MONSTERS & CREATURES
64 The Loch Ness Monster
67 Beware Bloodthirsty Redcaps
68 Morag Of Morar
70 What Lurks Beneath...
72 Out Of This World
76 The Grey Man Of Ben Macdui
78 A Tale With Bite
80 The Mystery Of Dog Death Bridge
82 Strange Tales

58 SCOTLAND'S LAST WITCH

18
THE SAUCHIE POLTERGEIST

83 CREEPY CASTLES
84 Terror Of Tantallon
86 Spooky Sanquhar
88 Deathly Duntrune
90 A Cursed Castle
92 Fairytale Castle Of Phantoms
94 The Mystery Of The Phantom Pipers

97 CHILLING CULTURE
98 Outlander Legends
100 Stoker's Dark Days
102 Gripping Plots
104 Screen Screams
106 Phantoms Of The Opera

109 FAIRIES & FOLKLORE
110 The Fairy Kingdom
112 Away With The Fairies
115 Fallen Angels
116 The Hidden World
118 The Queen Of Winter

121 HORRIBLE HALLOWE'EN
122 Bewitching Tales
124 Terror & Tradition

30
THE SPOOKY SEVEN

10
POLTERGEIST MANOR

ANDERSON & CO
THE SHETLAND WAREHOUSE

Anderson & Co produce an extensive range of classically styled high quality garments and accessories in genuine Shetland wool, renowned for its warmth.

Anderson & Co is a long established firm, founded in 1873 by Thomas Anderson. As a family owned firm we pride ourselves in a personal service and a great attention to detail.

For quality, value and service choose
ANDERSON & CO.
THE SHETLAND WAREHOUSE

60-62 Commercial Street, Lerwick Shetland Isles, ZE1 0BD
tel: 01595 693714 or email: enquiries@shetlandknitwear.com
www.shetlandknitwear.com

f @andersonandco **◯** @andersonsknitwear

Haunted Houses

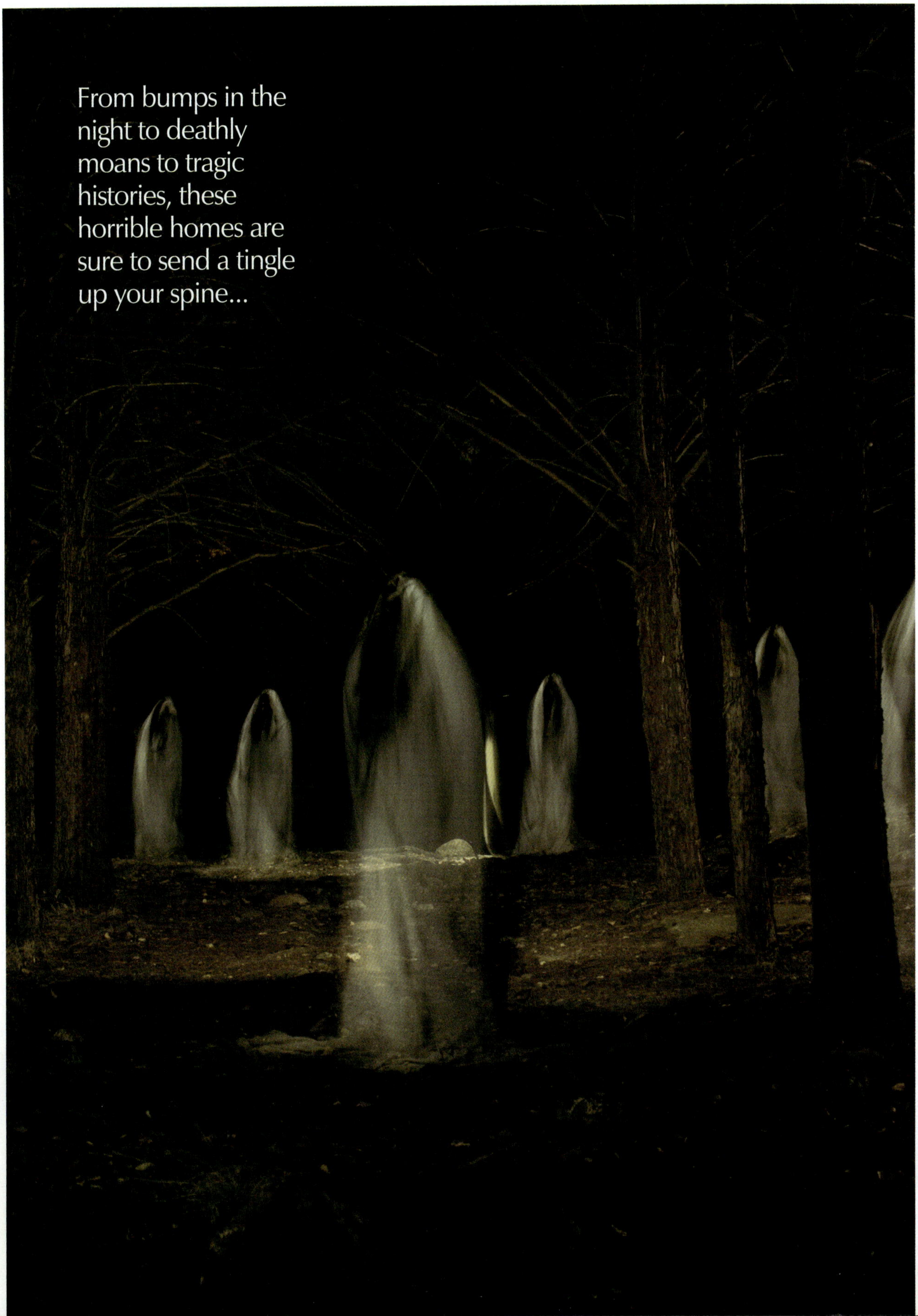

From bumps in the night to deathly moans to tragic histories, these horrible homes are sure to send a tingle up your spine...

House of Horror

Boleskine House on Loch Ness has had plenty of eccentric owners, but it's the permanent residents that will have your hair standing on end

Boleskine burial ground, Loch Ness

Boleskine House in 1912

Crowley allegedly created Nessie

The aftermath of the fire

IF you don't want your new home to have sinister vibes, our advice is simple – you shouldn't pick the site of a terrible tragedy as your plot.

Unfortunately, no one asked us back in the 1760s when Boleskine House, near Foyers, was being built.

Colonel Archibald Fraser's hunting lodge on the south-east shore of Loch Ness had an inauspicious start. Legend has it that the kirk that once stood there caught fire, killing the congregation who were trapped inside.

But that's not all – in the 17th century, there also was an unfortunate incident in the graveyard involving a bothersome wizard who insisted on raising the dead from their graves.

The minister at the time, Thomas Houston, had to wrangle these mischievous revenants back underground. Now, a tunnel allegedly links the house to the graveyard, which is patrolled by a coven of witches, naturally.

Boleskine House belonged to the Fraser family until the mid-1890s. Its most infamous owner, the English occultist and ceremonial magician Aleister Crowley, was handed the keys in 1899 after deciding it was the spot to perform the sacred magic of Abramelin the Mage. He hoped to conjure up his guardian angel, and Boleskine was exactly the sort of quiet location Crowley needed for six months of preparation, during which he had to summon the 12 Kings and Dukes of Hell.

The Highlands has had its fair share of inconsiderate visitors, but this demonic dozen were surely among the worst.

Unsurprisingly, a lot of eerie stuff started happening in the house and the surrounding area after the self-appointed Lord Boleskine's arrival.

One story tells of a priest visiting Crowley to warn him that Boleskine's lodgekeeper, who hadn't touched a drop of alcohol for 20 years, had been drunk for three days and had tried to murder his wife and children.

That drunken lodgekeeper might have been Hugh Gillies, who many believe bore the brunt of the misfortunes brought on by Crowley's rituals – according to local lore, he went on to lose two of his children in peculiar and tragic circumstances.

A butcher is also said to have cut off his hand, possibly because Crowley scrawled the names of

Words: LAURA BROWN
Pictures: REX/SHUTTERSTOCK, ALAMY, KHADI GANIEV

Supernatural Scotland

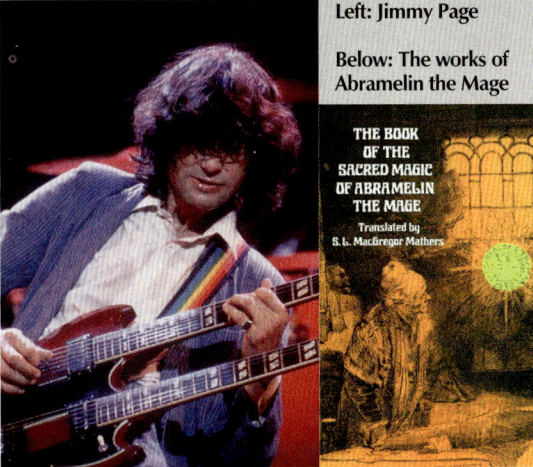

Left: Jimmy Page

Below: The works of Abramelin the Mage

> "Eerie stuff started happening in the house"

demons on a bill from his shop. A workman went mad, and a maid disappeared. The nearby loch was ripe for magical rumours, too – that he created the Loch Ness Monster, for example – though since the first sighting of Nessie dates back to the 6th century, it seems unlikely.

None of the strange happenings or disapproving gossip deterred Crowley – he saw them as a sign of success. He had to abandon his quest before it was completed, however, and didn't bother banishing the malevolent spirits he'd already raised.

Crowley left Boleskine for good before the First World War started and, in 1918, the house was sold. The following decades were, by all accounts, fairly uneventful – though in the 1960s, owner Major Edward Grant killed himself in Crowley's former bedroom.

Several years later, filmmaker – and follower of Crowley's religion, Thelema – Kenneth Anger rented Boleskine for a few months, and then Led Zeppelin guitarist and fellow Crowley enthusiast Jimmy Page bought it in the early 70s. And that seems to be when the weirdness ramped it up a notch – in fact, Anger soon had to help Page exorcise a headless ghost.

Page's friend Malcolm Dent became the caretaker of the house, and witnessed several spine-chilling incidents. Rugs would form a pile by themselves, furniture moved around and doors would slam of their own accord.

On one particularly terrifying occasion, he was awoken by the sound of a wild animal inside the house. He also reckoned that the head of the 11th Lord Lovat, a Jacobite rebel, could be heard rolling down the halls.

After being sold by Page in 1992, nothing untoward happened for a while, until ferocious fires in 2015 and again in 2019 threatened to burn the house down.

Work is under way to restore Boleskine, though there are undoubtedly those who wish the house and its spooky goings-on were gone for good. Others think that all this talk of ghosts is nothing but nonsense – one way to find out for yourself is to take a tour and see if the eerie feeling overwhelms you.

Aleister Crowley

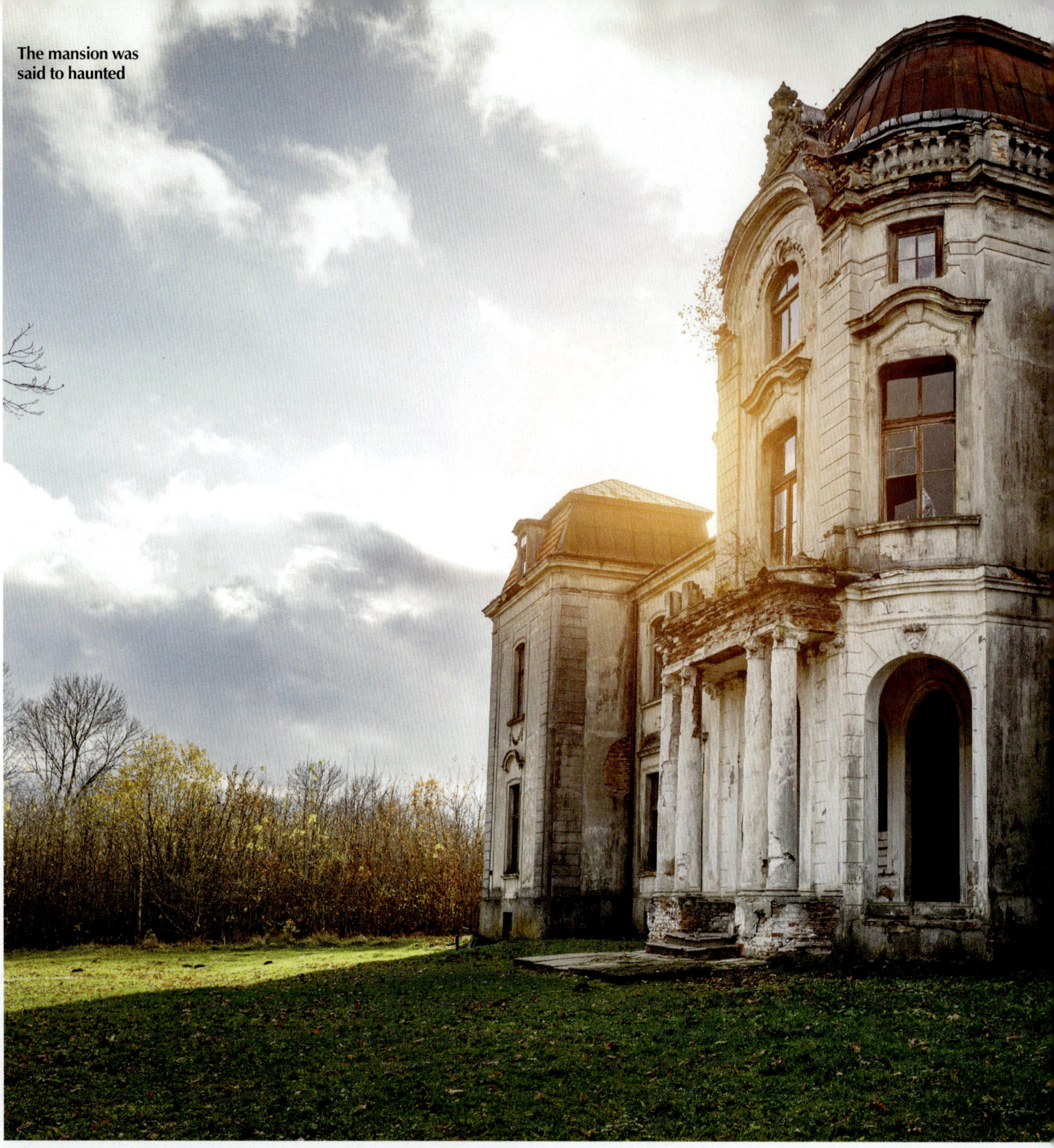

The mansion was said to haunted

Poltergeist Manor

A stately home in Fife was the site of numerous inexplicable events

"The range of manifestations in Pitmilly House near Kingsbarns was extraordinary"

Furniture was moved around

IN the 1930s and early 1940s, incidents at a Fife mansion produced the most intensive record of poltergeist haunting in recent times.

The range of manifestations in Pitmilly House, which stood in spacious grounds near Kingsbarns, was extraordinary.

It began with all the pictures in the house being found on the floor, many of them smashed. Furniture was moved about and upset. The family lawyer was called. As he sat on an armchair in the large three-window dining room, left to reflect on the story the owner and his wife had told him, he lit a cigarette and put the burnt match in an ashtray on the arm of the chair, noting that there were seven or eight matchsticks there already.

When, later, he turned to knock off the cigarette ash the tray was empty. He found the matchsticks neatly arranged in pairs further back on the arm of the chair.

He was awakened during the night by a crash outside his bedroom and found a piece of sculpture on the carpet outside the door, in fragments. A few days after a sculpture bust hurtled from its pedestal in the hall and smashed against the wall, narrowly missing the head of a member of the family.

The drawing-room furnishings were found in a heap. An eight-day clock, found by a maid on three successive mornings on its face, lay smashed to splinters on the fourth.

Billiard balls disturbed the sleep of the owners by rolling about the floor in the bedroom where they had no right to be. One morning the owner's wife took the balls, one red and two white, and buried them secretly in the grounds. That night they were disturbed again, and a red ball was found on the floor. She went to the spot where she had buried the balls and dug them up. The »

Words: J. W. HERRIES Pictures: SHUTTERSTOCK

Supernatural Scotland **11**

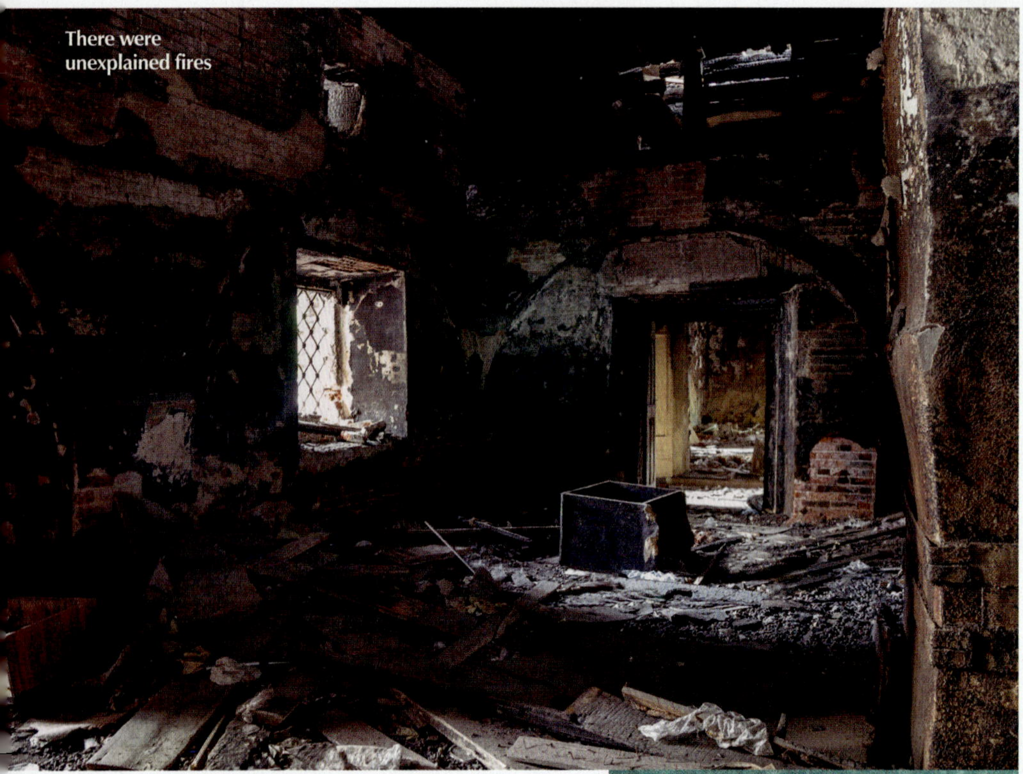

There were unexplained fires

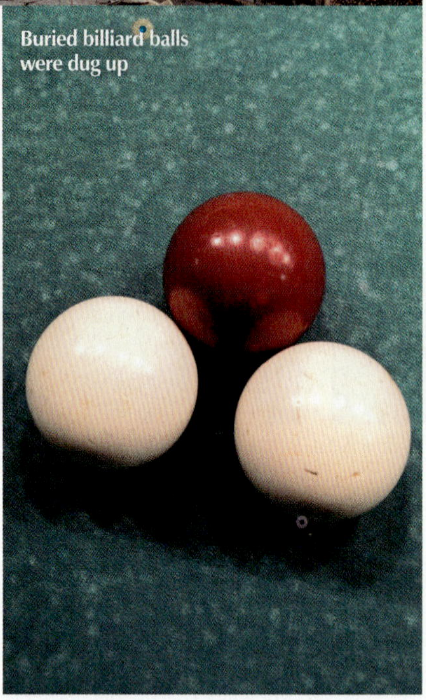

Buried billiard balls were dug up

two whites were there but the red ball was gone.

Finally, one afternoon, fire broke out in a number of rooms simultaneously, originating in every case in one of the corners at the height of the ceiling.

A claim for insurance was made and met by the insurance company, who made the fullest inquiry and were satisfied that no one in the household had any responsibility for the fires.

One of the London daily newspapers, coming out with a narrative of these events, headed the article, "Scottish poltergeist makes insurance company pay up."

Shortly after the fire the trouble completely ceased, but the reason for their occurrences – and why they stopped so abruptly – is unknown to this day.

> "*Finally, one afternoon, fire broke out in a number of rooms simultaneously*"

THE MOST Haunted House IN SCOTLAND

A similar manifestation occurred in the late 1800s in Ballechin House near Ballinluig, Highland Perthshire.

The Society for Psychical Research investigated in 1897, with observers staying in the building in turns. Among the observers were the Marquis of Bute John Crichton-Stuart, soon-to-be prime minister A J Balfour, and psychical researcher Ada Goodrich Freer.

Their reports were published in *The Alleged Haunting of Ballechin House* in 1899, which was serialised in *The Times*.

Reported incidents included a booming, bell-like sound that at times seemed to fill the house, associated with occasional apparitional appearances, the mysterious sound of footsteps, and the apparition of a nun.

The Society for Psychical Research later removed the reports from their proceedings on the investigation, and denounced Freer, but the house's infamy stuck.

Ballechin House was uninhabited by 1932 and finally demolished in 1963 – after a mysterious fire.

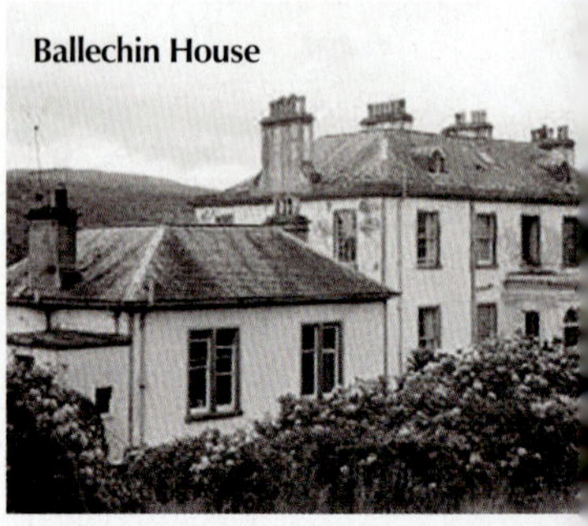

Ballechin House

Your must-have guide to
THE GREATEST SCOTS WHO EVER LIVED!

 YOUR MUST-HAVE GUIDE TO THE GREATEST SCOTS WHO EVER LIVED!

NEW!

100 Great Scots

Discover the true stories behind the remarkable men and women who shaped Scotland and changed the world

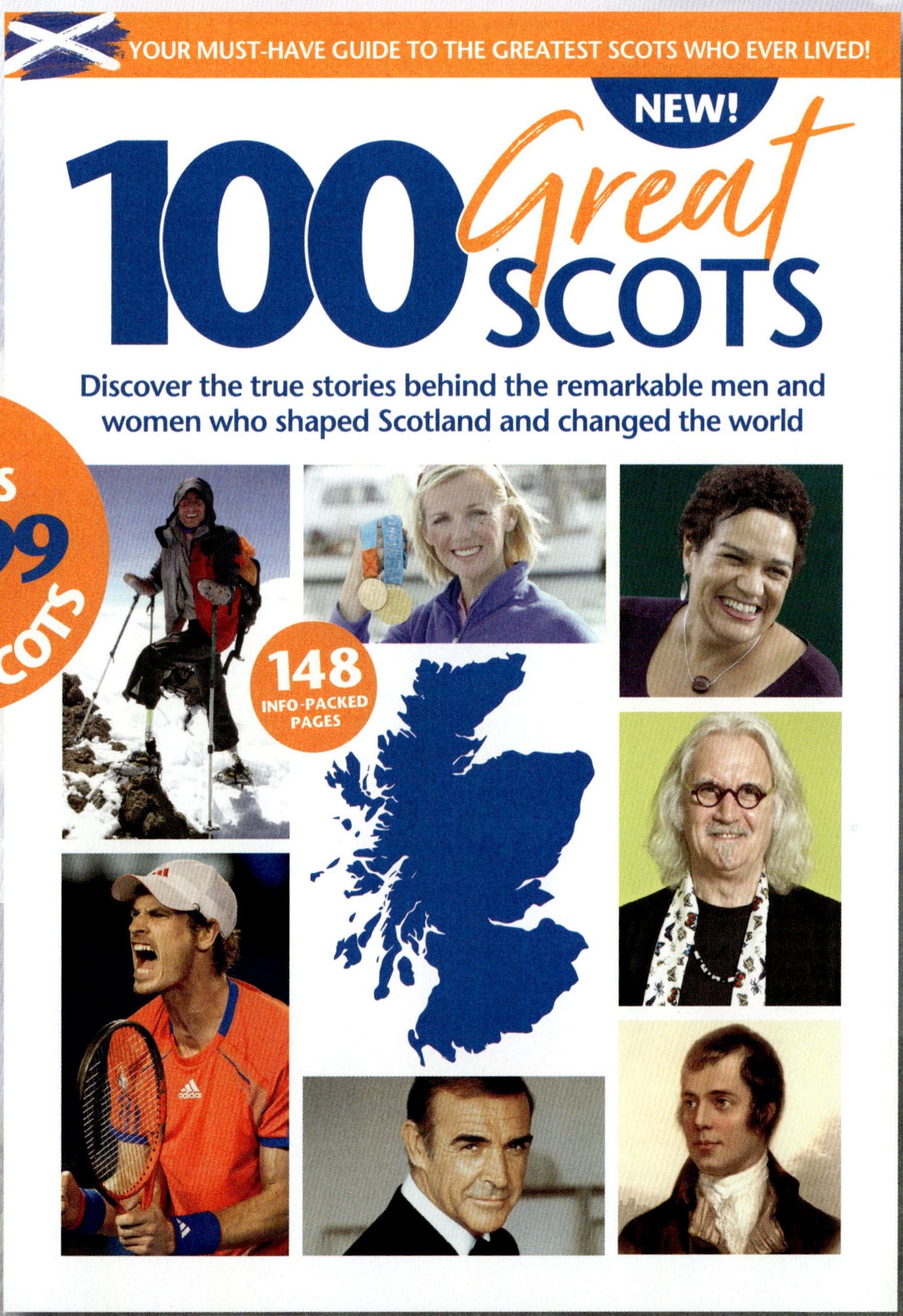

148 PAGES £9.99 OF GREAT SCOTS

148 INFO-PACKED PAGES

ORDER NOW!

Order online: www.dcthomsonshop.co.uk/100scots
or freephone 0800 318 846 (lines open Monday-Friday 8am - 6pm)
15% off with code 100SCOTS
Also available on Amazon and in WHSmith stores

The Haunting Of Ringcroft

The chilling tale of a poltergeist who terrorised a Galloway family

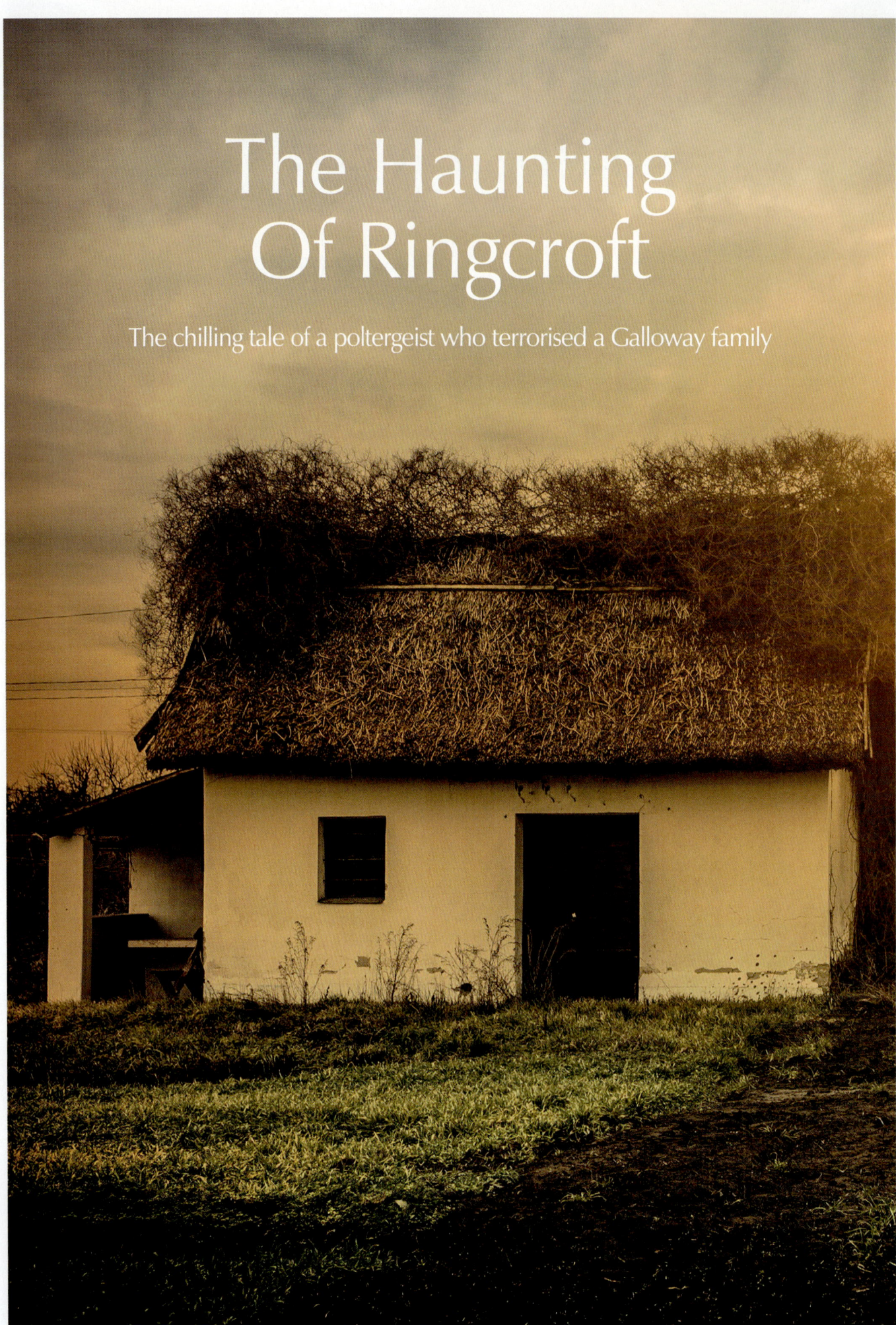

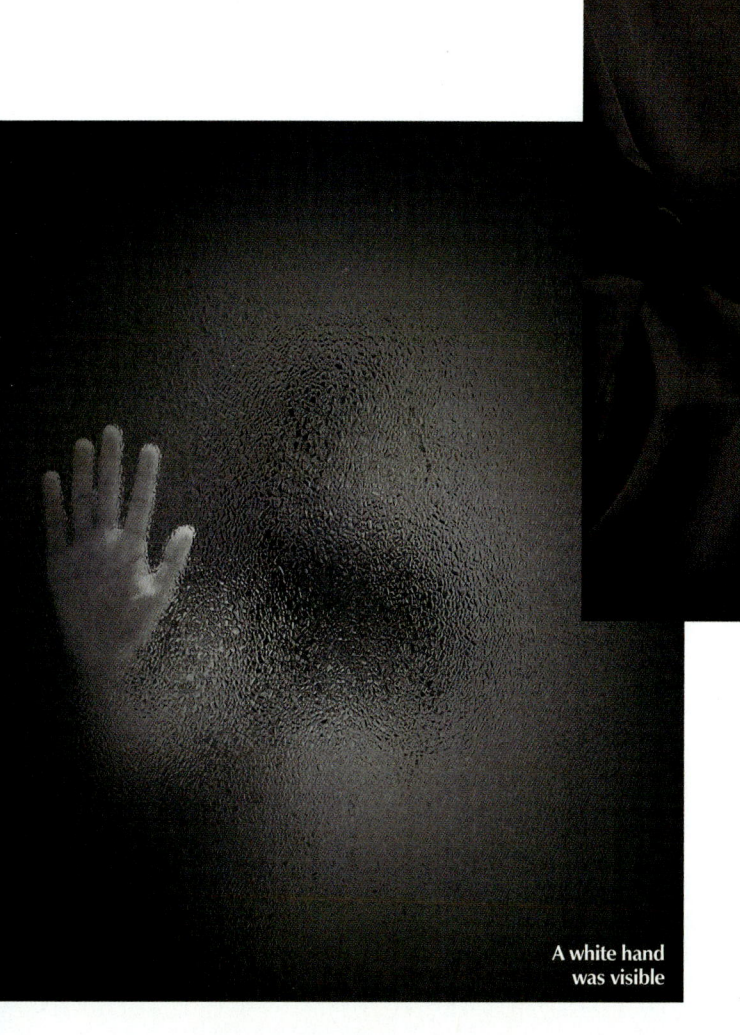

Ministers prayed at the house

A white hand was visible

THE Ringcroft case in Galloway is one of the earliest and most carefully detailed accounts of poltergeist manifestations.

In 1695, the Rev Alexander Telfair, minister of the parish of Rerrick in the Stewartry of Kirkcudbright, recorded his experiences. He wrote of the "apparition, expressions and actings of a spirit" that infested the house of Andrew Mackie, Ringcroft of Stocking, in the parish of Rerrick.

Andrew Mackie's troubles apparently began in February 1695, when he discovered that the bindings which secured his beasts had been loosened and broken overnight. Blaming the animals, he made stronger bindings, but they, too, were broken mysteriously.

He then moved his beasts to another outbuilding, and the first night thereafter found one of the animals bound with a "hair-tedder" to the back of the house in such a way that the feet of the poor animal scarcely touched the ground.

Shortly afterwards, when the family was asleep one night, a creel of peats were placed together in the middle of the floor by unseen hands and then set alight.

Fortunately, the smoke wakened Mackie and his family, otherwise both house and occupants would have been destroyed.

As time passed, the "manifestations" increased in frequency and severity. In March of that year stones were being hurled all over the interior of the house, – for four days and nights, witnessed by many people.

The matter was reported by Mackie to Telfair, the minister of the parish, who visited the house a day or two later. At first nothing happened and the minister was standing at the barn end, about to take his departure, when he saw two stones drop on the house.

Immediately, those inside the house began to cry out that the spirit was at it again. Telfair then went into the house and, as he prayed, several stones were thrown at him from unseen hands.

Later in the week, Telfair spent a night at the house and was greatly troubled. Stones and several other objects were thrown at him, and he was struck several times on the sides and shoulders very sharply with a great staff – with those who were present hearing the noise of the strokes. There was rapping on chests and boards, as if someone was calling for access.

That night, as Rev Telfair was at prayer, he felt something pressing on his arm and saw a little white hand and arm from the elbow down.

After that the spirit became more active and more abusive than ever – not only to the Mackie family, but also to neighbours who came to visit them.

Some were dragged up and down the house by their clothes. The local miller from Auchencairn, Keige by name, was gripped so forcibly that he called to his neighbours for help. At other times the door bar and other furnishings would move through the house as if being carried. Yet no person could be seen. »

> " He felt something pressing on his arm and saw a little white hand and arm "

Supernatural Scotland

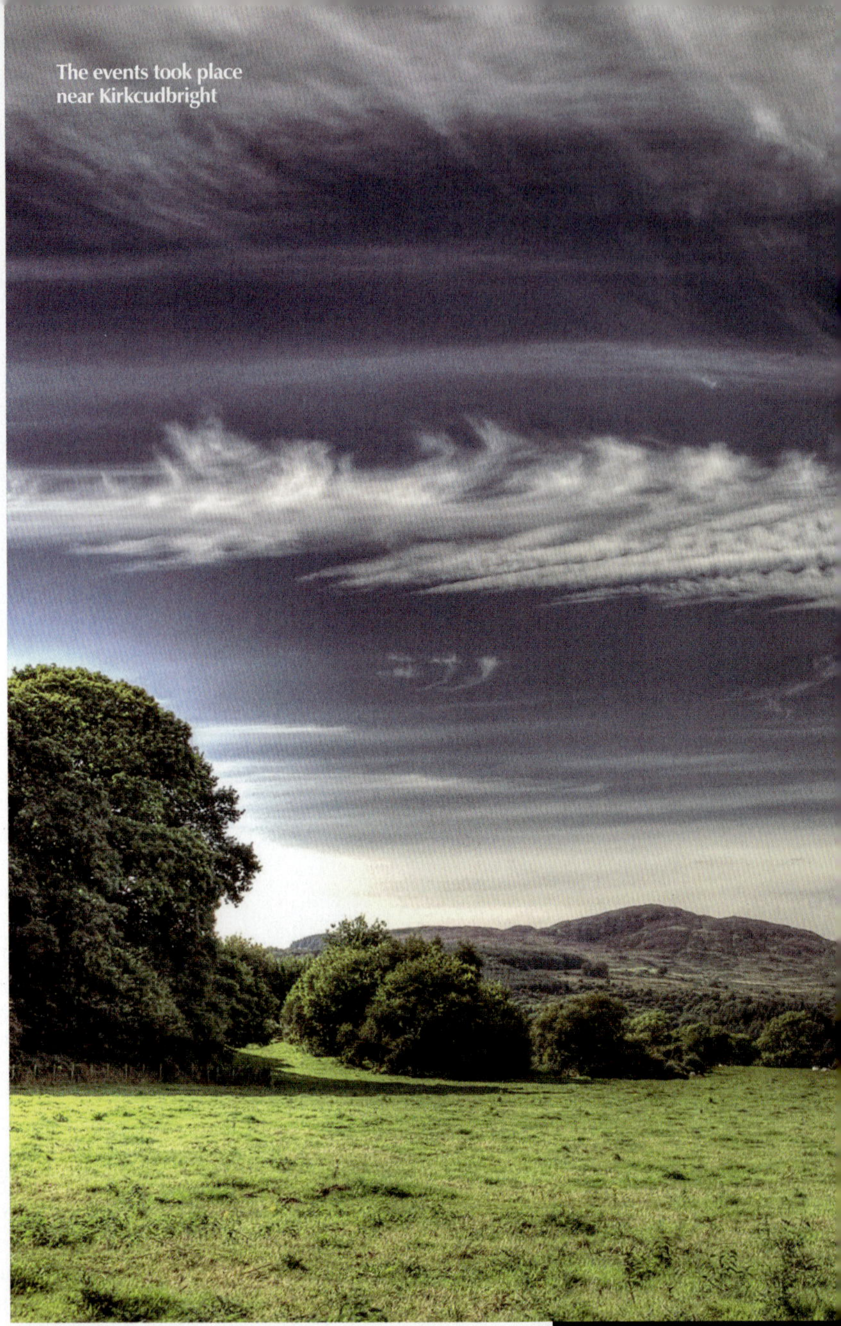
The events took place near Kirkcudbright

“Fiery peats were thrown at people”

Finally, Charles Macklelland of Colline, the landlord, and Mackie attended a meeting of ministers at nearby Buittle and gave them an account of the matter.

Two of the ministers, Andrew Ewart of Kells and John Murdo of Crossmichael, visited the house and spent a night there, fasting and praying. They, too, had a rough time. Great stones, some of them seven pounds in weight, were thrown at them.

No one in the house that night escaped from the spirit's fury and cruelty. Fiery peats were thrown at people and at dawn, when they rose from prayer, stones poured down on all who were in the house.

And so it went on. William Macminn, a blacksmith, was wounded on the head by a flying stone. A plough sock was cast at him, followed by a stone trough which landed on his back – though, remarkably, he was unhurt. Twice the house was set on fire, but luckily no serious damage was done.

As the local ministers were at that time meeting at Kirkcudbright, five of their number were appointed to go to the house with Telfair – to spend as much time as possible in fasting and prayer.

“No sooner did I begin to open my mouth,” records Telfair, “than it threw stones at me and all within the house.

“It came often with such force upon the house that it made all the walls to shake, it broke a hole through the timber and thatch of the house and poured in great stones, one whereof, more than a quarter weight, fell upon Mr Monteith's back – Rev John Monteith, minister of Borgue – yet he was not hurt. It threw another with great force at him when he was praying, yet he was neither hurt nor moved thereby.”

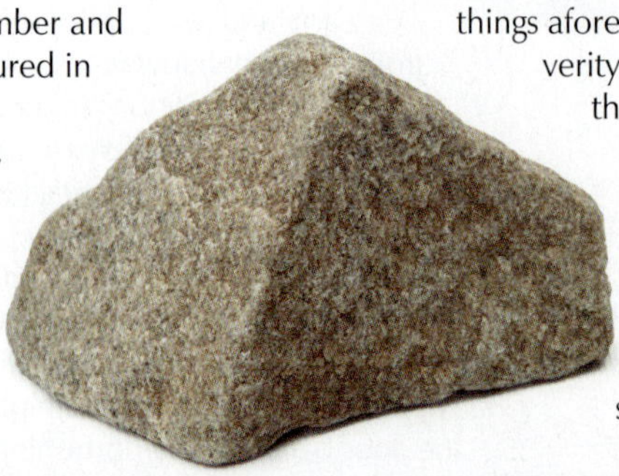

Once, a voice was heard warning all within hearing that it had been sent to warn the land to repent, and if the land did not repent it would go to its father and get a commission to return with a hundred worse than itself – and would trouble every family in the land. After many more acts of violence and fire-raising, mingled with spoken threats, the manifestations suddenly ceased. Alexander Telfair concluded his remarkable narration with the following words, “Now all things aforesaid being of undoubted verity, therefore I conclude with that of the Apostle, 1. Peter v., 8-9 – Be sober, be vigilant, because your adversary the devil, as a roaring lion, walketh about seeking whom he devour. Whom resist steadfast in the faith.”

The location of the Ringcroft cottage, which has long since vanished, was marked by a row of four trees conspicuous on the skyline near Auchencairn.

Of the four, one remains – a single, dead tree guarding the site of the cottage, the foundations of which are still there.

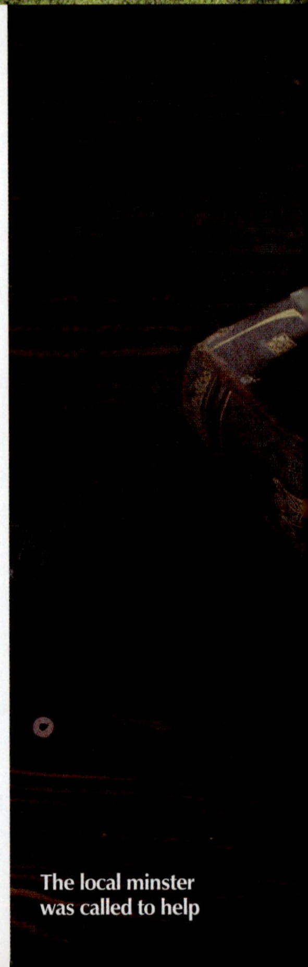
The local minster was called to help

Stone-throwing is a common feature

Showers OF Stones

The throwing of stones, as in the Ringcroft case is a theme reported at supposed poltergeist hauntings around the world.

Lithobolia: Or, The Stone-Throwing Devil is a 7,000-word narrative folk tale by Richard Chamberlayne, first printed in 1698.

It records the apparently true events of New Castle in the US where hundreds of stones mysteriously rained down on George Walton's tavern over the entire summer of 1682.

There have been various reports of stone-throwing poltergeists across the centuries, but the most recent to have made headlines was in Birmingham in 1981, when even a police inquiry could not identify the source of stones being thrown at residents of Thornton Road.

"Even a police inquiry couldn't find the source"

Supernatural Scotland   17

The Sauchie Poltergeist

The terrifying tale of the spirit which left two girls and their families living in fear…

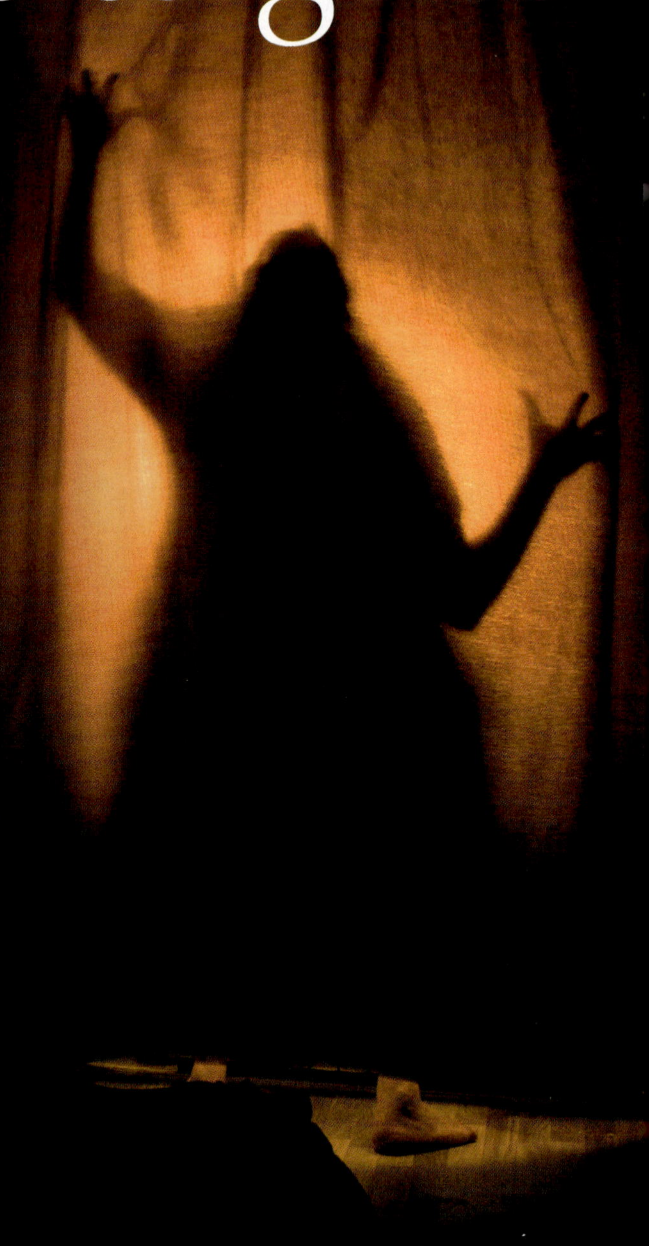

IT was during November of 1960 when two young Sauchie girls became convinced a poltergeist was in their house.

Virginia Campbell (11) had just moved to town with her mum to live in a family home. She'd been struggling to fit in after leaving her home, dog and friends in Donegal, Ireland, where her father also stayed to look after the family farm.

While her mother worked in Dollar most days, Virginia spent time with and grew close to her younger cousin Margaret, with whom she shared a room at her aunt and uncle's house. But something felt odd.

By November 22, they started hearing noises in the dead of night.

First it was banging while they both lay in bed – they couldn't figure out where it was coming from given that it sounded like a ball bouncing off the walls. As they both got up to investigate, they swore the sound followed them down the stairs. Alas, nothing came of it, and they went back to bed.

Little time passed before both Margaret and Virginia jolted awake again, this time disturbed by what sounded like a headboard banging. Surely not – they could see nothing in the darkness to scare them. But they both moved to another room, just to be safe.

Virginia heard the banging continue right up until she fell asleep – and only once she'd woken up had it stopped. Some nights the girls could even hear faint scratching all over the house.

Wherever they went and however hard they tried to block it out, as they slept or kept themselves busy with something else, they grew increasingly unsettled. But this was only the beginning.

Items around the house started disappearing. A linen basket had its lid open one morning – after no one had touched it. And parts of furniture seemed to move as if of their own accord. It wasn't long before the adults started noticing.

One day Thomas and Isabella – Virginia's aunt and uncle – watched incredulously as their sideboard moved several inches

"It sounded like a ball bouncing off the walls"

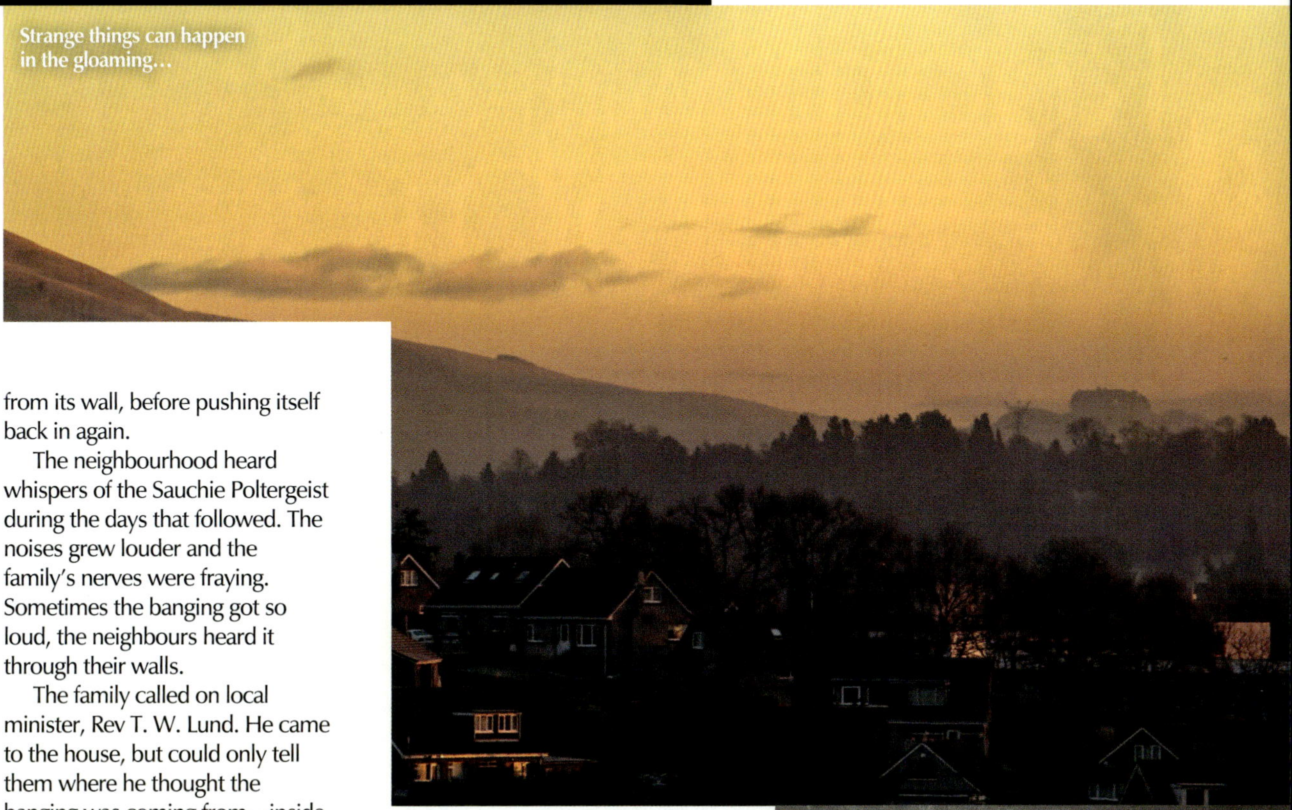

Strange things can happen in the gloaming…

from its wall, before pushing itself back in again.

The neighbourhood heard whispers of the Sauchie Poltergeist during the days that followed. The noises grew louder and the family's nerves were fraying. Sometimes the banging got so loud, the neighbours heard it through their walls.

The family called on local minister, Rev T. W. Lund. He came to the house, but could only tell them where he thought the banging was coming from – inside the headboard and from the wooden bed frame. But by then Margaret, who was terrified of what she'd witnessed, had fled.

For whatever reason, Virginia found that the poltergeist was attached to her. She could not escape the oddities, even when she went to school.

One day, sitting in her classroom, the young girl found it near impossible to open her desk lid. Her teacher noticed Virginia struggling by herself and asked her to remove her hands. To the horror of the class, the desk lid flew open and flapped around on its own.

Virginia grew gradually more hysterical as time went on – soon it was up to Dr Nesbit of the Tillicoultry medical practice to medically sedate her. But strange things kept happening.

Ministers, doctors,and Virginia's family all said they noticed her pillow rotate at night as they checked in. Dr Nesbit even set up a cine camera to capture the peculiarities on film.

By December, the story had hit the press. More strange occurrences were being reported all the while – Virginia's aunt was supposedly pushed out of her bed, and more clergymen arrived at the scene to help pray for the family.

It was not until March the following year that Virginia and her family seemed finally free from the grasp of the apparent poltergeist. The unexplained events had become more and more rare until they stopped altogether, but by then the story had become legend.

The family are understood to have left Sauchie thereafter.

To this day, the town remembers the story of the Sauchie Poltergeist. It's one of the most interesting and intriguing Halloween stories in the country but remains unexplained.

Residents can visit the area in Park Crescent where it all happened today – but it's not known whether the original house remains standing.

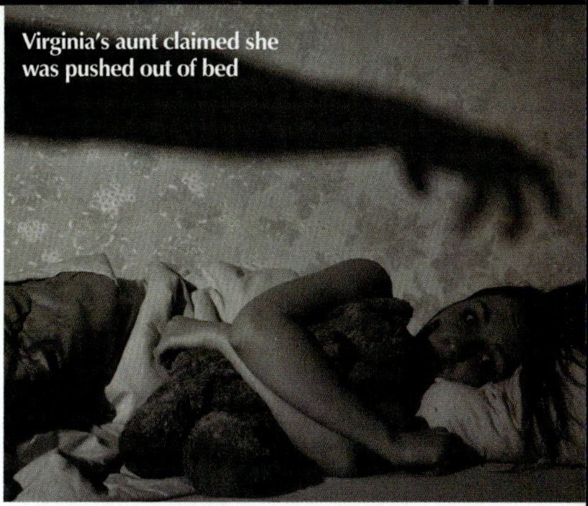

Virginia's aunt claimed she was pushed out of bed

"Virginia grew gradually more hysterical as time went on"

Words: SOPHIE MCVINNIE
Pictures: SHUTTERSTOCK

Room With A BOO!

Scotland's haunted hotels offer chills and thrills in equal measure

SCOTLAND has a rich history, much of which is gory and full of bloodshed, so there is no shortage of spirits, ghouls and ghost stories.

The walls of our centuries-old structures attract ghost hunters from across the world. Riddled with disembodied sounds, knocks and creaks, and faint, forgotten cries, the chances of spotting an apparition are high.

So to whet your appetite for supernatural encounters, here are just a few of the old haunts around Scotland where you can stay the night and put the ghostly tales to the test.

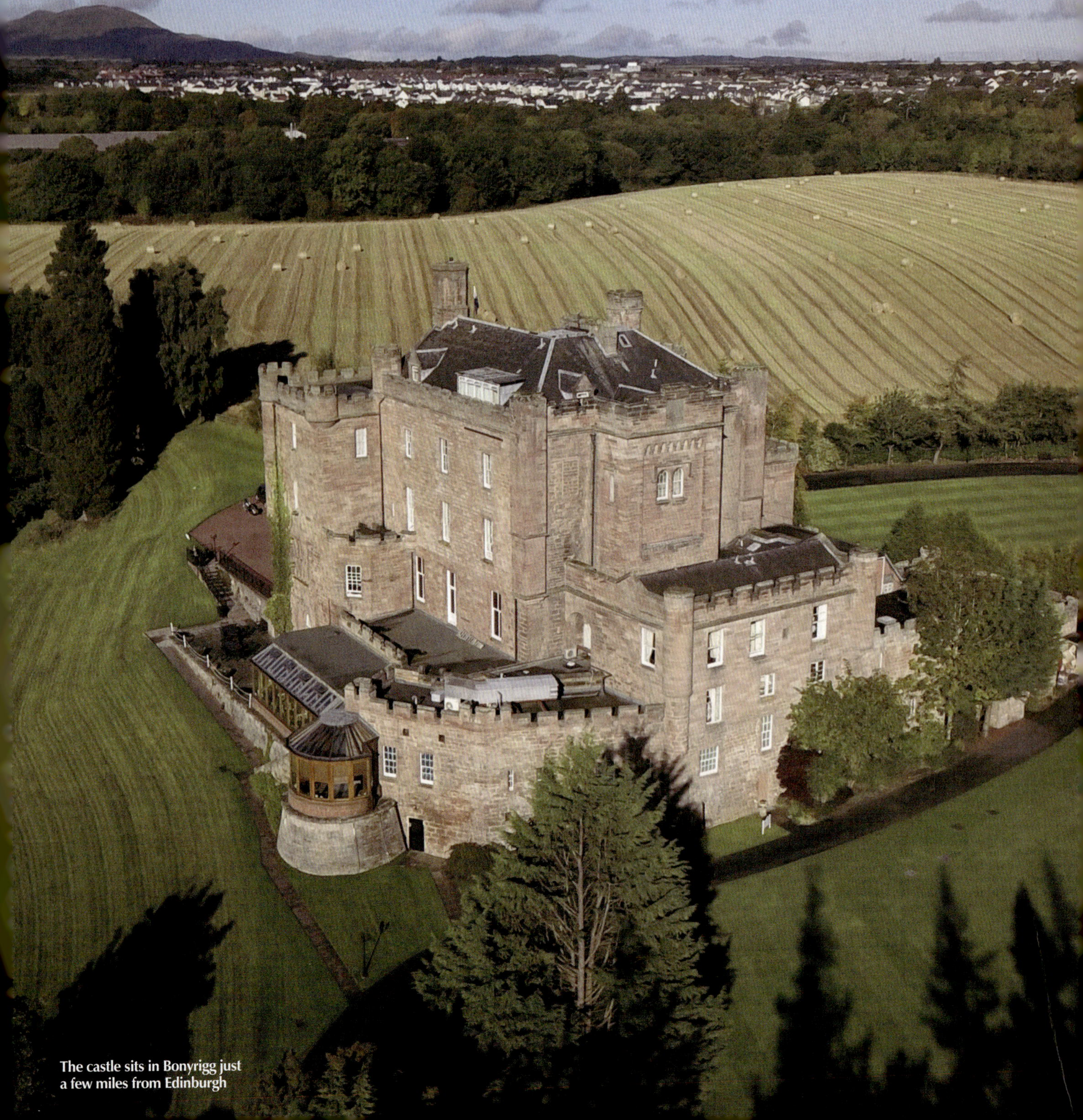

The castle sits in Bonyrigg just a few miles from Edinburgh

Popular with guests and ghosts alike!

Dalhousie Castle Hotel
Haunting elegance from centuries past

LOCATED near Edinburgh, Dalhousie Castle Hotel stands as a testament to Scotland's tumultuous past. With roots dating back to the 13th century, this majestic fortress has witnessed a rich history of royal alliances, battles and political intrigue. Yet, behind its grand façade and luxurious interiors, the hotel harbours a darker side – a realm of ghostly apparitions and unexplained occurrences.

Among its spectral inhabitants, the most renowned is Lady Catherine, once owner of Dalhousie Castle. Legend has it that she tragically fell to her death from the tower, and her spirit has since roamed the halls, clad in a flowing white gown. Guests and staff claim to have seen her wandering through the castle, her presence accompanied by a sense of sorrow and unease.

Another haunting tale surrounds Sir Alexander Ramsay, also a previous owner, who was imprisoned within the castle's hidden room and left to starve to death.

His restless spirit is said to linger, and some visitors have reported hearing faint cries and moans from the concealed chamber.

Despite the eerie stories, Dalhousie Castle Hotel offers a luxurious and comfortable stay for modern guests, with top-notch amenities and superb views of the surrounding countryside.

For those with a love for history and the supernatural, a stay at Dalhousie Castle Hotel promises an unforgettable experience, bridging the gap between past and present.
dalhousiecastle.co.uk

> "Visitors have reported hearing faint cries from the concealed chamber"

A luxurious stay is still guaranteed

"It's not just the inn itself that's haunted, but the grounds, too"

The inn was established in 1705

The quirky reception area

The Drovers Inn

Ghosts around every corner

THIS old inn in Inverarnan is named after the Highland drovers who once used it as a stop point when taking their cattle down the side of Loch Lomond to the markets for sale. Today it is a wonderful pub and restaurant, as well as cosy place to stay.

However, be warned – it is said to be one of the most haunted hotels in the country, and Room 6 has been noted as an especially haunted place. A young girl who drowned in the loch after a particularly heavy rainfall has appeared throughout the hotel but especially this room where her recovered body was laid for the family to grieve. There have been reports of an icy presence lying close to guests, as well as sightings of the girl's favourite doll, Annabel, searching for its owner. Photographs taken in the room have also shown orbs and ghostly figures, which are said to be the young girl.

It's not just the inn that's haunted, but the grounds, too. A young drover named Angus is said to wander late at night, screaming and in search of the thieves who stole his cattle one night as he drank at the inn. After falling foul of the chieftan whose cattle he lost, he set off to hunt down the thieving clan rivals but, as luck would have it, they found him first and murdered him – hanging him from the old tree behind the inn.

Ghosts and horror stories aside, the inn is a wonderful place to rest your weary head after exploring the Loch Lomond area. It's also dog-friendly with various room types available, including family and twin.
droversinn.co.uk

The Falls of Falloch are a nearby attraction

The Coylet Inn
Lakeside beauty meets ghostly enigmas

NESTLED on the tranquil banks of Loch Eck in the enchanting region of Argyll, The Coylet Inn exudes olde-worlde charm and offers a perfect escape from the hustle and bustle of modern life.

Yet, beneath the peaceful exterior of this picturesque inn lies a history filled with whispers of the paranormal, making it an ideal destination for those seeking tranquillity – and the odd spine-tingling encounter.

Local legends surround The Coylet Inn, where ghostly figures and apparitions are said to wander the halls and linger by the water's edge.

The most famous ghostly inhabitant is "The Phantom Piper", whose eerie bagpipe tunes have been heard echoing through the inn during the stillness of the night. It is believed he met a tragic fate while trying to find his way back to the inn on a stormy night, and now his spirit seeks eternal rest.

Another enigmatic figure is the ghost of a drowned young boy who appears near the shores of Loch Eck. "The Blue Boy" is thought to have been a young boy who drowned after sleepwalking into the loch during a stay at the inn. In other versions of the story, he froze to death whilst outside it.

The Coylet Inn's history as a smuggler's den adds an extra layer of intrigue, as some guests claim to have heard the clinking of glasses and murmurs from long-lost patrons, giving a glimpse into the inn's colourful past.

Today, The Coylet Inn provides a cosy retreat for travellers seeking relaxation amidst breathtaking natural beauty. For those intrigued by the paranormal, a stay promises a unique blend of history and ghostly tales within the serenity of Loch Eck.
thecoylet.co.uk

Keep an ear out for the Phantom Piper

> "*A stay here promises a unique blend of history and ghostly tales*"

Loch Eck

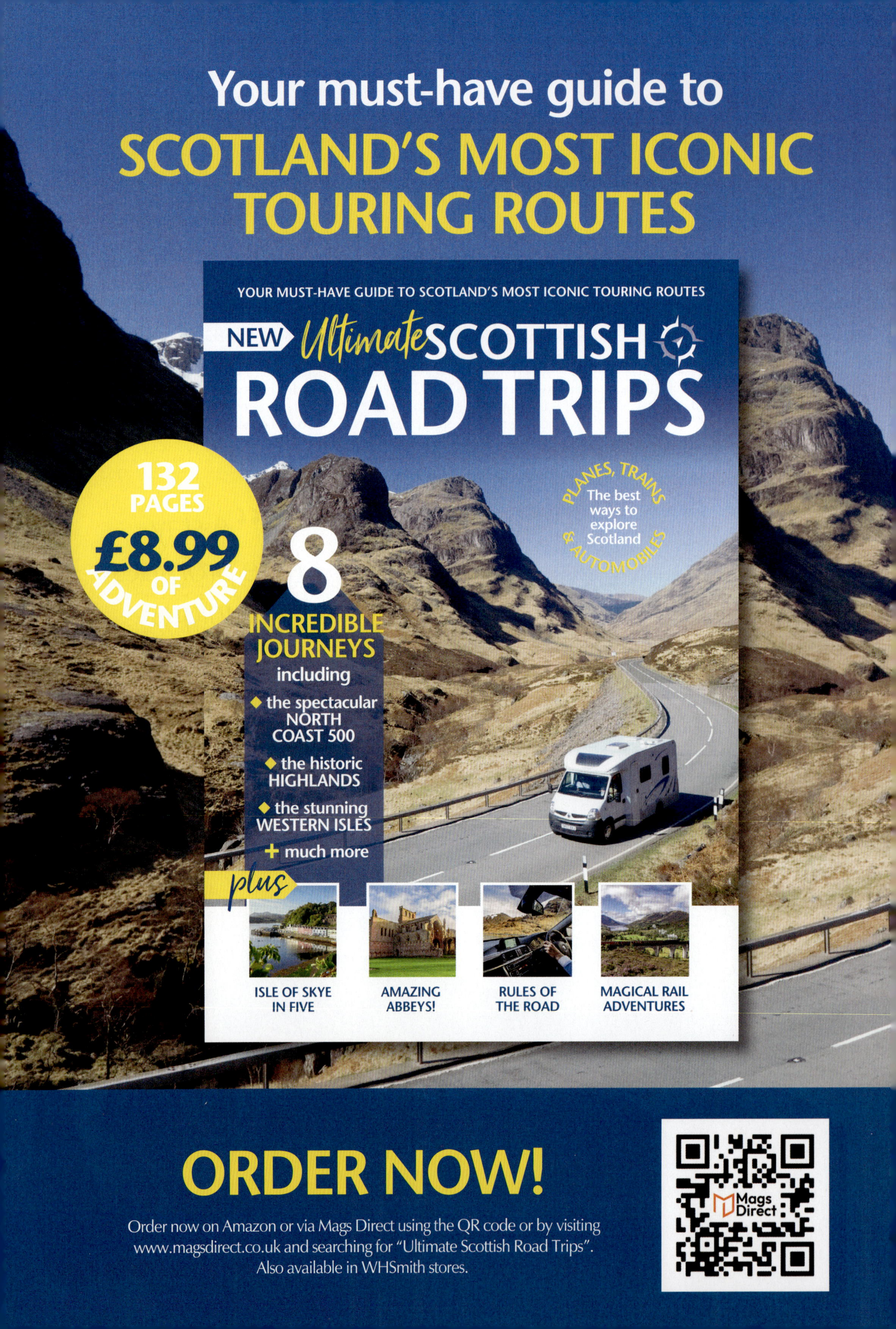
Your must-have guide to
SCOTLAND'S MOST ICONIC TOURING ROUTES
YOUR MUST-HAVE GUIDE TO SCOTLAND'S MOST ICONIC TOURING ROUTES
NEW
Ultimate SCOTTISH
ROAD TRIPS
132 PAGES
£8.99 OF ADVENTURE
PLANES, TRAINS & AUTOMOBILES
The best ways to explore Scotland
8 INCREDIBLE JOURNEYS
including
◆ the spectacular NORTH COAST 500
◆ the historic HIGHLANDS
◆ the stunning WESTERN ISLES
+ much more
plus
ISLE OF SKYE IN FIVE
AMAZING ABBEYS!
RULES OF THE ROAD
MAGICAL RAIL ADVENTURES
ORDER NOW!
Order now on Amazon or via Mags Direct using the QR code or by visiting www.magsdirect.co.uk and searching for "Ultimate Scottish Road Trips". Also available in WHSmith stores.
Mags Direct

Ghastly Graveyards

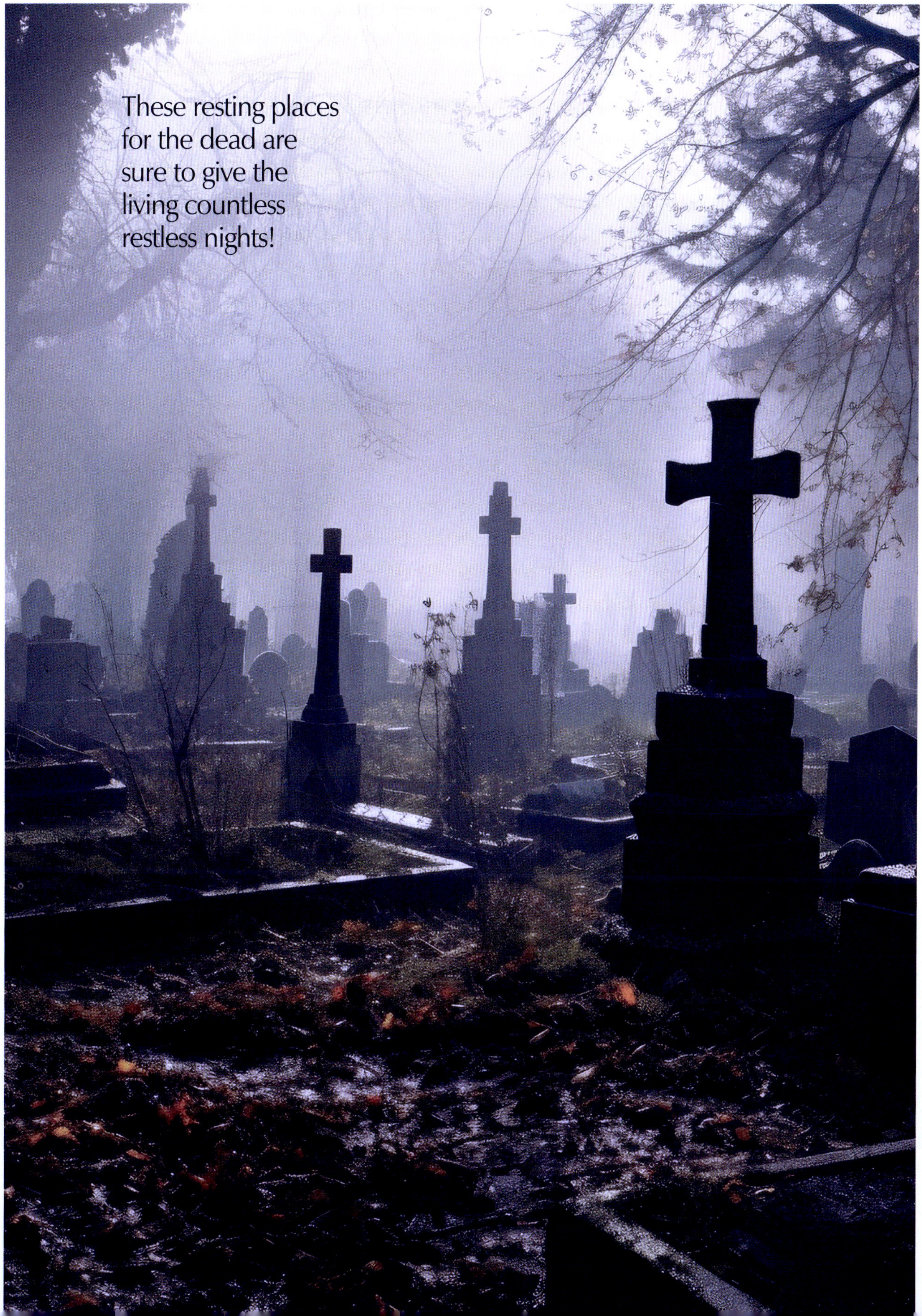

These resting places for the dead are sure to give the living countless restless nights!

City Of The Dead

Greyfriars Kirkyard in Edinburgh is said to be one of the most haunted places in the UK

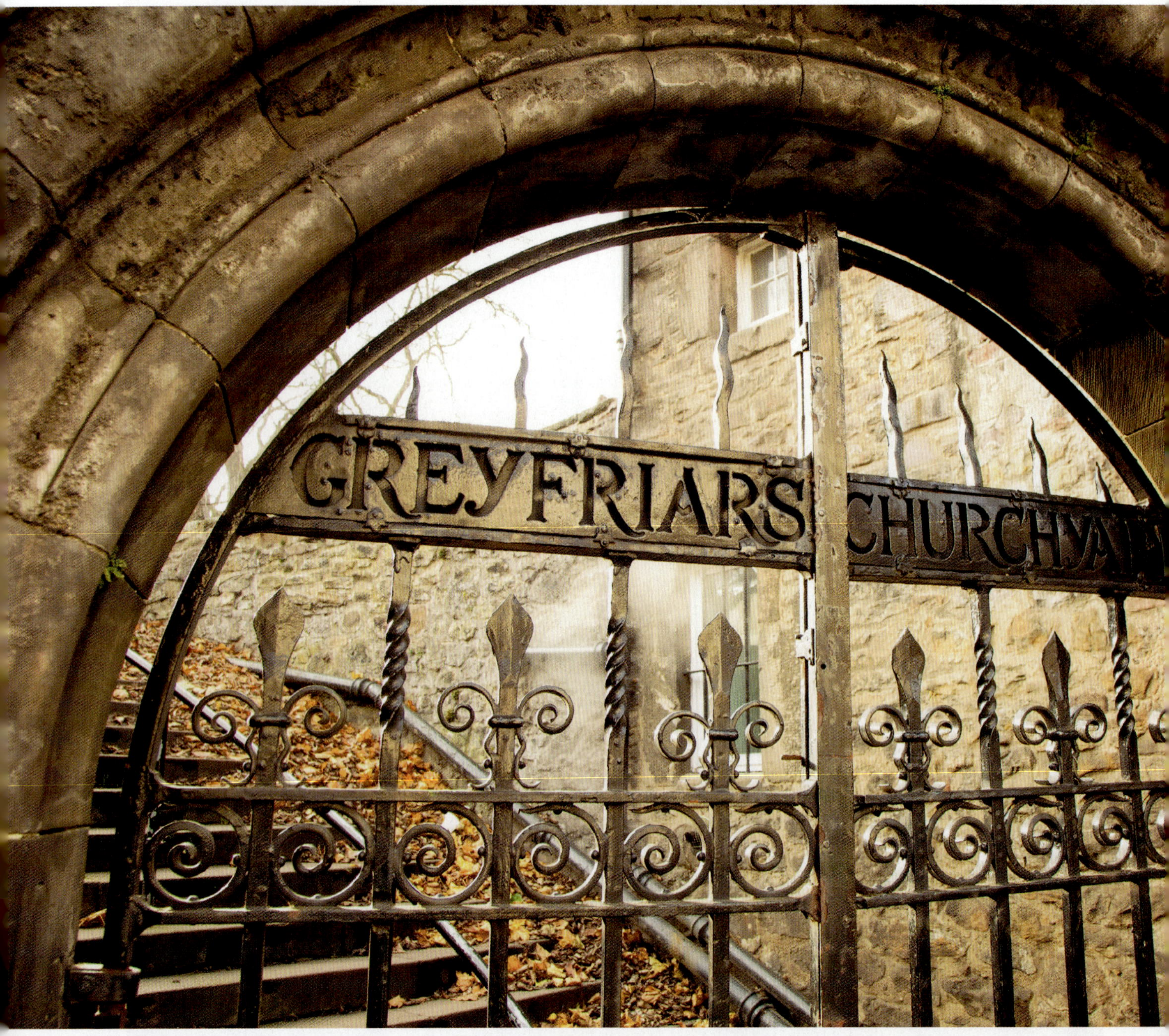
GREYFRIARS

The kirkyard entrance

Bluidy Mackenzie

NO-ONE can say for sure just how many dead lie in the soil of Greyfriars Kirkyard in Edinburgh's Old Town, but between 1562 when Mary, Queen of Scots, established the kirkyard and 1900 the figure has been estimated at 100,000.

The vast majority of those died of illness and the miseries of poverty, and could not afford the dignity of a casket. They were piled in mass graves, with many human remains now lying less than an arm's length below the topsoil.

Little wonder, then, that Greyfriars is consistently ranked among the most haunted locations in Britain.

There are also a morbidly fascinating array of murals and monuments in the kirkyard, with the motif of a skull and crossbones waiting to spook you around every bend.

These are not the graves of pirates, nor are they intended to frighten you. Instead, the often visceral depictions of the dead, alongside innocent looking cherubs, are reminders that death awaits us all.

It's not an especially uplifting place.

Some of the most striking carvings can be found on the the gravestone of James Borthwick, against the eastern wall of the kirk. Borthwick was a surgeon who died in 1840, and his gravestone is decorated with carved surgical instruments such as syringes and bone chisels alongside an alarmingly lifelike skeleton – reminders of Edinburgh Medical College's role as a beacon for the study of medicine and anatomy.

This expertise was made possible by a steady supply of cadavers disinterred by grave robbers from the city's kirkyards in the 17th to 18th centuries. This is why there are cages over some graves, known as mortsafes, to stop folk digging up bodies to sell to the college.

There are many tales of one culprit who seems to be responsible for the majority of the ghostly accounts at Greyfriars Kirkyard – Bluidy Mackenzie.

Sir George Mackenzie – c.1636-1691 – had a penchant for summary executions before any trial could take place, which earned him his grisly epithet.

Under his supervision upwards of 1,000 Covenanters, who rebelled against the monarchy's influence over the church, were held in a roofless prison in appalling conditions, and the chained-off area of the kirkyard where this occurred – a stone's throw from Mackenzie's mausoleum – has sent many a self-proclaimed psychic and medium running from the ground in terror.

Mackenzie is said to stalk the kirkyard searching for the souls of Covenanters to torment. By Robert Louis Stevenson's time, the legend of Bluidy Mackenzie was so firmly entrenched in Edinburgh's psyche, he wrote in 1897, "When a man's soul is certainly in hell, his body will scarce lie quiet in a tomb however costly; sometime or other the door must open, and the reprobate come forth in the abhorred garments of the grave".

Accounts of Mackenzie's wrath range from people being forcefully pushed, having sudden onsets of extreme terror, and even discovering inexplicable scratches on their bodies after leaving the kirkyard. »

Covenanters were persecuted

Supernatural Scotland

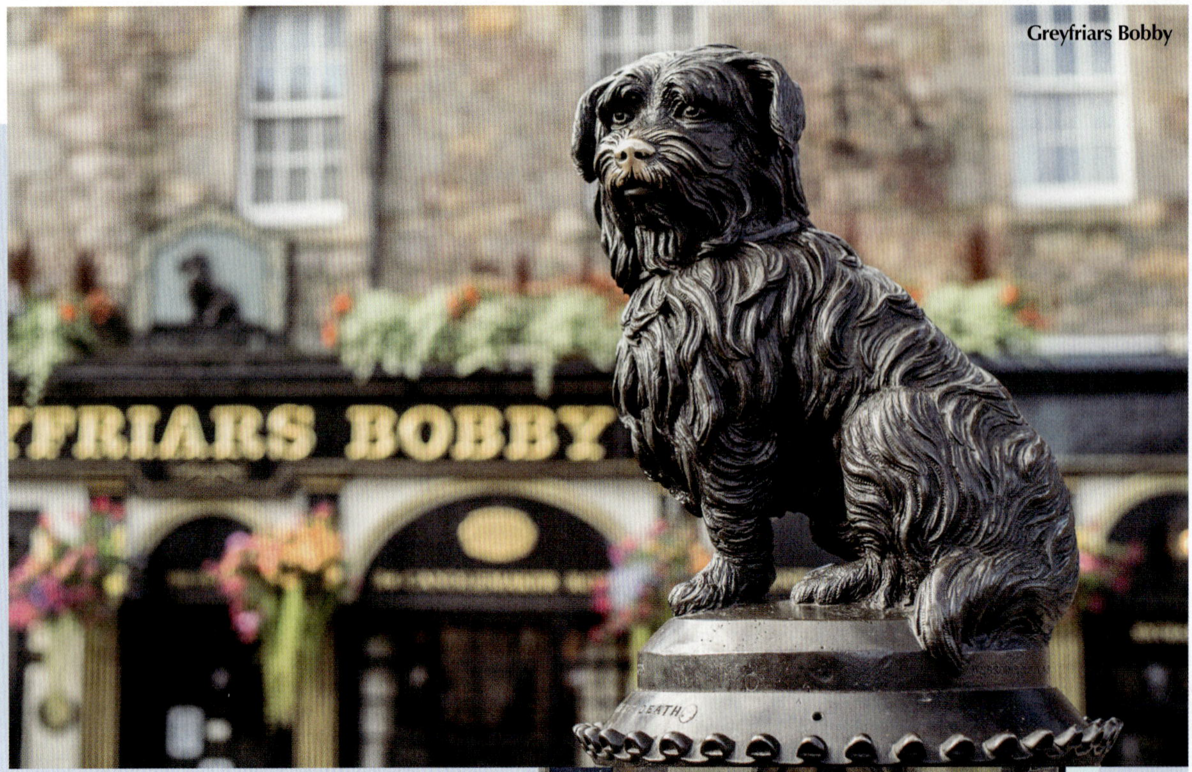
FRIARS BOBBY

Greyfriars Bobby

NO account of Greyfriars Kirkyard would be complete without a stop to greet the statue of Greyfriars Bobby, a 19th-century Skye terrier known as Edinburgh's best friend.

His master was John Gray, a night watchman who sought a canine companion.

John died of tuberculosis in 1858 and was buried in the kirkyard.

It is said Bobby stood vigil at his master's grave for 14 years.

He was cared for by locals who would bring food to the kirkyard gates every day at the firing of the One O'Clock Gun.

Some details have surely been embellished over the years, but, regardless, little Bobby has found an enduring place in the city's heart.

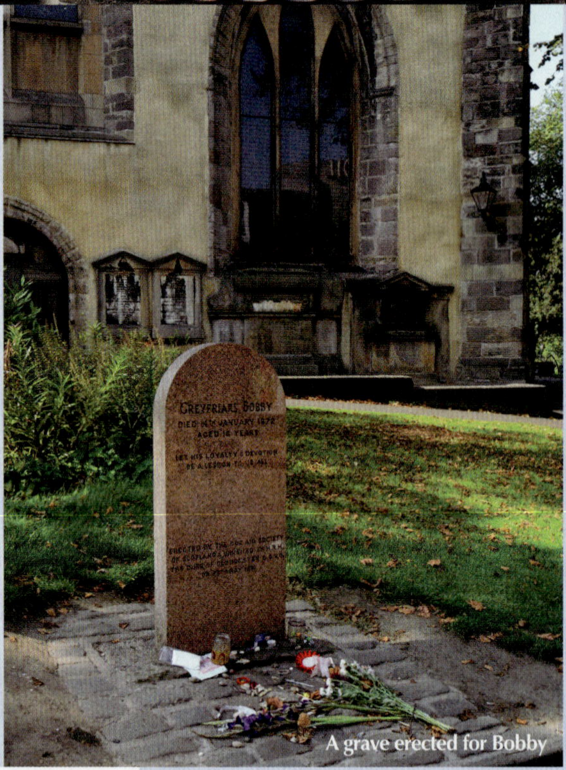
GREYFRIARS BOBBY

A grave erected for Bobby

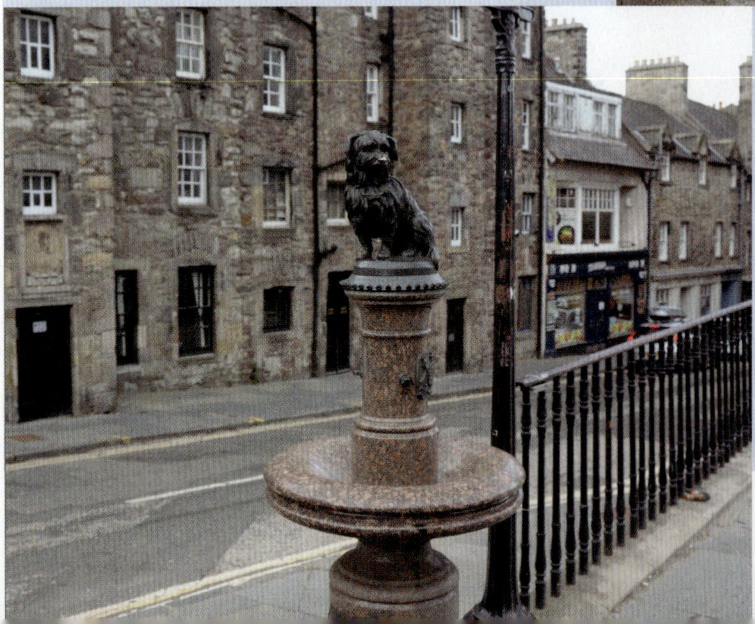

"Stood vigil at his master's grave for 14 years"

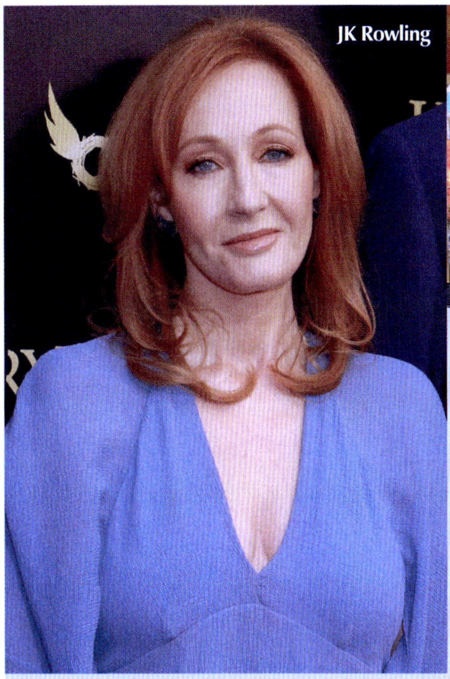

JK Rowling

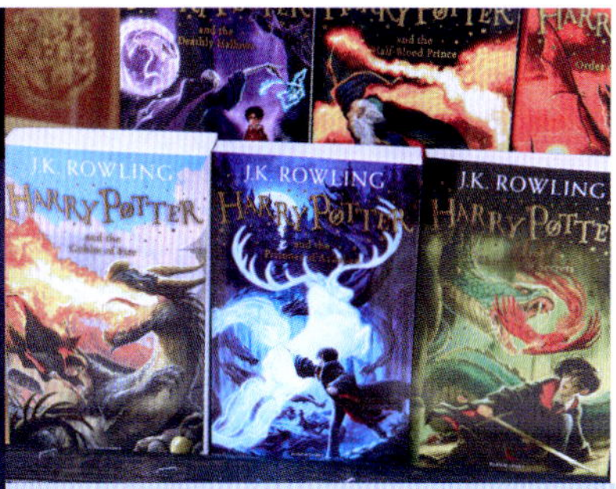
J.K. ROWLING
HARRY POTTER
J.K. ROWLING
HARRY POTTER
J.K. ROWLING
HARRY POTTER

"Continues to be a muse for many to this day"

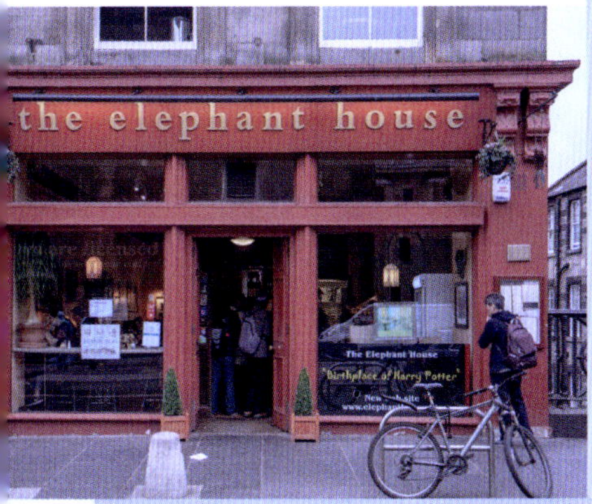
the elephant house

Potter Mania

A SPELL has been cast over Greyfriars Kirkyard giving a massive increase in visitors in the last few years. It was cast by none other than the boy wizard, Harry Potter.

JK Rowling wrote the majority of the Harry Potter books in Edinburgh, with several cafés boasting of their connection to what has become the world's third most widely-read work of literature. The Elephant House cafe is the most prominent with seats overlooking the Kirkyard.

Rowling has never directly confessed to it, but tour guides insist that names on graves throughout the Kirkyard inspired those of her characters – and you can see why. The cemetery boasts Thomas Riddell, William McGonagall, Elizabeth Moodie, and Robert Potter.

It must be said that views from the Kirkyard of the stands used for the Royal Military Tattoo on the Castle Esplanade bear a distinct resemblance to the wizarding world's quidditch stadiums. Pushing the parallels past the point of coincidence, George Heriot's School, adjacent to the Kirkyard, is thought to be an architectural inspiration for Hogwarts – its pupils are even sorted into one of four houses.

The kirkyard continues to be a muse for many to this day.

In the twilight hours especially, it is not uncommon to see artists capturing the colours and writers perched atop the mausoleums scrawling what could be the next great Scottish novel.

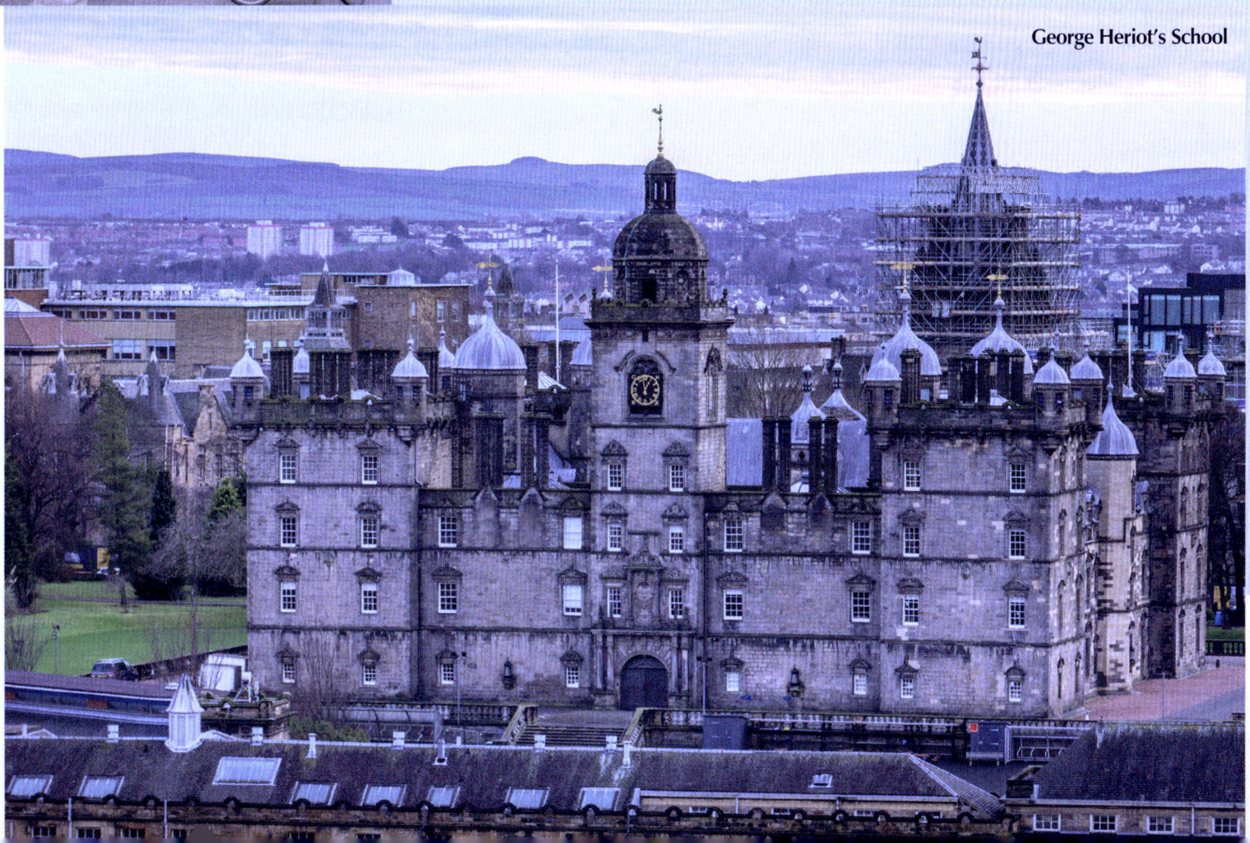

George Heriot's School

The Howff

The Spooky Seven

Scotland's burial grounds can be fascinating sites of historical interest where you can unearth ghostly and ghoulish tales

THE graveyards and cemeteries of Scotland can be many things to many people.

For some, they're sombre places to pay one's respects or fascinating sites steeped in history. For others, they are retreats from the hustle and bustle of a city centre.

The stories they tell, of course, are even more varied than the motives of those who visit – from the macabre to the heartrending.

From north to south, east to west, here are seven of the spookiest Scottish burial grounds.

The Howff, Dundee

This takes its name from a Scots word for "meeting place". The Nine Trades of Dundee used to convene there to discuss matters concerning their various crafts. Mary, Queen of Scots, granted the city the land in 1564. Before then it had housed the ruins of Greyfriars Monastery, destroyed in 1548. Stone No.502 is a favourite among visitors. It depicts a young family standing in an archway with an angel above them. John Galloway, a flax-dresser, raised the stone in memory of Margaret Duncan, his spouse, who died aged 23 on September 11, 1795. The cemetery closed to interments in 1857.

30 Supernatural Scotland

Reilig Odhrain, Iona

Reilig Odhrain, or Oran's graveyard, is the burial ground at Iona Abbey. St Columba founded the abbey in AD 563, and Oran was one of his companions. The site is said to be the final resting place of a number of Scottish kings. Clan chiefs were also buried there, including those of the MacLeans, MacLeods and MacKinnons. The abbey museum contains gravemarkers dating back hundreds of years. Reilig Odhrain continues to be an active graveyard and, in 1994, former Labour leader John Smith was interred here. »

The chapel at Reilig Odhrain

"*The final resting place of a number of Scottish kings*"

Aberlemno Kirkyard

Five miles from Forfar, off the B9134, lies Aberlemno Kirk. The kirkyard is a modest affair with a number of 19th-century gravestones. It is most famous for is its magnificent Pictish cross-slab, at more than seven feet tall. One side reputedly illustrates the Battle of Dunnichen – in which the Pictish king Bridei, son of Beli, defeated and slew Ecgfrith, son of Oswiu, king of Northumbria, in AD 685. View it in the summer – in winter it is covered to preserve the carvings. It is among several Pictish stones found in the area, with another discovered last year.

The cross-slab at Aberlemno

"The Necropolis sprung up around the statue of the Scottish reformer John Knox"

Glasgow Necropolis

Glasgow Necropolis is a Victorian garden cemetery established by the Merchants' House in 1831. The interdenominational burial ground sprung up around the statue of the Scottish reformer John Knox, which continues to dominate the hill. Something in the region of 50,000 burials have taken place at the 150-hectare (370-acre) cemetery that is home to around 3,500 tombs. One notable monument is the Monteath Mausoleum. It was built for Major Archibald Douglas Monteath, who served in the East India Company before returning to Glasgow. It stands out from the broadly classical monuments through being neo-Norman in design and bearing neither letters nor numerals. »

Dryburgh Abbey

The green, serene landscape that surrounds Dryburgh Abbey and its graves is the legacy of David Steuart Erskine, 11th Earl of Buchan. The Scottish antiquarian bought the abbey and surrounding estate in 1786, and set about planting exotic parkland trees.

When he died in 1829, he was laid to rest in the sacristy.

The novelist Sir Walter Scott – Erskine's close friend and fellow antiquarian – was buried here three years later, on September 26, 1832.

His tomb is in the north transept, known as St Mary's Aisle.

A third great Scot, Field Marshal Earl Haig, was interred beside Scott in 1928.

"The novelist Sir Walter Scott was buried here in 1832"

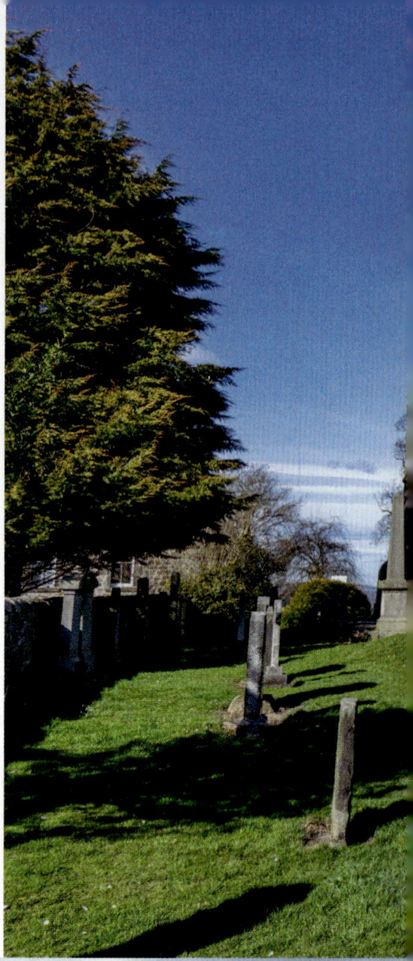

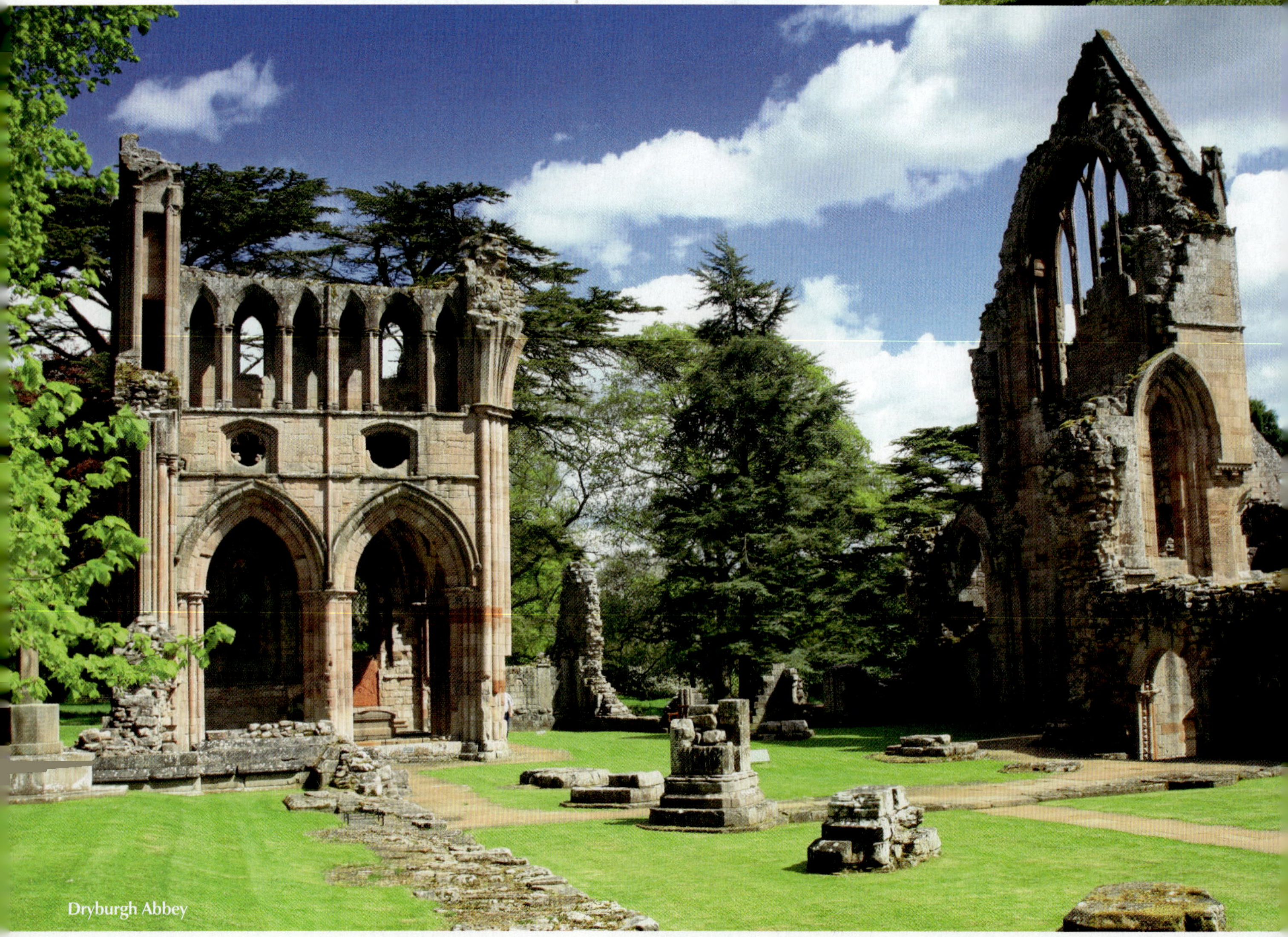

Dryburgh Abbey

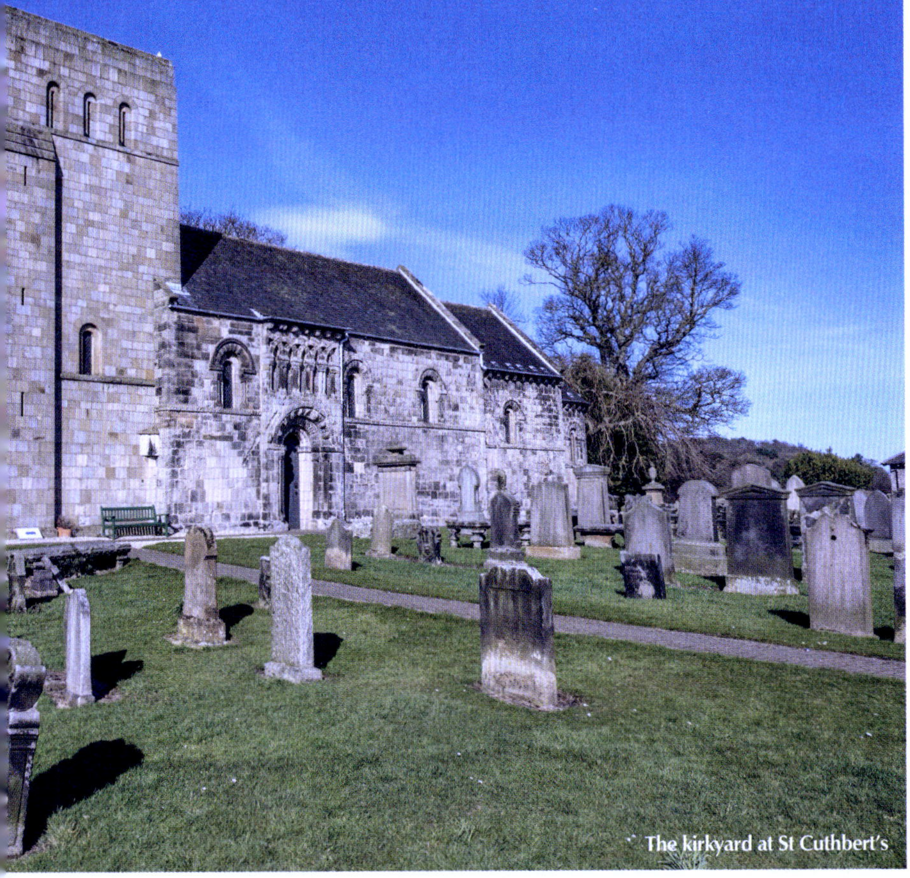
The kirkyard at St Cuthbert's

St Cuthbert's Kirkyard, Edinburgh

A church dedicated to this popular saint, who died in AD 687 has probably been on the site since at least the 8th century. However, the earliest known record of a building dates to the 12th century, when it is recorded that King David gifted St Cuthbert's to the Abbey of Holyrood.

The kirkyard contains around 747 headstones, monuments, tombs and other structures.

One interesting feature is the crenellated watchtower built in 1827 to ward off bodysnatchers like Burke and Hare.

People of note interred in the kirkyard include William Macao, the first naturalised Chinese citizen of Scotland, and father of logarithms John Napier.

Osmondwall Cemetery, Hoy

The statue of a lifeboatman looking out to sea dominates Osmondwall Cemetery in Hoy, Orkney. It is a memorial to one of the island's darkest days.

On March 17, 1969, the lifeboat TGB was launched from Longhope to aid the Liberian steamship Irene off South Ronaldsay. Coxswain Daniel Kirkpatrick and his seven crewmen battled rough seas and a south-easterly gale but, tragically, the lifeboat capsized. None survived.

Irene ran aground near Grim Ness and her crew was brought ashore.

A plaque on the memorial reads, "Greater love hath no man than this, that he lay down his life for his fellow men."

"The statue is a memorial to one of the island's darkest days"

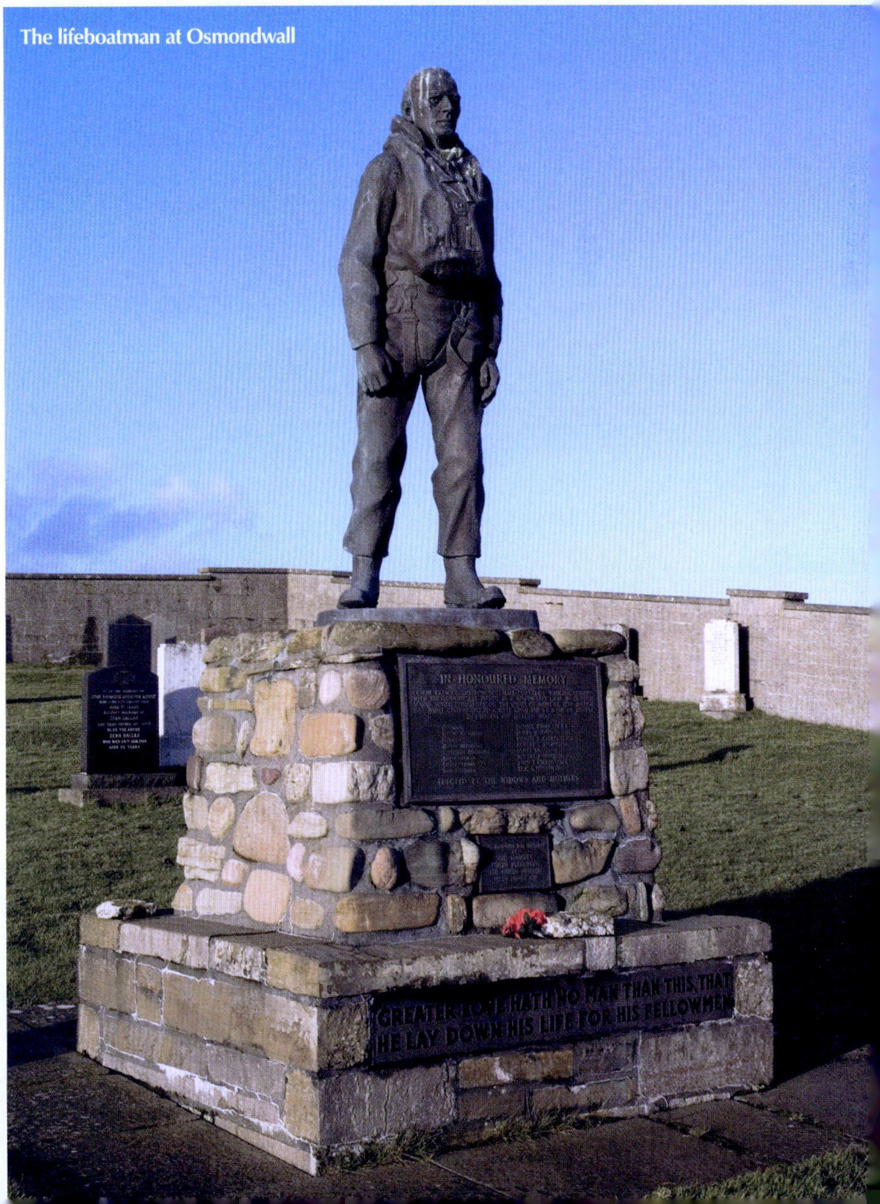
IN HONOURED MEMORY
HATH NO MAN THAN THIS THAT
HE LAY DOWN HIS LIFE FOR HIS FELLOWMEN
The lifeboatman at Osmondwall

Hideous History

There's always something – or someone – chilling round the corner in Scotland's supernatural past...

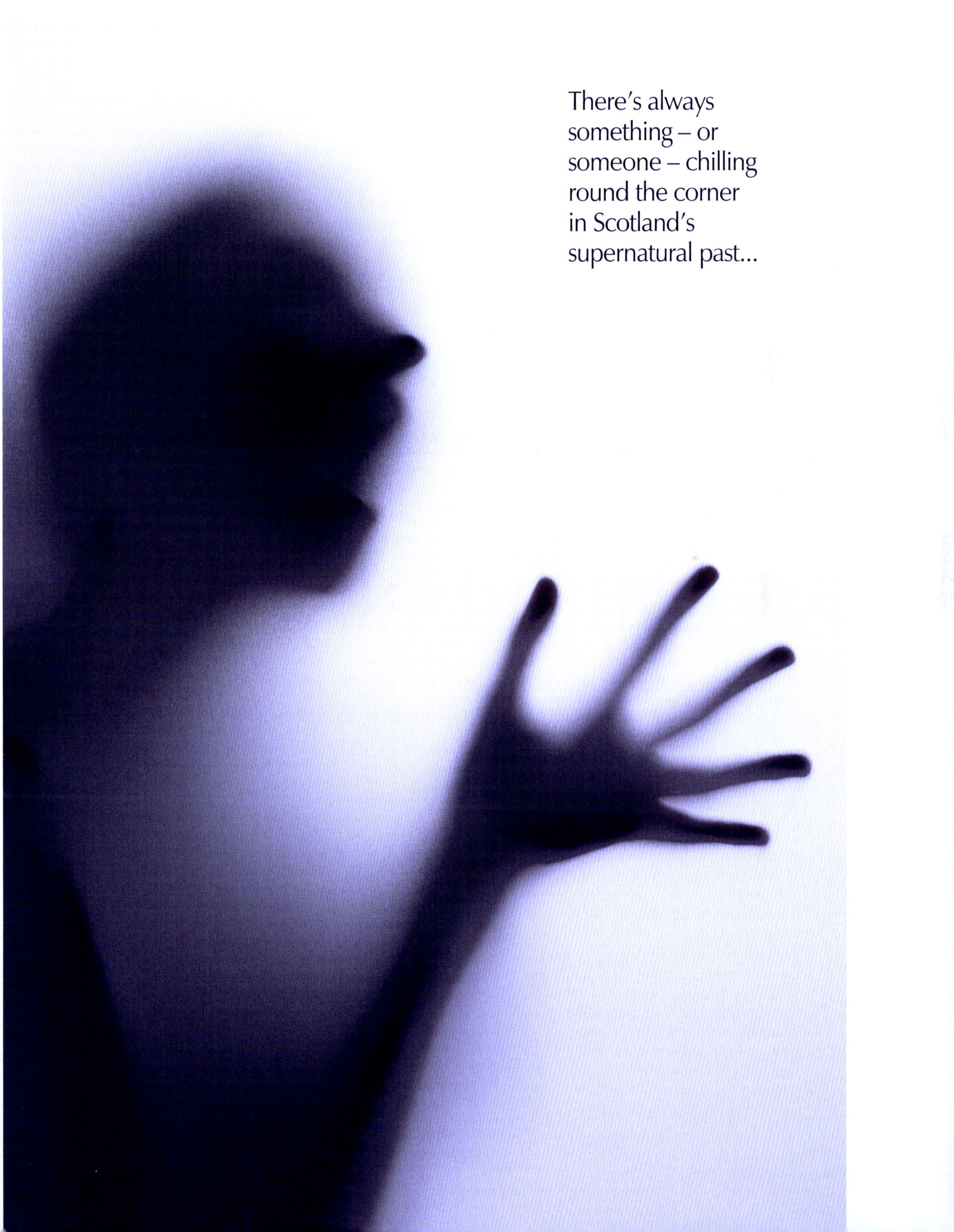

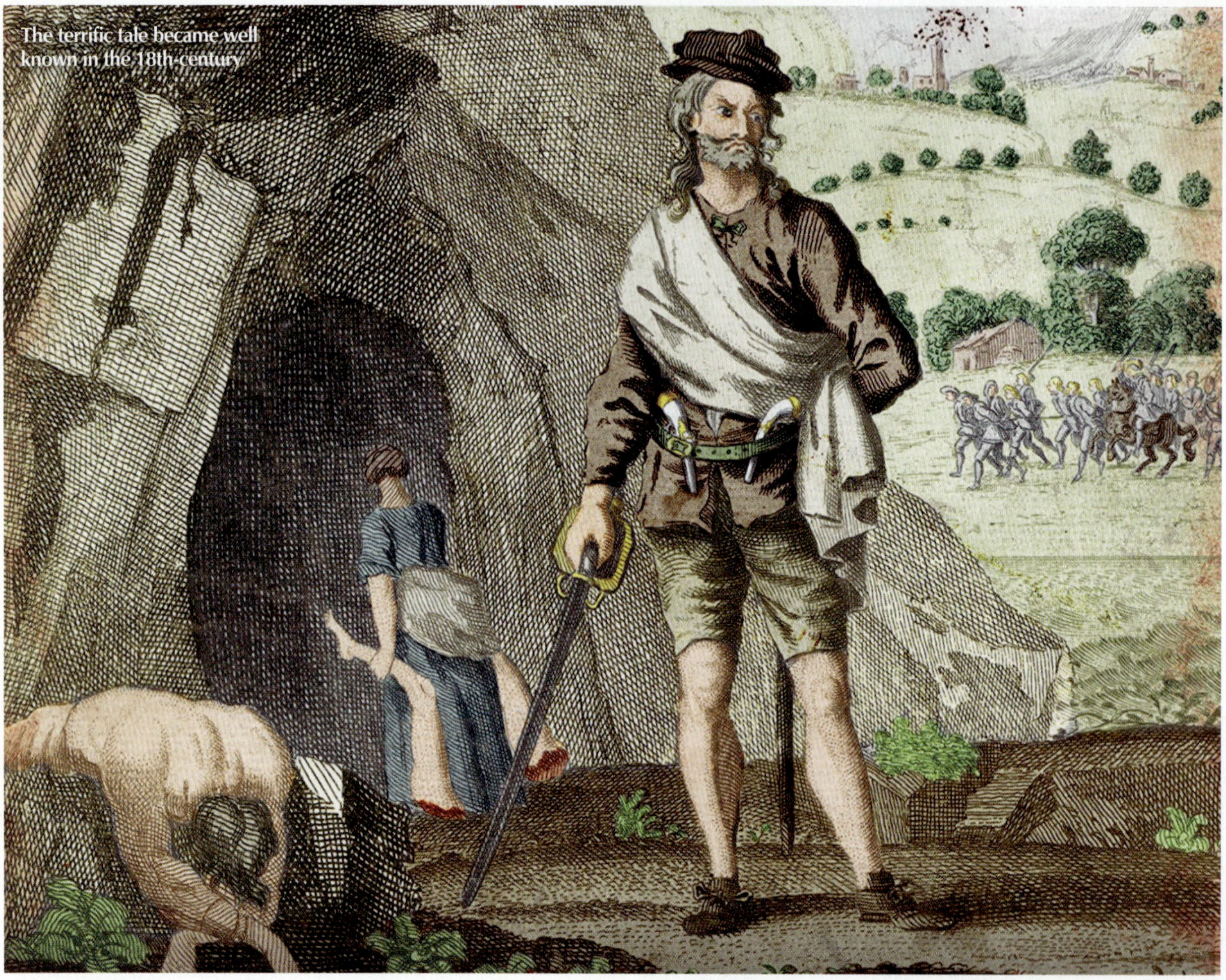
The terrific tale became well known in the 18th-century

The Cannibal Clan

The details are debatable, but the horrific legend of murderous Sawney Bean and his family has persisted for centuries

Words: NICK DRAINEY Images: SHUTTERSTOCK, ALAMY

MURDERING and eating 1,000 people in a cave on the coast of south-west Scotland might sound like the fantastical storyline of a Hollywood movie, but many believe that is exactly what Sawney Bean and his many offspring once did.

Over 25 years, Bean and his clan are said to have continued a reign of terror in the area around the village of Ballantrae in what is now South Ayrshire.

The story is so fascinatingly gory and gruesome that it has become part of Scottish folklore.

Sawney Bean became the most despicable man on earth around the turn of the 17th century, but he had rather humble and obscure beginnings.

It is said he was born in East Lothian but was unsuited to his father's trade of a "hedger and ditcher" – someone who repairs hedgerows and digs ditches – so became a tanner.

Could it be that this knowledge of dissecting bodies led to his later behaviour?

He left the east of Scotland with his wife – called Black Agnes Douglas – and ended up near Ballantrae, where they set up home in a cave, as you do. The cave was a good place to hide as it had tunnels going into the sea cliffs and its entrance was flooded by the tide twice a day.

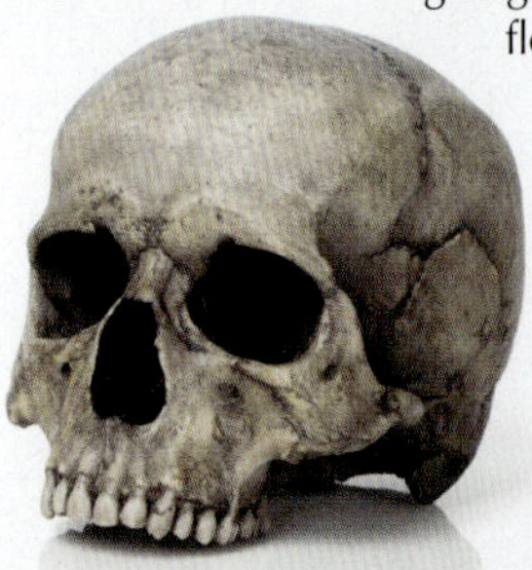

Bean and his wife had many offspring – 14 children who produced 32 grandchildren. But this was no early version of the Swiss Family Robinson – the progeny came through incest, as none of the children were allowed to leave the cave.

> *"Under the cover of darkness he would lead his family out of the cave onto surrounding roads"*

Now with so many mouths to feed and an apparent aversion to hard work, Sawney Bean took to drastic – very drastic – measures.

Under the cover of darkness he would lead his family out of the cave onto surrounding roads and tracks, attacking and murdering unsuspecting travellers. The bodies of the victims were hauled back to the cave. They provided a good source of protein, albeit not the type of sustenance advised by dieticians now or then. When the bodies started piling up, it is said the family pickled parts for later consumption.

But surely they would have been discovered? Most accounts say they scattered body parts all along the coast, making villagers believe it must have been animals attacking and devouring the unfortunate dead.

Some locals became suspicious of the disappearances and vigilante groups were set up to hunt the perpetrators. Often, however, innkeepers ended up being blamed as they had been the last to see the unfortunate victims.

Eventually the cannibal family's luck ran out – or perhaps natural justice finally caught up with their unnatural deeds. The beginning of the end is said to have come one night when the Beans attacked a couple returning from a country fair.

Female members of the clan pulled the woman from her horse and began to disembowel her at the scene. The husband, meanwhile, had managed to keep the male attackers at bay just long enough »

Dare you brave the cave?

The cave lies hidden along the Ballantrae coast

to fire a pistol – according to some accounts – and ride his horse at them.

Although the husband also perished, he had managed to distract the family long enough for witnesses to arrive. Other revellers returning from the fair came upon the grisly scene.

The Beans were outnumbered and fled, leaving the body behind as evidence for the local magistrate.

Some sources say that Glasgow magistrates were involved in the resulting manhunt, but most agree it was a force of around 400 of King James's men who were assembled to track the Bean clan down.

At first they could not be found, such was the isolation of their cave, especially with the tides to protect them. However the men had brought bloodhounds, who immediately picked up the scent of something gory. They set off, racing along a trail to the cliffs, at what is now known as Bennane Head.

Soon the stench of putrefied flesh in the sea air became unbearable – but that was nothing compared to the scene that was about to unfold for the troops around the next corner.

Piles of bloody clothes and jewellery from the victims were strewn around the entrance to the cave, interspersed with discarded, rotting body parts.

The clan was done for.

With their cave surrounded, they fell into the hands of the King's men.

As with so much of the story, what happened next is subject to debate.

The clan – numbering nearly 50 – were taken to the tolbooth in Edinburgh. There was no trial, as the evidence was seen as too compelling.

The men were hung, drawn and quartered the next day – a slow, painful death thought to be justice for the way the victims had died. After being forced to watch their kin die in excruciating pain, the women were burned as witches.

But did it really happen?

Some say the Bean clan were causing havoc around 1400, but most believe that the events took place 200 years later. It could be either that the King James whose soldiers tracked down the family was James I of Scotland (around 1400), or James IV of Scotland and I of England (around 1600).

Most accounts originate in pamphlets – kind of tabloid newspapers of their day but containing far more fiction than fact – written towards the end of the 18th century.

It has even been suggested the stories surfaced as part of an anti-Scottish sentiment following Culloden and the end of the Jacobite Risings.

Unsurprisingly, the local tourist industry would prefer the grisly events which may or may not have taken place here were forgotten, and there are no signposts to the cave today. Yet the gruesome tale of Sawney Bean, like the best Scottish legends, continues to endure.

Occasionally, the bravest – or most foolhardy – horror hunters will scale the dangerous cliffs to clamber into the cave, returning with tales of bloodstains on the stone walls and the lingering scent of putrid flesh…

The family lived near Ballantrae

> **"With their cave surrounded, they fell into the hands of the King's men"**

> "The bravest horror hunters will scale the dangerous cliffs"

Snib's Cave, home of Henry Ewing Torbert

Bean On Screen

HISTORIANS may struggle to find the basis of a true story in the Bean clan but that has not stopped Hollywood and other writers having a go.

The 1977 horror film *The Hills Have Eyes*, written and directed by Wes Craven, is said to have been based on the legend of Sawney Bean, although it was set in Nevada.

Harry Tait said his novel *The Ballad Of Sawney Bain* was a "kind of historiographical meta-fiction retelling of the tale of Sawney Bean". It went on to win the Saltire Society's prize for Scottish First Book of the Year in 1990.

Scots actor David Hayman starred in *Sawney: Flesh Of Man* in 2012. It is based on the terrible deeds of the Bean clan, although in this modern-day twist his character uses a black cab to abduct his unsuspecting victims.

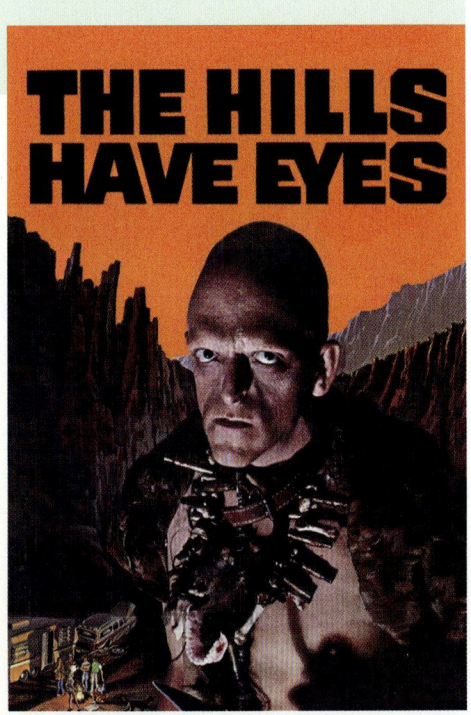

Dare You Find The Cave?

NORTH of Ballantrae, Bennane Head is a pleasant stretch of rocky coast backed by fields, popular with walkers on Ayrshire Coastal Path. The cave, looking out to Ailsa Craig, now seems a nice place for a picnic, which no doubt many unsuspecting visitors have enjoyed there.

Snib's Cave, home of hermit Henry Ewing Torbert until his death at 71 in 1983, is not the Beans' abode. The horror scene is further north.

Sawney Bean's Cave (aka Bennane Cave) is hard to reach. Blocked by a boulder, the entrance is down near the waterline and requires visitors to descend treacherous rocks.

It is only accessible at low tide – so check both a map and tide times before going, and set an alarm on your phone so you don't get cut off!

Strange Visions

The Brahan Seer's uncanny predictions are still coming to pass – though there's no proof he actually existed!

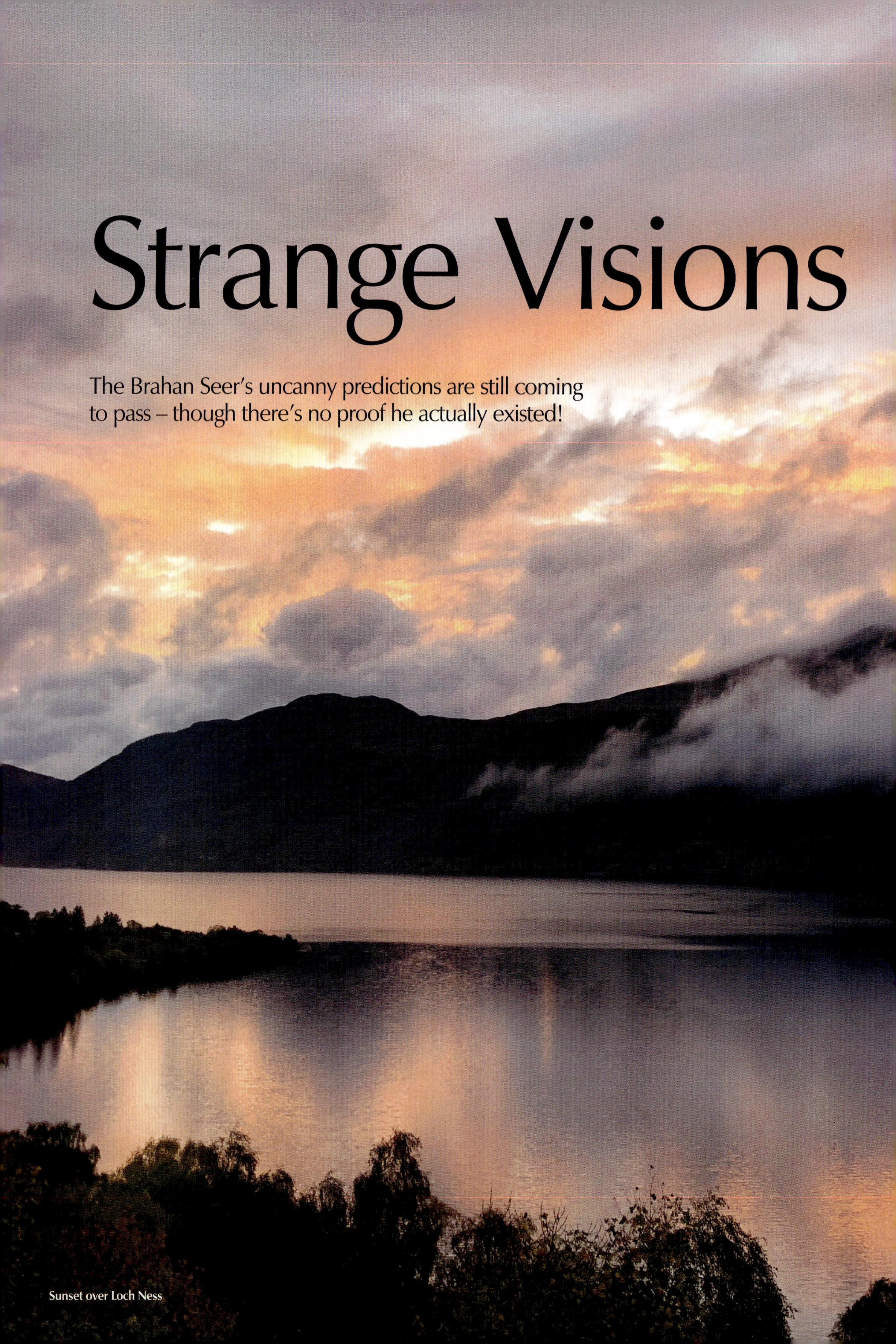

Sunset over Loch Ness

THE
PROPHECIES
OF THE
BRAHAN SEER
(Coinneach Odhar Fiosaiche)
BY
ALEXANDER MACKENZIE.

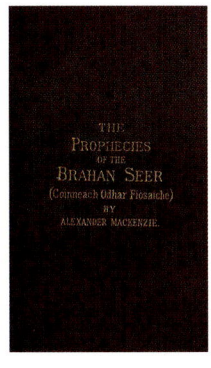

"THE day will come," predicted the Brahan Seer, "when fire and water shall run in streams through all the streets and lanes of Inverness." Before residents of the Highland capital start panicking, fear not – Scotland's answer to Nostradamus was, in fact, simply foreseeing the installation of gas and water pipes.

This is one of the less dramatic prophecies that Kenneth Mackenzie is said to have made in the 17th century. Born on the Isle of Lewis, he ended up working for the 3rd Earl of Seaforth on the Brahan Estate near Dingwall. As well as his day job as a labourer, he had a successful sideline in second sight.

Some say he gained his gift when his mother struck a deal in a graveyard with the ghost of a Scandinavian princess. Others reckon his powers took hold as he slept on a fairy hill. Waking to find a hagstone in his pocket, he realised that if he looked through the hole piercing this powerful pebble, he could see more than the landscape.

Feats of engineering and fierce battles lurked within, set to happen at some point in the future.

Many of the scenes he saw took years, even centuries to be fulfilled, while others are still threatening to come true.

Known as Coinneach Odhar in Gaelic, translated as Dark Kenneth or Kenneth the Sallow, he had a knack for forecasting not only local events involving foxes and deer, but national and international incidents.

He insisted that once five bridges crossed the River Ness, chaos would be unleashed across the globe. A fifth bridge was temporarily constructed in 1939 and completed that August; on the first day of September, Hitler invaded Poland.

Other startling revelations included accurately predicting the Battle of Culloden in 1746 and the Highland Clearances. Coinneach also spoke mysteriously of black, bridleless horses drawing carriages, a premonition of steam trains.

However, as the first printed version of his prophecies didn't appear until 1877, courtesy of folklorist Alexander Mackenzie, a pertinent question might be: did he, aye?

It's certainly a source of speculation among historians. It's likely Kenneth's story benefited from a hefty dose of hindsight. By the time *The Prophecies Of The Brahan Seer* was written, several predicted events – such as the creation of the Caledonian Canal, which saw ships sail around the back of Tomnahurich Hill in Inverness for the first time, as our canny prophet foretold – had happened.

What's more, there's no official record of him actually existing, though a "wizard" named Coinneach Odhar did live in Easter Ross the century before.

But he couldn't possibly have been employed by the 3rd Earl of Seaforth, unless his spells granted him a preternaturally long life.

We'll never know. The passing down of stories, mistranslations of Gaelic, false memories and poetic licence all play a part in warping history and weaving a new thread through the tapestry of tales we cherish.

Many of us can't help but get swept up in the legend of Coinneach Odhar, not least because he's still hitting the mark to this day, having predicted the Piper Alpha disaster, the construction of the Channel Tunnel, and the opening of the Scottish Parliament.

According to Alexander Mackenzie, Kenneth met a grisly end when he let slip one of his most believable visions – that while in Paris, the Earl of Seaforth (his boss) was carrying on with a woman who wasn't his wife. On hearing this, Lady Seaforth ordered that he be burned alive in a barrel of tar at Chanonry Point.

Today, a memorial to the Brahan Seer stands there, and whether you think he was real or just a myth, he'll always be a fascinating part of our past – and our future.

Kenneth Mackenzie, 3rd Earl of Seaforth

"A fascinating part of our past – and future"

The memorial cairn at Chanonry Point

62005
The Seer foresaw the advent of steam trains

A depiction of the Battle of Culloden

Words: LAURA BROWN Images: SHUTTERSTOCK, ALAMY

A Quartet Of Curses

Can bones, stones and words really lead to death and destruction?

The Curse Of The Pharaohs

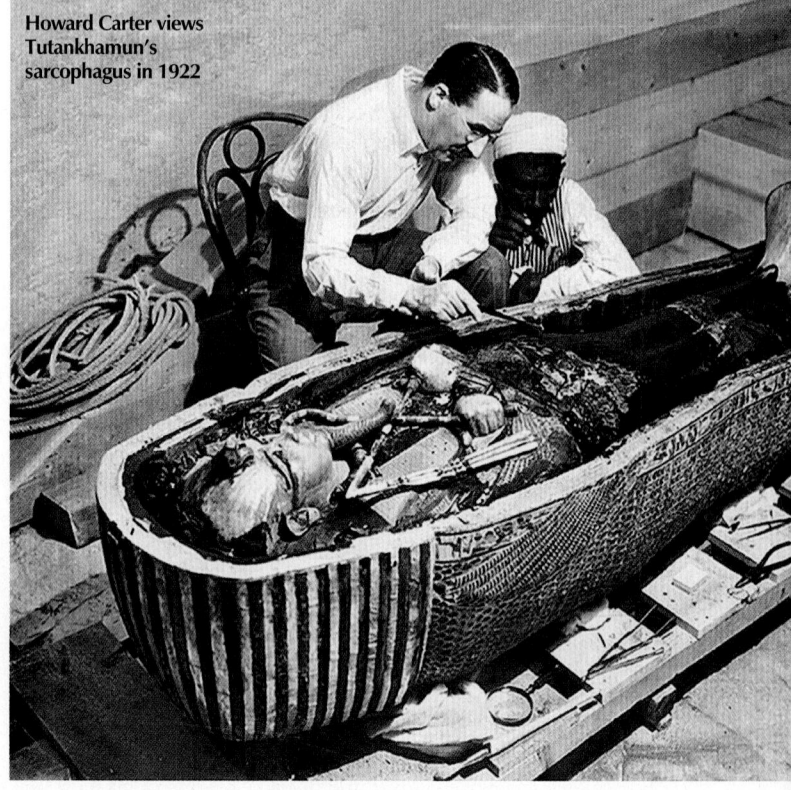

Howard Carter views Tutankhamun's sarcophagus in 1922

WHEN Howard Carter opened King Tutankhamun's tomb 101 years ago, it sparked a craze for all things Ancient Egyptian. So, when Sir Alexander Seton and his wife Zeyla holidayed there in 1936, they were thrilled when their guide offered an exclusive extra visit – to a newly opened tomb.

There they saw the partial skeleton of what they were told was a princess. Later Seton found his wife had helped herself to a bone as a souvenir. He didn't think much of it – "to my eyes it looked like digestive biscuit" – but that changed back at their home in Learmonth Gardens, Edinburgh. The bone was put in a glass case to show dinner guests – who were lucky to survive when a piece of roof parapet crashed to the ground as they were leaving.

The family began being woken during the night "and none of us could explain the noises". Tables were overturned and books flung about in the locked room where the bone was, and a mysterious figure was seen walking about the house.

Nerves were frayed and Seton confided in his friends at his club. Next thing the newspapers had hold of it, and the story had become "the Curse of the Pharaohs".

Eventually the bone was disposed of – the papers claimed Lady Seton had returned it to Egypt in 1937, but Seton later said he had burned it. But the Setons did not seem to escape its curse.

Their marriage broke up in 1939 but neither found happiness, which Seton put down to the bone.

"From 1936 onward, trouble, sometimes grave, seemed to be always around the corner," he later wrote.

"Tables were overturned and books flung about in the locked room where the bone was, and a mysterious figure was seen walking about"

Words: JUDY VICKERS Pictures: ALAMY, SHUTTERSTOCK, GREY GRANITE BLOGGER

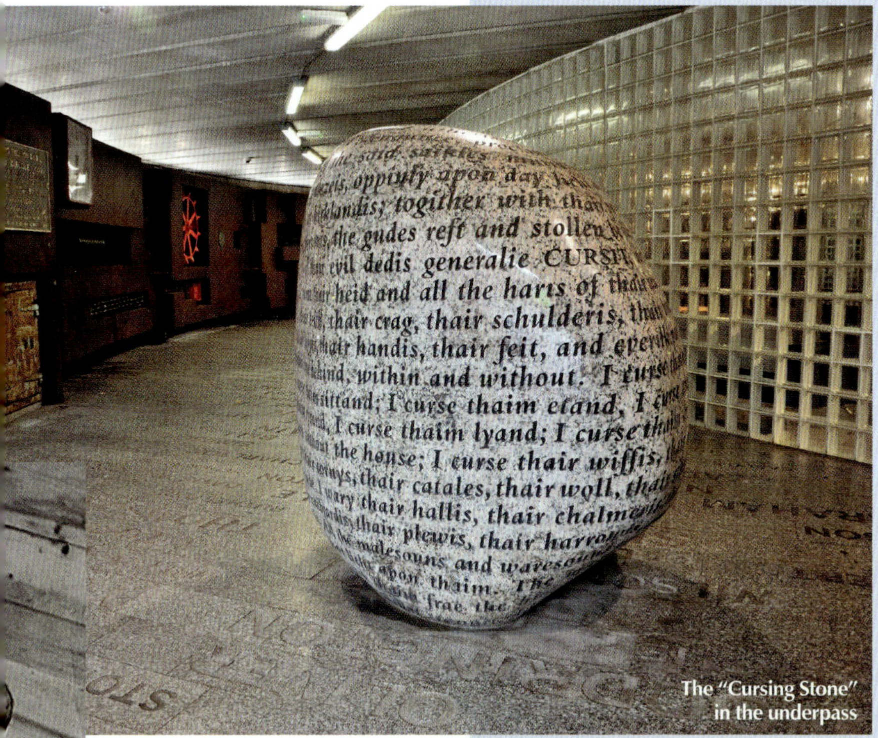

the gudes reft and stollen
evil dedis generalie CURSE
heid and all the haris of
thair crag, thair schulderis,
thair handis, thair feit, and
within and without. I curse
I curse thaim etand,
I curse thaim lyand; I curse
the house; I curse thair wiffis,
thair catales, thair woll,
thair hallis, thair
thair plewis, thair
and
upon thaim.

The "Cursing Stone" in the underpass

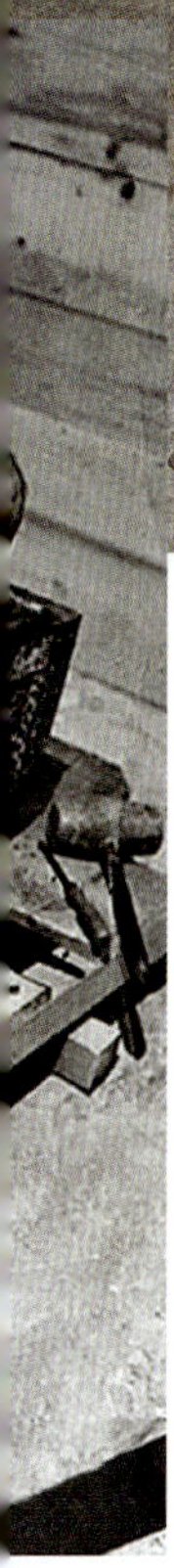

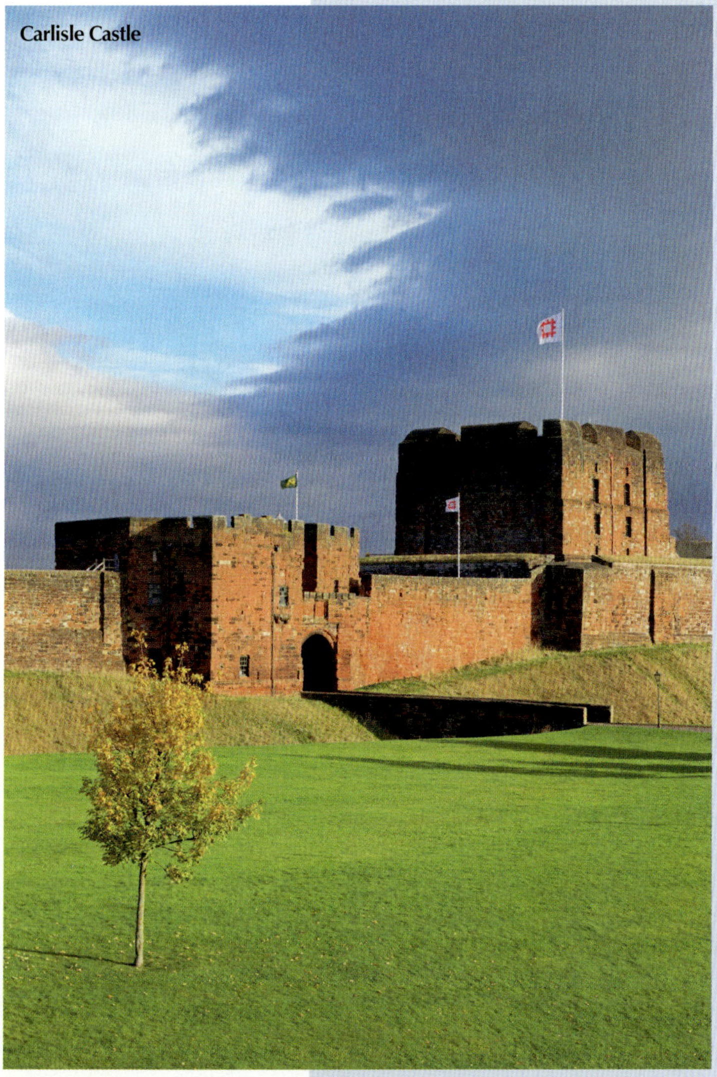
Carlisle Castle

The Curse Of The Border Reivers

MURDER, theft, rape, kidnap, blackmail – everyday life for hundreds of years in the lands around the Scottish-English border. Reivers ruled – clans with more loyalty to family than distant king or country and for whom cattle and sheep rustling was the main career option.

Understandable then that in 1525 the Archbishop of Glasgow, Gavin Dunbar, completely lost his rag with the lawless gangs and issued a spectacular and remarkably detailed 1,069-word curse in Scots designed to be read out by priests in churches in the border lands.

It starts with their body parts – "I curse thair heid and all the haris of thair heid… to the soill of their feit" – then curses them whatever they and their families are doing, and everything they owned, down to cabbage patches.

He then calls for a range of Biblical horrors, including the flood of Noah, the fires of Sodom and Gomorrah and the plagues of Egypt, to fall on them. The curse failed to have any effect and only when James VI became king of England as well as Scotland were the reivers clamped down on, with many hanged or banished to Ulster.

The cleric's curse has a modern-day aftermath, though. In 2001, artist Gordon Young carved 383 words of it on a stone that was placed in an underpass between Carlisle Castle and the Tullie House museum. Four years later, there were calls for it to be removed amid rumours it was to blame for calamities including the 2001 foot-and-mouth outbreak. The stone, however, remains. »

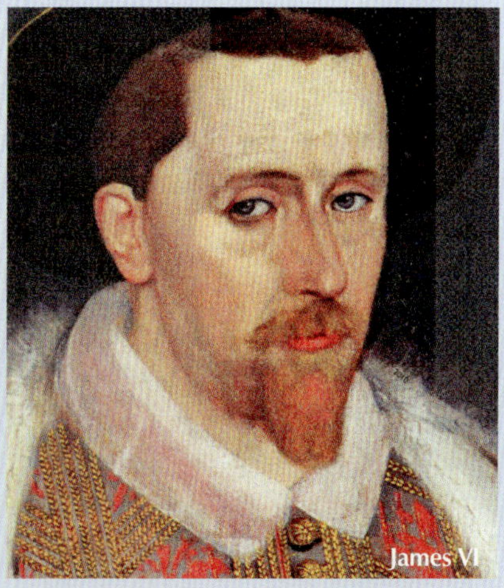
James VI

The caged grave

The Cursed Stones

A METAL cage sits on top of a grave in the kirkyard of St Tuchaldus in Rothiemurchus. But unlike most mortsafes, this was not created in the age of Burke and Hare to deter resurrectionists – it was put there in the 1980s to protect five ancient marshmallow-shaped stones which sit on the tomb.

The grave is that of Seath Mor Sgorfhiaclach ("Bucktooth"), chief of the Clan Shaw, who lived at the Doune, a nearby hill fort. He was chosen to lead the Clan Chattan (of which he was a part) at the Battle of the Clans or Battle of North Inch at Perth in 1396, a fight between 30 champions from each side to settle a feud.

The Chattans were victorious, with 11 left standing – the single Cameron survivor fled. Sgorfhiaclach died in 1405 and the stones are said to represent the survivors of the battle – it is believed there were once more of them. They are said to be cursed, with anyone who interferes with them being doomed.

A footman in 1800s was said to have thrown one of the stones into the Spey to prove the curse was a fiction. Four days later, the stone was back and the footman was dead. In the 1940s a similarly sceptical journalist lifted one of the stones only to die in a car crash hours later. In the late 1970s and early 80s there was a spate of the stones vanishing, and the mortsafe was place over the tomb.

The Battle of the Clans

46 Supernatural Scotland

Mar's Wark, Stirling

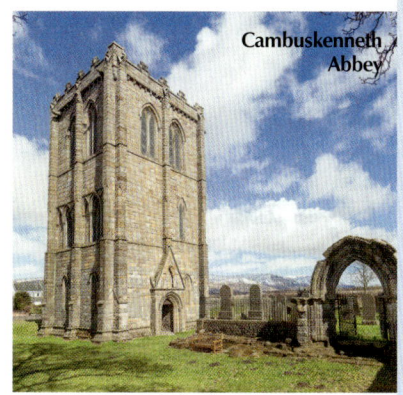

Cambuskenneth Abbey

The Curse Of Alloa Tower

THE Abbot of Cambuskenneth allegedly cursed John Erskine, Earl of Mar, in the 16th century after he took stones from the ruined Cambuskenneth Abbey to build a mansion, Mar's Wark, near Stirling Castle.

This curse was far more cryptic than the Glasgow archbishop's forthright damnation. Known as the "doom of Mar", the (again rather lengthy) curse says, "Thy work shall be cursed and shall never be finished … Thy lands shall be given to a stranger, and thy titles shall lie amongst the dead… The branch that springs from thee shall see his dwelling burnt, in which a King was nursed, his wife a sacrifice in that same flame; his children numerous but of little honour; and three born and grown who shall never see the light… Thine ancient Tower… shall be a ruin and a beacon until an ash sapling shall spring from its topmost stone. Then … the sunshine of Royalty shall beam upon thee once more."

According to the National Trust for Scotland, which looks after Alloa Tower, some parts of the curse did come true. While Mar's Wark was finished, the 6th Earl Mar threw his lot in with the Jacobites in 1715 and lost his land. They weren't given to a stranger, but bought back by his younger brother from the Crown for his heir. His titles, though, did indeed lie with the dead for 100 years.

In 1800, there was a fire at Alloa House, the mansion once attached to the tower, where four kings had been nursed, after a maid accidentally set a curtain alight. The family fled in their nightclothes and the mansion burned to the ground; only the tower survived.

Lady Erskine did not perish in the fire but had died previously. Of the couple's eight children, the eldest was disinherited and suffered an opium-related death in 1828. Three, born blind, "never saw the light".

And, crucially, an ash sapling was spotted growing from the roof in 1815 – shortly before George IV visited Scotland in 1822 and spread his royal sunshine by restoring the title of Earl of Mar.

> "Only the tower survived"

Alloa Tower

Supernatural Scotland

Royal Revenge

James VI started a Scottish witch-hunt with the North Berwick trials

MAY DAY eve is Walpurgis Night, the date when witches are said to fly on broomsticks to the peaks of the Harz Mountains in Germany to celebrate the arrival of spring.

In Scotland, the supernatural was seen as just another part of life, but witches were a phenomenon only peasants believed in. There was a shift in perception, however, after a collection of German superstitions were published, named Malleus Maleficarum. The popular book and its ideas filtered through Europe, influencing the public and the church.

People started to become wary of witches, believing that they might put their powers to devilish use. This fear grew and witchcraft was officially outlawed in Scotland in 1563. Thousands of horrific trials took place between the 16th and 18th centuries, as neighbour turned on neighbour and accusations flew.

It might be more than 300 years since the last person accused of being a witch in Scotland was executed, but the macabre period has not been forgotten. The first major witch trial in Scotland took place at North Berwick in 1591. The trial lasted two years and once Geillis Duncan was burned at the stake the country became obsessed.

Geillis worked as a maid for the local deputy bailiff, David Seaton, in Tranent near North Berwick. When Geillis started to sneak out at night, David became suspicious. When she suddenly seemed to have the power to heal the injured and cure the ill, he accused her of being a witch, and demanded that she explain her strange behaviour and new-found skills.

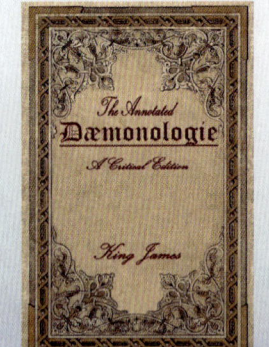

When no explanation was forthcoming, he had the poor maid tortured. Geillis refused to admit to her alleged crimes, but her tormentors – who used despicable devices such as pilliwinks, or thumbscrews, to force a confession – found what they said was the Devil's Mark on her neck.

She was immediately thrown into prison. News reached King James VI that a witch had been

Witches are believed to fly to the Harz mountains on Walpurgis night

caught in the area. He and his wife Anne has just been caught in a fierce storm in the North Sea, and the royal couple immediately accused Scotland's witches of summoning the storms to destroy their ship.

James launched a witch hunt, inspired by those he'd heard about in Norway and Denmark, and arrived to interrogate Geillis himself. She revealed the names of several other people she claimed had been practising the dark arts alongside her.

Geillis spoke of having been on a boat named the Grace of God with the Devil and other members of the alleged coven, where merrymaking and mayhem ensued. She also admitted to casting a spell on a hat belonging to the laird of Balnaird. After months of torture, she was sentenced to death.

On December 4, 1591, the day of her execution, she was taken to Castle Hill in Edinburgh. In a final statement, she announced that everything she'd said about her co-accused was untrue, and that she'd made it all up because the horrors inflicted on her by David Seaton had been too much to bear.

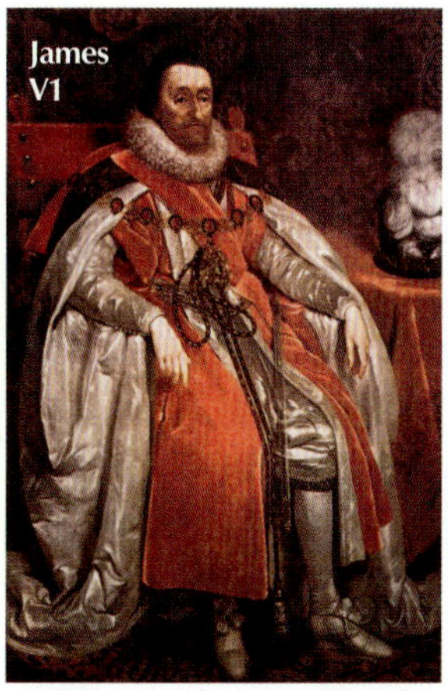
James V1

Sadly, it was too late for two of her co-accused, Euphame and Barbara, as both are thought to have already been executed, and it was too late for Geillis herself. Historians widely believe that the torture of Geillis and the other alleged witches was so brutal, they would have been left with little choice but to confess.

The North Berwick Witch Trials continued for two years, and more than 70 people were investigated.

This was far from the end of James's crackdown, however. In 1597, he published *Daemonologie* – or to use its longer title, *Daemonologie, In Forme Of A Dialogue, Divided Into Three Books: By The High And Mighty Prince, James &C.*

It was split into three sections: magic and necromancy; witchcraft and sorcery; and spirits and spectres. It wasn't a handbook, of course. James didn't want to help budding witches and wizards learn their craft – instead, he wanted to drum up as much fear as possible.

It's thought that his unhealthy obsession with the occult was triggered by the violent death of his mother, Mary, Queen of Scots, who was beheaded. He saw the book not only as a warning to the people of Scotland, but a call to arms for witch-hunters. His mission was successful in the country – convictions of witchcraft increased exponentially.

When he became King of England, however, as James I, he was disappointed to discover that witch-hunts and executions were on the decline there – in fact, the English had started to doubt witches existed at all. He had *Daemonologie* reprinted twice in the first year of his reign, and decided to revise English law while he was at it.

The Witchcraft Act of 1604 took a zero tolerance approach to the dark arts, making hanging the punishment for even first-time offenders.

This was eventually replaced with the Witchcraft Act of 1735, which seemed to acknowledged that witchcraft wasn't real – it only enforced penalties on those was claimed the "pretence of witchcraft".

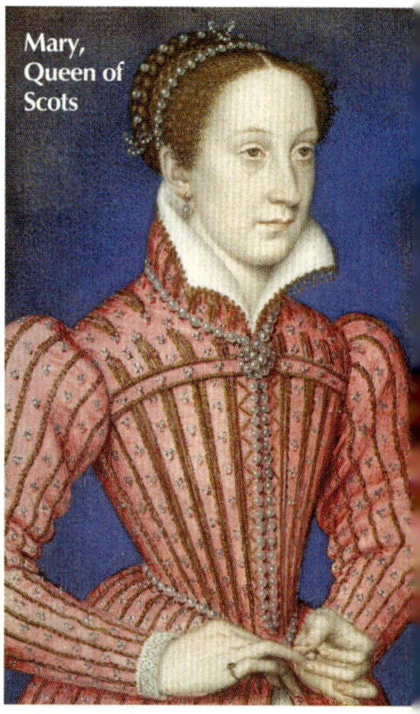
Mary, Queen of Scots

"The alleged witches had no choice but to confess"

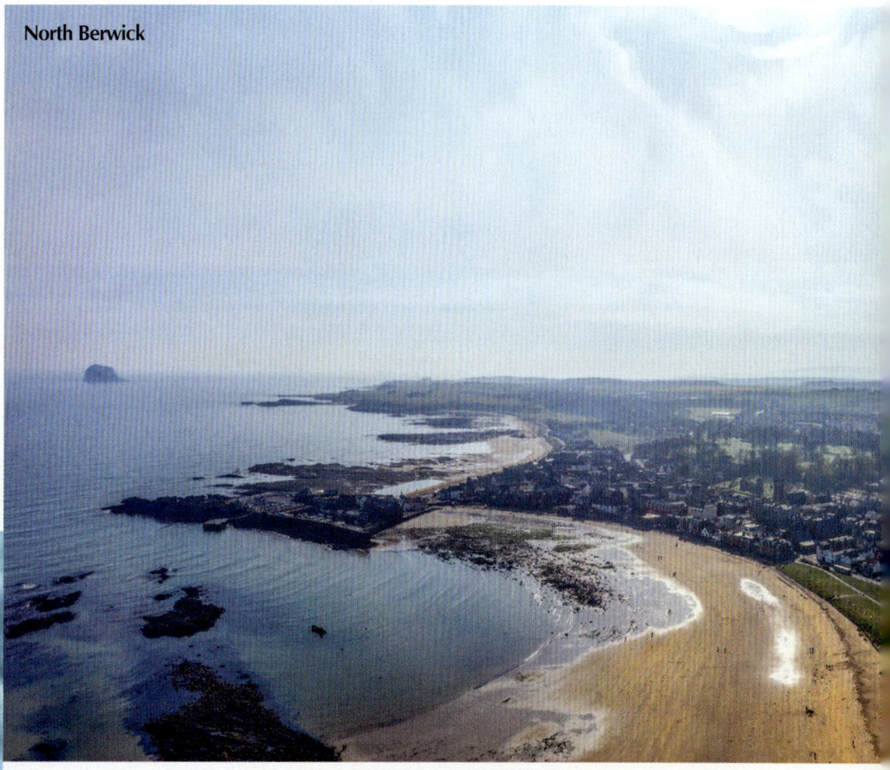
North Berwick

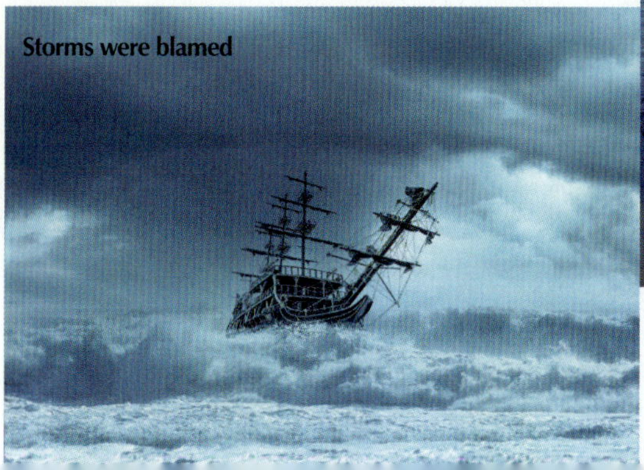
Storms were blamed

Back To The Future

The unsuspecting RAF pilot who allegedly became a time traveller during a routine flight to Edinburgh

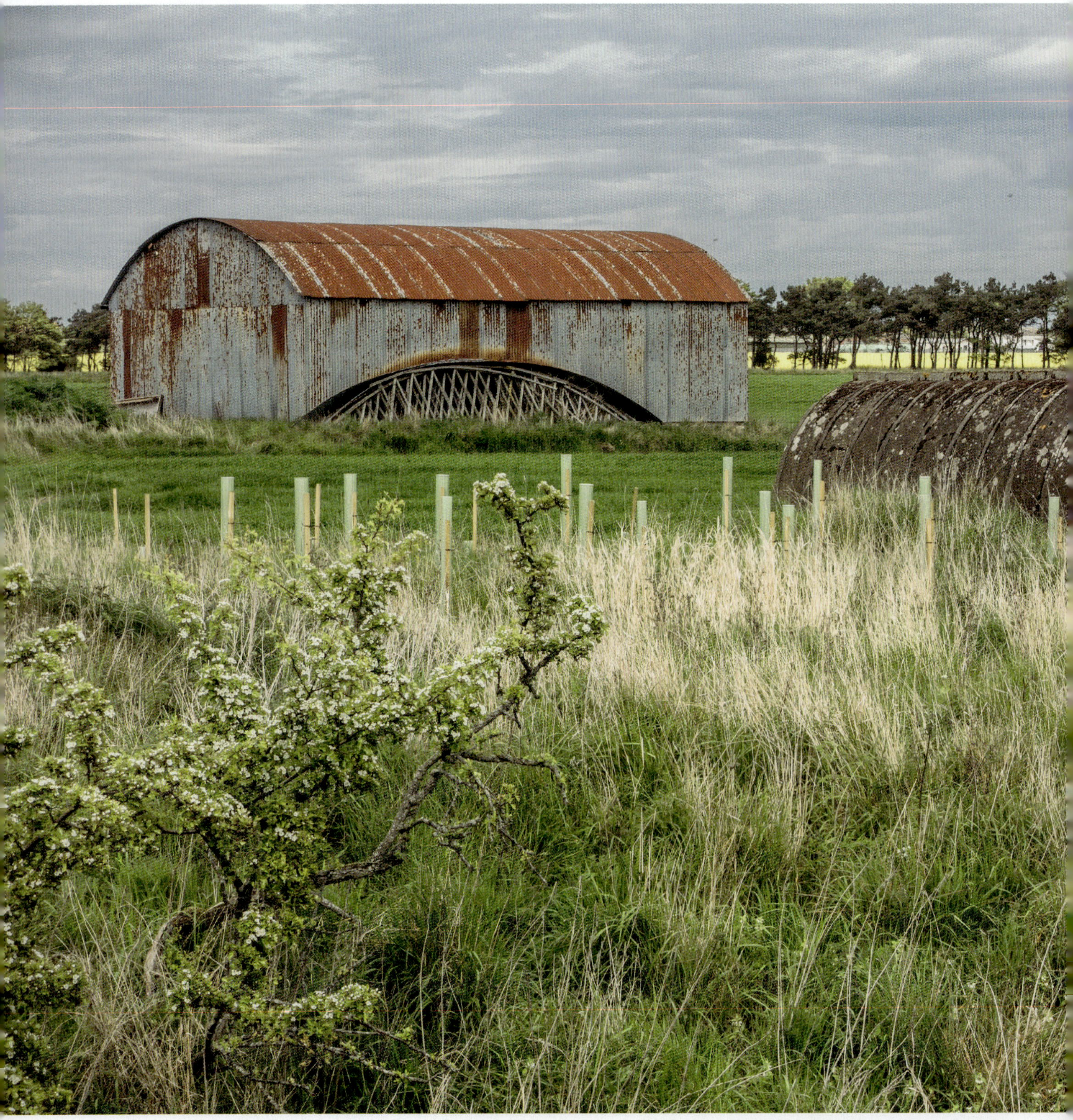

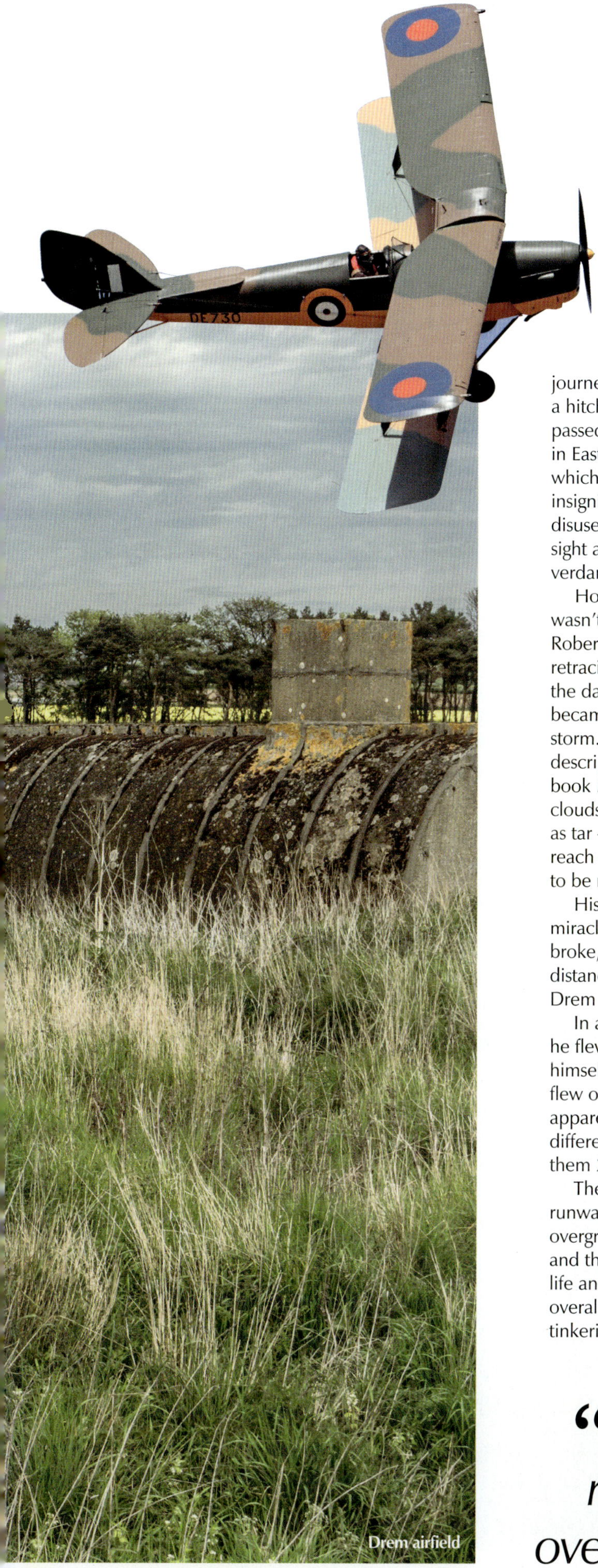

Drem airfield

IN 1935, RAF Air Marshal Sir Robert Victor Goddard returned from a trip between Andover and Edinburgh with a strange story to tell.

The pilot had completed the outgoing journey the previous day without a hitch. On his travels he had passed over the airfield at Drem in East Lothian – something which at the time had seemed insignificant. The dilapidated disused airfield was not a notable sight among the east coast's verdant scenery.

However, his return journey wasn't so straightforward. Sir Robert set off from Edinburgh, retracing the route he had flown the day before, but he soon became caught up in a peculiar storm. According to Sir Robert's description in his subsequent book *Flight Towards Reality*, the clouds appeared yellow and thick as tar – he flew upwards to try to reach clear sky, but they seemed to be never-ending.

His plane began to fall when a miracle occurred. The clouds broke, the sun shone and in the distance he could just about spot Drem airfield.

In an attempt to recalibrate, he flew towards the airfield to set himself back en route – but as he flew over the site it became apparent that things were very different to how he remembered them 24 hours before.

The cows that roamed the runways had vanished, the overgrown greenery was gone and the airfield was now full of life and industry. Men in blue overalls were hard at work, tinkering with planes the likes of which Sir Robert had never seen. Yellow aircraft dotted the runways and he was left bemused.

The pilot returned to Andover and felt compelled to regale his RAF colleagues with his bizarre story, which was met with disbelief. At the time, not only was Drem airfield disused, but the details of the story were baffling – RAF engineers sported tan overalls, not blue, and a yellow plane was certainly unheard of.

The final strange twist to the tale – by 1939 the scene that Sir Robert witnessed had become reality. The overalls were indeed changed to blue, the RAF began to paint their training planes yellow and the airfield at Drem was recommissioned.

Had the unsuspecting pilot experienced a time slip or was there a simple explanation for what he witnessed on that flight? That question remains unanswered, but Sir Robert certainly believed he was an inadvertent time traveller.

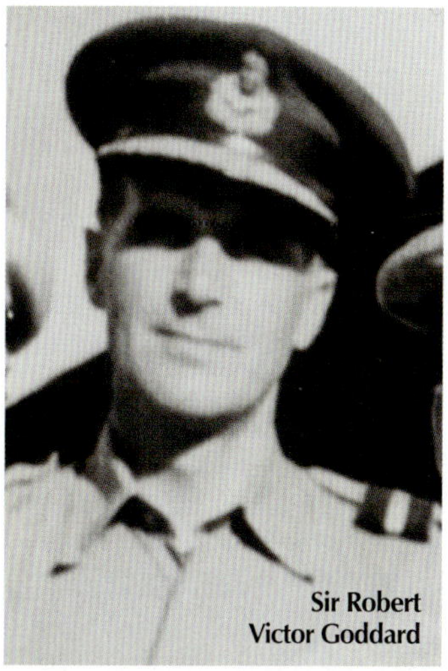

Sir Robert Victor Goddard

"The cows that roamed the runways had vanished, the overgrown greenery was gone"

Words: GEORGINA MCKENZIE-SMITH images: SHUTTERSTOCK, ALAMY

Route of Evil

Sad spirits, vanishing vehicles, evil beasties – is any road or track across Scotland unhaunted?

Ghost Train

Suspended just above the old Highland railway line, a phantom grey steam locomotive has been reported as appearing to lone travellers near Dunphail Station since at least the 1920s. Confident that the last train had long since departed, terrified walkers taking a shortcut along the tracks were suddenly forced to scramble up the embankment to escape as the fearsome engine bore down on them from nowhere, belching steam and sparks, yet with no driver on the footplate, and no passengers in the brightly lit carriages. Not even Dr Beeching's axe could stop the train, which continued to appear after the line was closed and broken up in 1965.

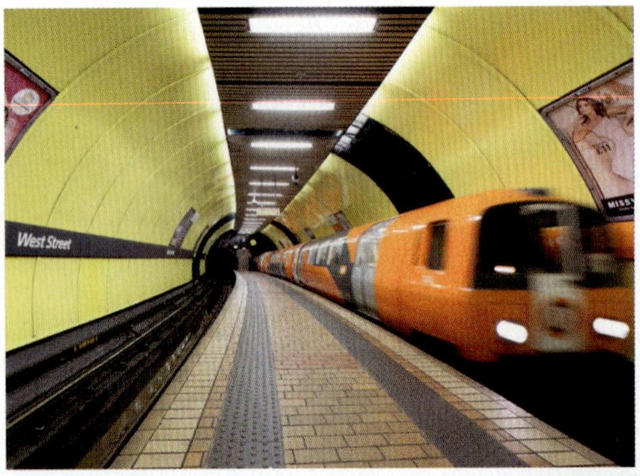
West Street

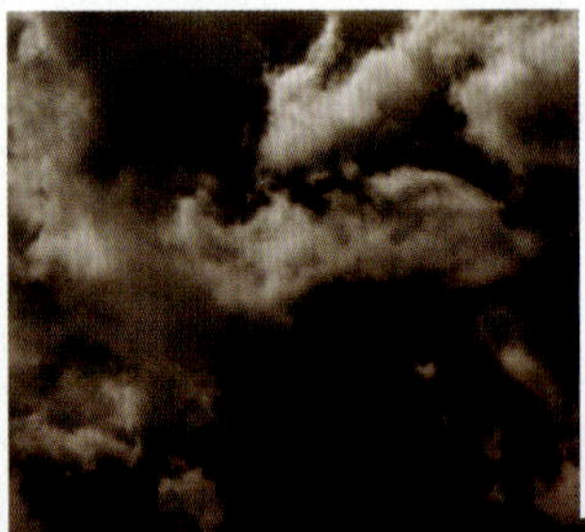

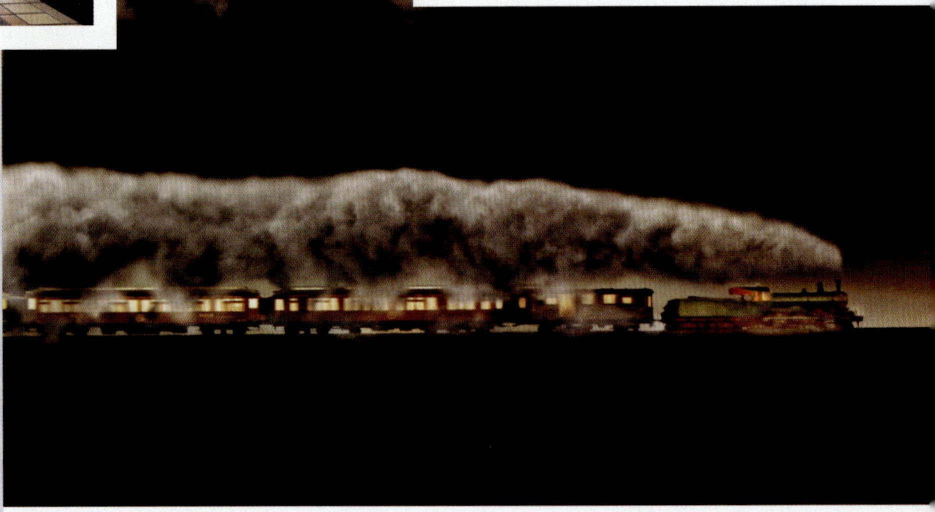

Going Underground

Down in Glasgow's subway stations at midnight, something stirs... A shivering figure hunched by West Street station is believed to be the ghost of Robert Cobble. The riches-to-rags local character was left blind after an attack while sleeping rough. He died of the cold outside the station in 1900.

At Shields Road, running footsteps may be heard on the platform as lights flicker. It's said to be the ghost of a girl who died on the tracks in 1922.

And north of the river, a beautiful woman in 1930s evening dress wanders the platform at Hillhead station, occasionally singing and laughing.

Words: MARION McGIVERN Pictures: SHUTTERSTOCK, ALAMY

"A ghostly, cowled monk roams the roads"

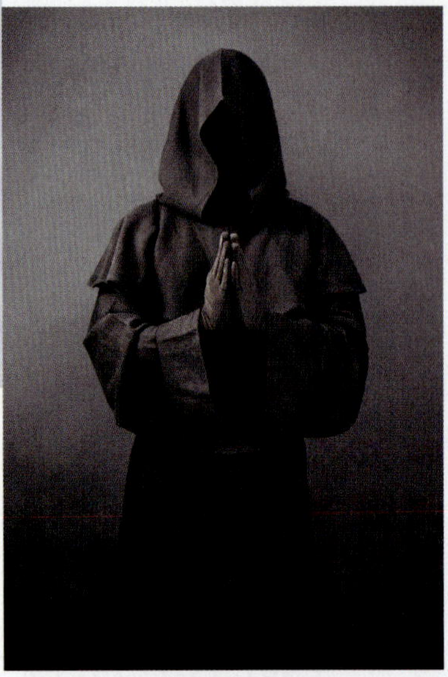

Oh, Brother

In Aberdeenshire, between Banchory and Crathes, a ghostly, cowled monk is reputed to roam the roads, sometimes emerging into traffic in front of unsuspecting motorists. Drivers have reported braking hard, sure of an impending collision, only to find the apparition dissolving into air just before impact.

There is speculation that the monk may have been associated with the college or "banchor" founded by St Ternan in the fifth century, remnants of which can still be seen in Banchory's old churchyard. There is no clue as to the identity of the unfriendly friar, though he does seem to have learned some dangerously bad habits.

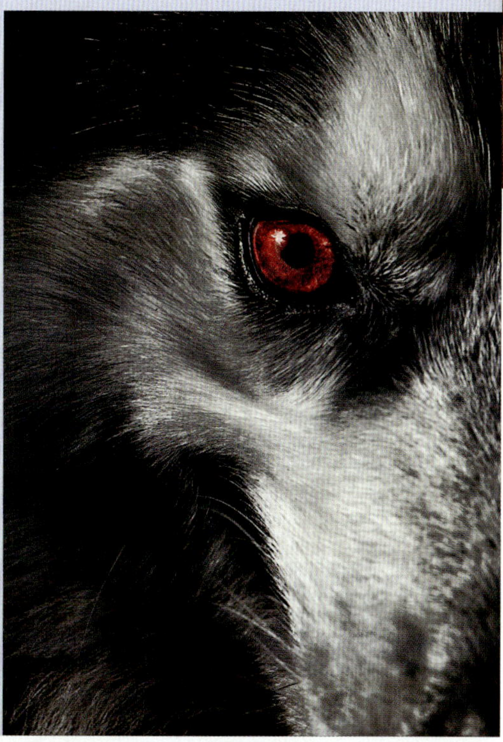

Aw, Shucks

A shuck, or to give it its Scottish name, cù sìth ("fairy dog") is a huge black canine (sometimes dark grey or dark green) with a shaggy coat and red eyes. They're found throughout Britain and Ireland.

While it's generally bad luck to meet one, what with their habit of presaging death, rarely they are said to guide lost travellers to safety. The scary kind prowl locations including the A93 north of Blairgowrie, the B7009 between Selkirk and Langholm and the A939 near Grantown.

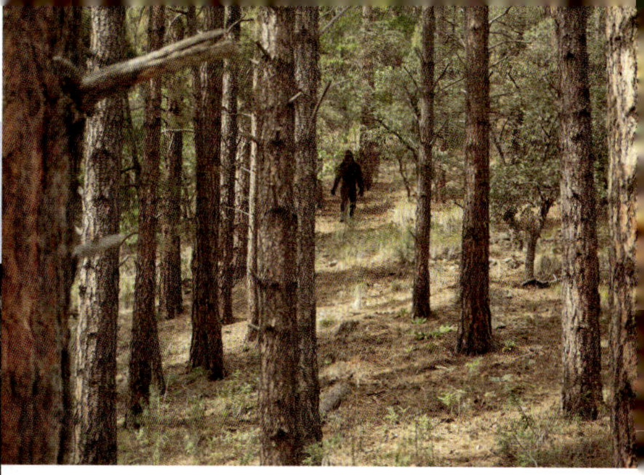

Not McYeti?

Bigfoot-seeking cryptozoologists usually locate their searches in the snows of the Himalayas or America's Pacific Northwest. Yet it would appear Tayside has its own version of the giant, ape-like creature, with sightings reported since the late 20th century.

After several appearances in Arbroath woodland, our McYeti seems to have favoured Dundee's A92. In 2005, a driver approaching the Five Roads Roundabout had to brake to avoid hitting a 2-metre (7ft), dark brown, hairy figure, which crossed the broad carriageway in three strides. In the same year, near the Tay Road Bridge, another driver reported that he had seen a giant, hairy man-like apparition in trees by the roadside.

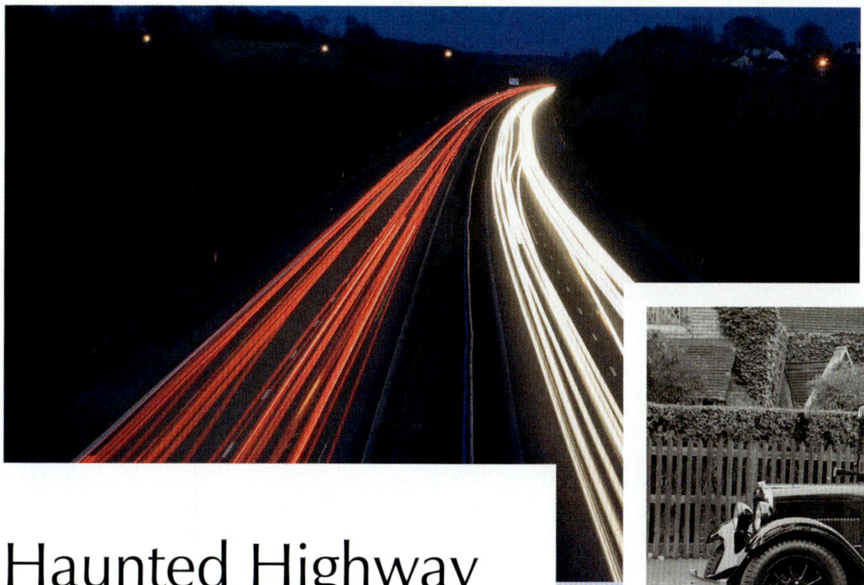

Haunted Highway

Take a deep breath and stay calm as you approach the A75 between Gretna and Dumfries. Known as Scotland's most haunted road, for years drivers have encountered myriad manifestations along its length, with the largest concentration in the notorious four-mile stretch known as the Kinmount straight.

Phantom animals, a wandering witch and an imminent head-on collision with a disappearing white van have all been reported by terrified motorists. Approaching Annan, be alert for pedestrians stepping out suddenly – several drivers claim to have struck a man wearing a red jumper and dark trousers, only to find no sign of anyone in the vicinity when they stopped to check.

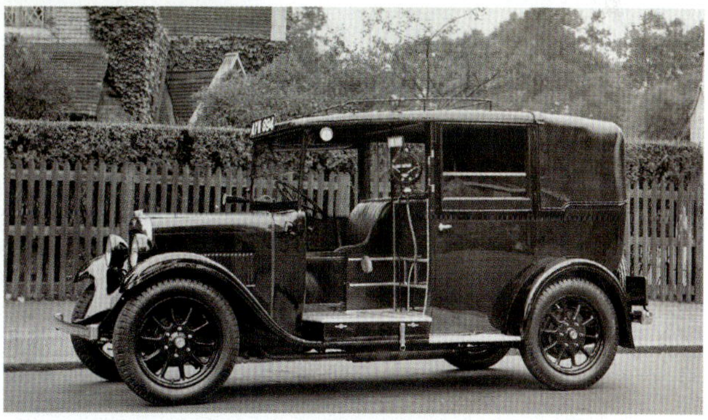

Austin Powers

Motorists on Skye are advised to stay alert on the roads by Sligachan. Drivers have warned of a speeding 1934 Austin approaching, lights blazing, only to vanish. The first incident was reported in 1941 when a doctor driving the then single-track road had to pull over to let the car pass... except it never arrived. A local policeman claimed a similar experience while other witnesses (apparently) included wildlife writer Seton Gordon, who wrote of his encounter in *The Scots Magazine* in 1959.

The Pittenweem Trials

Villagers imprisoned, tortured and killed over a teenager's accusation

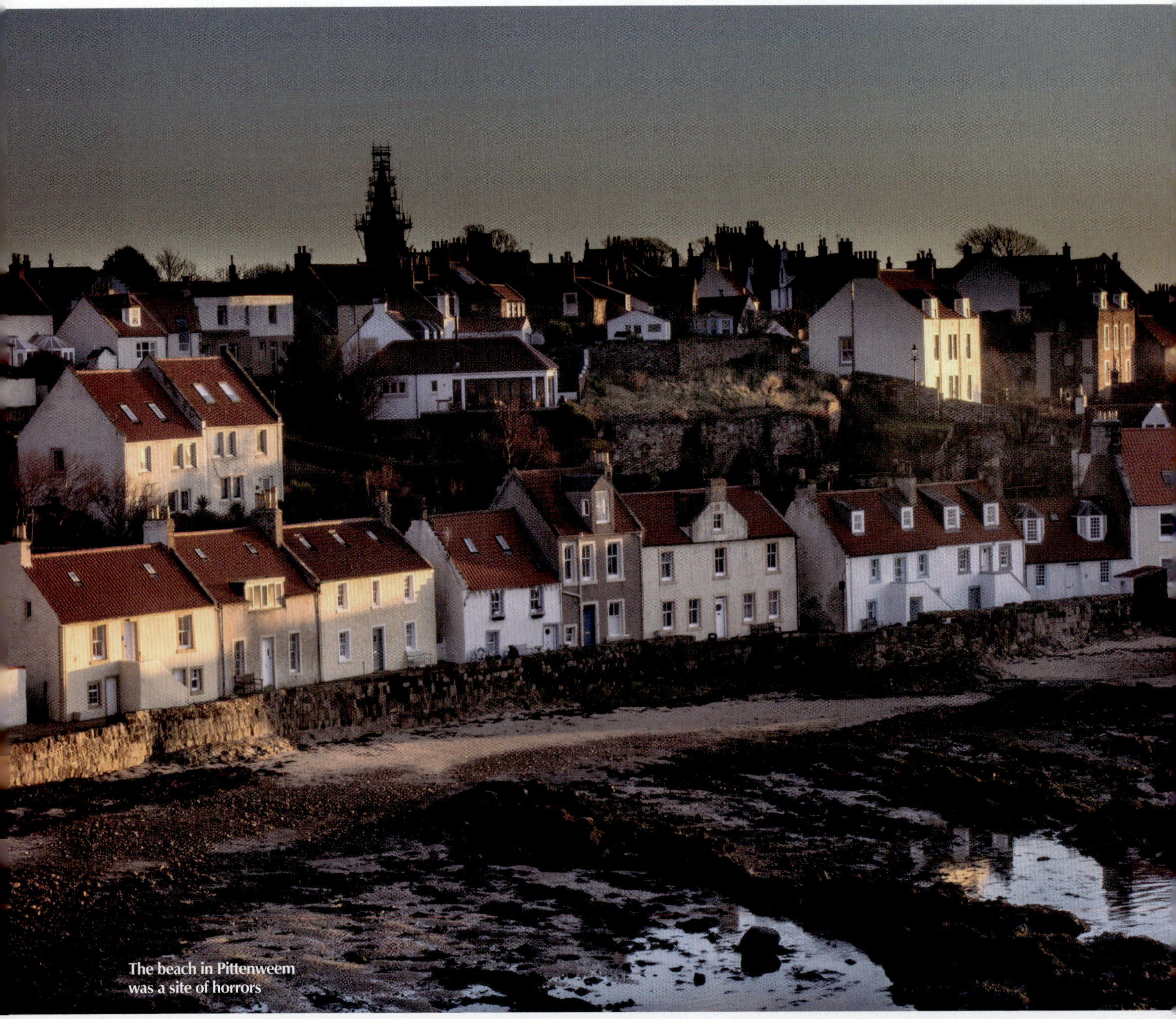

The beach in Pittenweem was a site of horrors

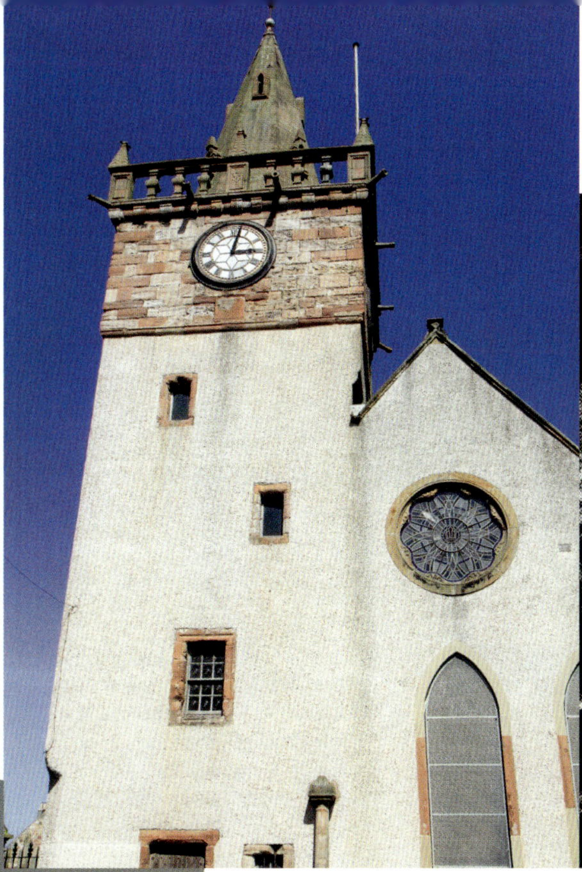

Left: Pittenweem Tolbooth

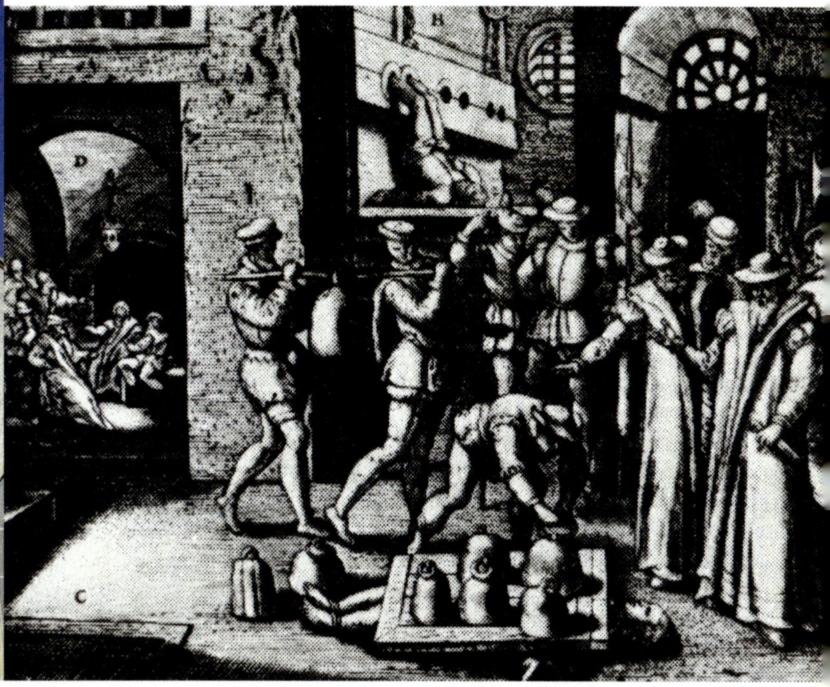

Below: *Peine forte et dure* torture

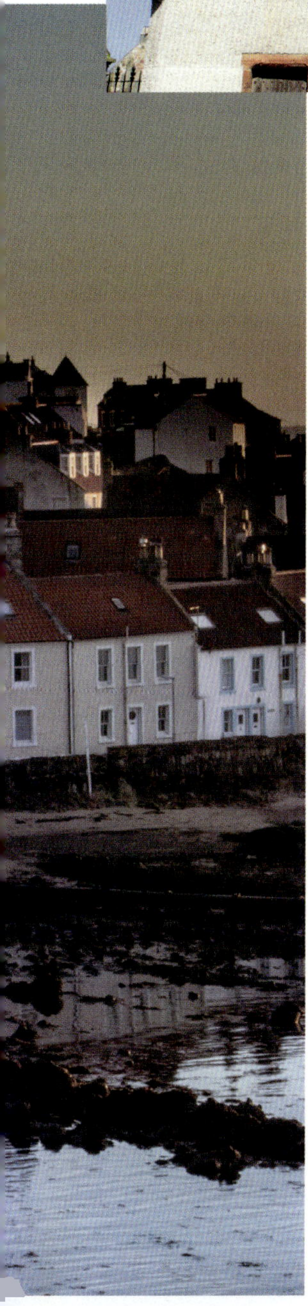

IN 1704 in Pittenweem, Fife, a 16-year-old apprentice blacksmith, Patrick Morton, was asked by his neighbour Beatrix Laing, to make some nails.

When Patrick cheekily replied that he was too busy, Beatrix walked off in a huff, furiously muttering something under her breath – presumably along the lines of "kids these days."

When Patrick became ill just a few days later, however, he suspected that Beatrix's mutterings were in fact a curse.

As his illness progressed he became convinced that she had cast a spell and was sending evil thoughts to torture him. He confided his worries to local minister Patrick Cowper, who persuaded the boy to report Beatrix to the authorities.

The minister, who must have been one nasty piece of work, also managed to convince the lad to accuse several other villagers along with Beatrix. No one thought to investigate the reasoning behind the boy's accusations and the suspected witches were imprisoned in Pittenweem Tolbooth.

Beatrix was confined to a dark cell for five months while subjected to horrific torture. On being released with a fine, she was chased out of town by the locals.

She found safety in nearby St Andrews, but she died alone shortly after her arrival.

Another of the accused, the elderly Thomas Brown starved to death in his cell. The Pittenweem witch case was eventually dismissed by the Privy Council in Edinburgh, but when one of the accused, Janet Cornfoot, escaped from prison, an angry mob seized her and dragged her down to Pittenweem Beach.

> *"An angry mob dragged her to the beach"*

Janet was pelted with stones, then covered by a door, which was weighed down by heavy boulders.

This method of torture, known as *peine forte et dure*, was also used to execute accused Giles Corey at the Salem Witch Trials just over a decade before.

When Janet had died, a horse and cart was driven over her repeatedly to make sure the devil's soul was squashed out of her and wouldn't return. Refused a Christian burial, her body was thrown into a communal grave with that of Thomas Brown at the spot in Pittenweem known as Witch Corner.

It was intended that when the rest of the accused were found guilty and burned at the stake, the bodies would be exhumed and thrown to the flames.

Thomas Brown's family and friends smuggled his body out of Witch Corner and reburied it in consecrated grounds. All the other accused were eventually freed, however, and the apprentice blacksmith Patrick Morton was later exposed as a liar.

Despite this, neither he nor the mob that killed Janet Cornfoot were ever brought to justice.

Words: DAWN GEDDES Images: SHUTTERSTOCK, ALAMY

The Queen of Witches

Confessions of flying, making potions and meeting with the devil

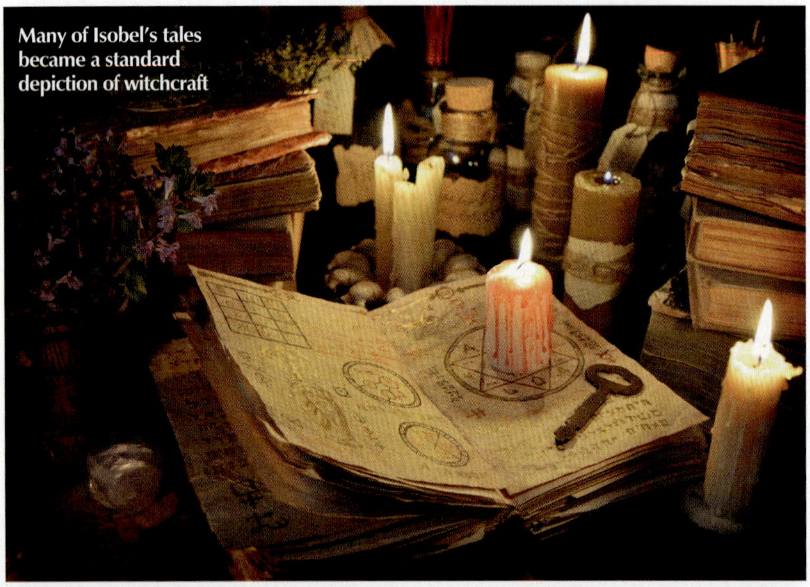
Many of Isobel's tales became a standard depiction of witchcraft

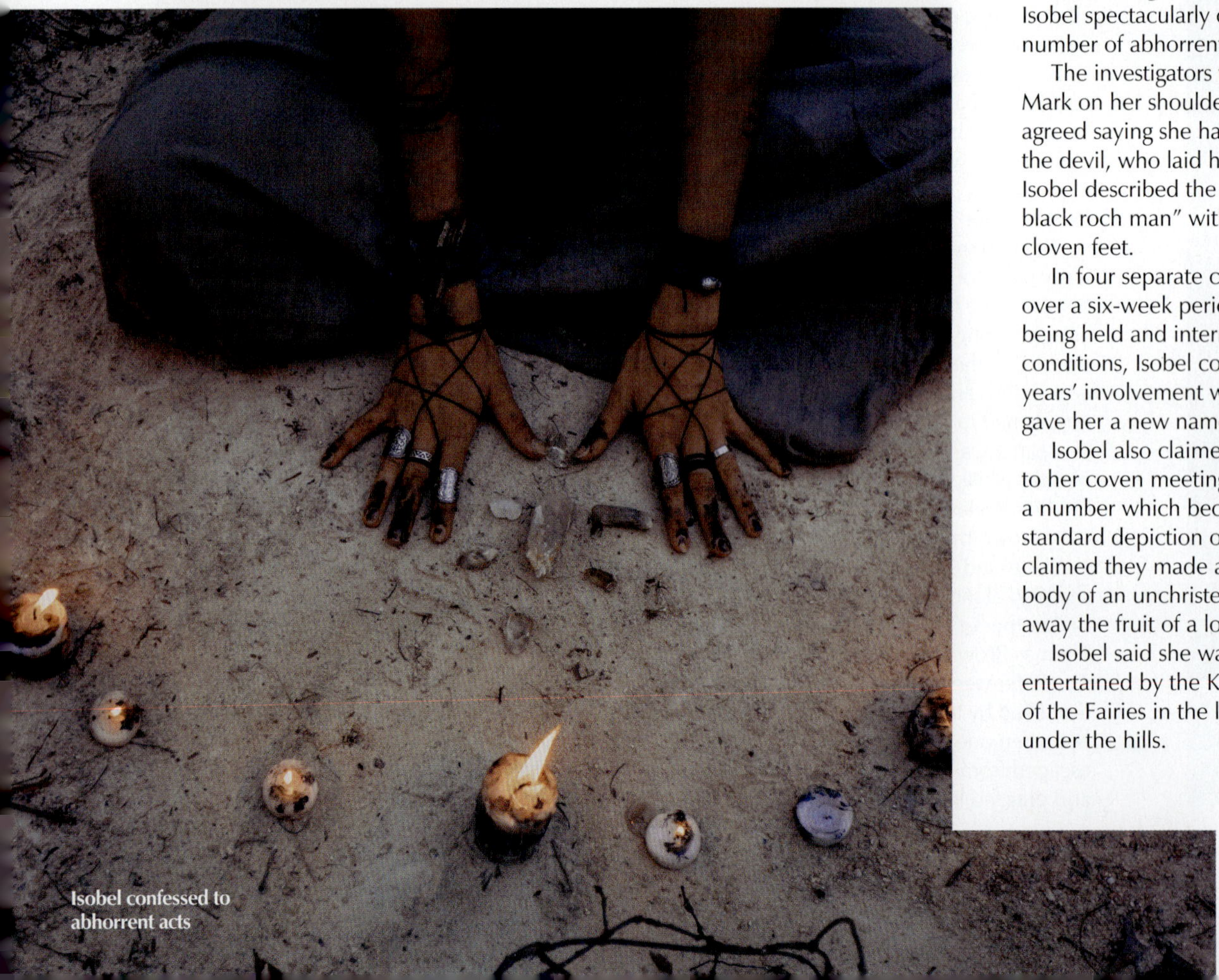
Isobel confessed to abhorrent acts

ISOBEL GOWDIE, a young housewife from Auldearn, Nairnshire, was one of Scotland's most infamous witches. While most of the evidence against her presented can now be easily dismissed as nonsense, Isobel's admissions during her trial in 1662 started the myths that still surround witches today.

Isobel and her husband led an unremarkable life in the area around Loch Loy, just north of Auldearn. Isobel was illiterate, and spent her days doing basic household chores and tasks such as milking, making bread, and weaving.

It is unclear how Isobel first came to trial, but it is thought that the local minister Harry Forbes, a zealous extremist who feared witches, accused her of conspiring against him.

After being accused of witchcraft, Isobel spectacularly confessed to a number of abhorrent acts.

The investigators found the Devil's Mark on her shoulder, and Isobel agreed saying she had been baptised by the devil, who laid his mark on her. Isobel described the devil as a "meikle black roch man" with forked and cloven feet.

In four separate confessions given over a six-week period, no doubt while being held and interrogated in dreadful conditions, Isobel confessed to 15 years' involvement with the devil, who gave her a new name – Janet.

Isobel also claimed to be able to fly to her coven meetings, a group of 13 – a number which became absorbed into standard depiction of witchcraft. She claimed they made a potion with the body of an unchristened child to take away the fruit of a local farmer's corn.

Isobel said she was regularly entertained by the King and Queen of the Fairies in the land of the elves under the hills.

"The investigators found the Devil's Mark on her shoulder"

The transcripts of her confessions feature many inclusions of "et cetera" which cut short her lengthy monologues of fantasy, suggesting even the witchfinders were unsure of her stories.

The source of Isobel's tales have been debated over the years. Many believe Isobel was mentally ill, while others speculate that she created the tales based on folklore of the time as a way of avoiding further questioning.

On April 10, 1662, the Privy Council in Edinburgh issued a proclamation prohibiting torture being used as a means of securing confessions from witches – unless it was specifically authorised by the Council.

Although probably imprisoned for the six-week duration of her confessions, it would appear that Isobel spoke freely without being under duress.

The Council advised she should be found guilty only if the confessions had been volunteered without torture, that they were sane and without a wish to die.

Whatever the real story, Isobel's fantastical confessions earned her the nickname the Queen of Scottish Witches, and although subsequent records have been lost, it is presumed that she was burned at the stake shortly after her trial.

Many Christian authorities considered witchcraft a post-Christian Satanic cult – rather than the surviving religion of pre-Christian Europe – and Isobel's confessions about the devil helped them start a new wave of persecutions in Scotland during the reign of Charles II.

Many characteristics we associate with witches today come from Isobel's detailed, spectacular and inexplicable confessions.

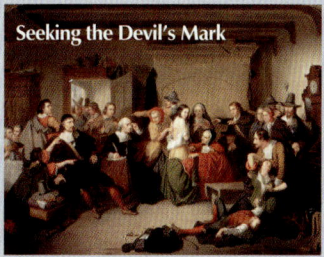

Isobel was likely burned at the stake after her trial

The Devil's Mark

SEARCHING for the Devil's Mark – also known as the Witches' Mark – was one of the many ways witch-hunters convinced themselves, and the jury, that they had found their prey. Those accused of witchcraft had their bodies scrutinised for such marks, which would then be pricked to test if they were sensitive.

If no pain was felt or the wound did not bleed, their abusers took it to mean they had caught a witch.

Seeking the Devil's Mark

To add to the humiliation, this was usually carried out in front of a crowd of braying onlookers, and the women were often shaved from head to toe. Eyelids, armpits and private places were inspected, and if the alleged witch happened to have no blemishes, the accusers were undeterred. They simply said that the devil had left an invisible mark, and so they pricked her all over with a pin until they found a tough area of skin that didn't bleed.

Some believed that the devil created each mark with his claws or a hot iron. Others thought he licked his followers, and the contact would leave a mysterious blemish.

Except, of course, these were not mysterious blemishes but moles, skin tags, birthmarks or scars – but to the hunters, they were irrefutable proof they had caught a witch.

Words: DAWN GEDDES Images: SHUTTERSTOCK

Scotland's Last Witch

The trial of the "Blitz Witch" Helen Duncan caused a stir during the Second World War

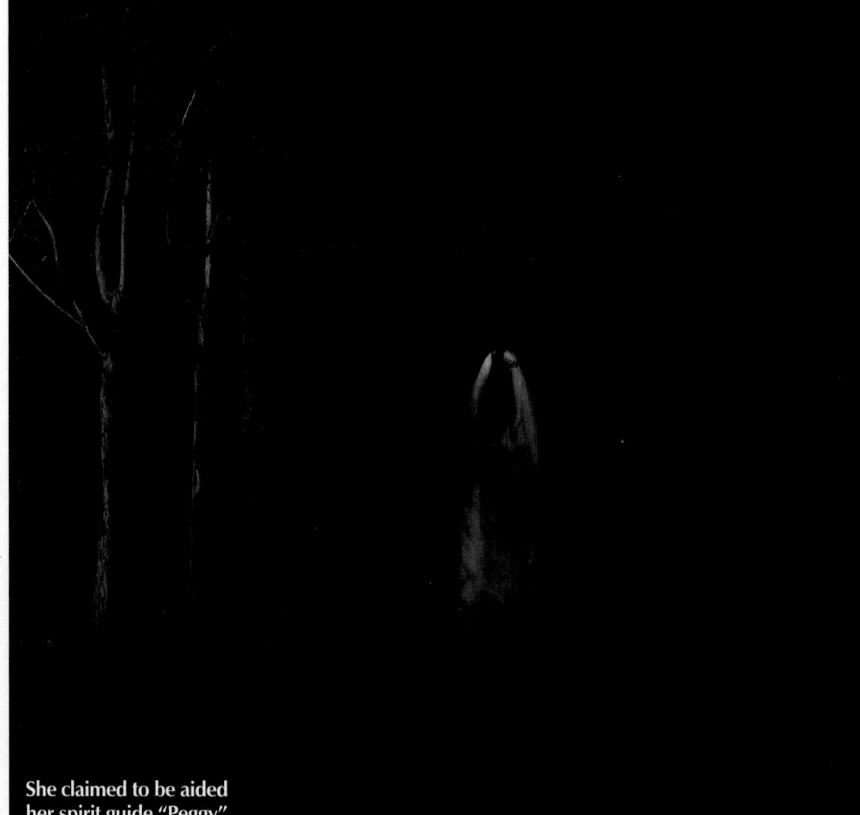

Communing with spirits

ACROSS Scotland you'll find monuments to victims of witch hunts that saw thousands jailed and put to death over two centuries.

Janet Horne was the last woman executed for witchcraft in Britain in 1727 (see right), but the Witchcraft Act wasn't abolished until the 1950s and before this there was to be one final victim.

Helen Duncan was the last "witch" imprisoned in the UK over government fears she might reveal military secrets during the Second World War. Born in Callander in 1897, Helen Duncan's dark prophecies to classmates earned her the nickname "Hellish Nell". She worked at Dundee Royal Infirmary and married war veteran Henry, who supported her psychic endeavours. In the 1920s, she began holding séances for extra money to feed their six children.

Aided by her spirit guide, Peggy, spirits manifested as ectoplasm spewing from Helen's mouth. The London Spiritualist Alliance investigated in 1931 and found the ectoplasm to be made of paper, cheesecloth and egg.

Some apparitions had faces fashioned from magazine covers. In 1933, police were called when it was discovered that "Peggy" was a white vest.

She claimed to be aided her spirit guide "Peggy"

Helen was fined £10 for fraud, but despite this, the war was a busy time for her. Families of soldiers killed in battle attended her séances in the hope of contact. At one meeting in Portsmouth in 1941, she claimed to have spoken to a sailor named Sid who drowned when *HMS Barham* sank in the Mediterranean.

The Navy were alarmed – the sinking hadn't been announced. The 862 men aboard perished, but relatives were asked to keep quiet to help morale.

From then on, Helen was on the radar. A lieutenant attending a séance in 1944 was outraged when she conjured up the spirits of his dead aunt and sister. Helen was arrested. The trial of the "Blitz Witch" caused a stir in London. She was sentenced to nine months in Holloway under the Witchcraft Act of 1735, where she became popular for séances in her cell. Her sentence was harsh, due perhaps to wartime paranoia; even Winston Churchill sent a memo to the home secretary calling her charge "obsolete tomfoolery".

It's a tale more heretic than heroic, but her case led to the abolition of the Witchcraft Act in 1951 and campaigners are still calling for Helen to be pardoned.

Helen Duncan

Words: LAURA BROWN Images: SHUTTERSTOCK

Suspicion And Speculation

JANET HORNE lived in Dornoch with her daughter, who was born with a disability affecting the shape of her hands and feet.

Her neighbours gossiped about the lone elderly woman, speculating that her daughter's feet looked just like hooves.

They accused poor Janet of turning the young woman into a pony so that she could ride her through the countryside carrying out the work of the devil.

Janet and her daughter were swiftly arrested and tried for the crime of witchcraft.

Captain David Ross, sheriff-depute of Sutherland, quickly found both women guilty, and sentenced them to death by burning the next day.

Fortunately, the younger woman managed to escape, but poor Janet was tarred and feathered then paraded through the streets of Dornoch to her execution.

The elderly woman, who is now thought to have been suffering from dementia, warmed her hands by the very flames that were waiting to consume her.

She smiled and called them "a bonny blaze".

This was 1727, and the methods that had been used to confirm the guilt of thousands of witches began to be scrutinised and rejected. Janet was the last to be executed for the crime of witchcraft, and the law was eventually completely abolished in 1736.

In Dornoch today there is a stone marker, erected in the 1900s, in the spot where Janet met her end.

Although the days of burning accused witches at the are thankfully long over, it's important that we never let the mistakes of our past slip far from our minds.

The Scottish witch trials may just be one chilling chapter in our country's great history, but while we continue to live in a world where suspicion, speculation and gossip can easily escalate into fear and terror, the mistakes of our past will never truly leave us.

Below: A stone memorial to Janet in Dornoch

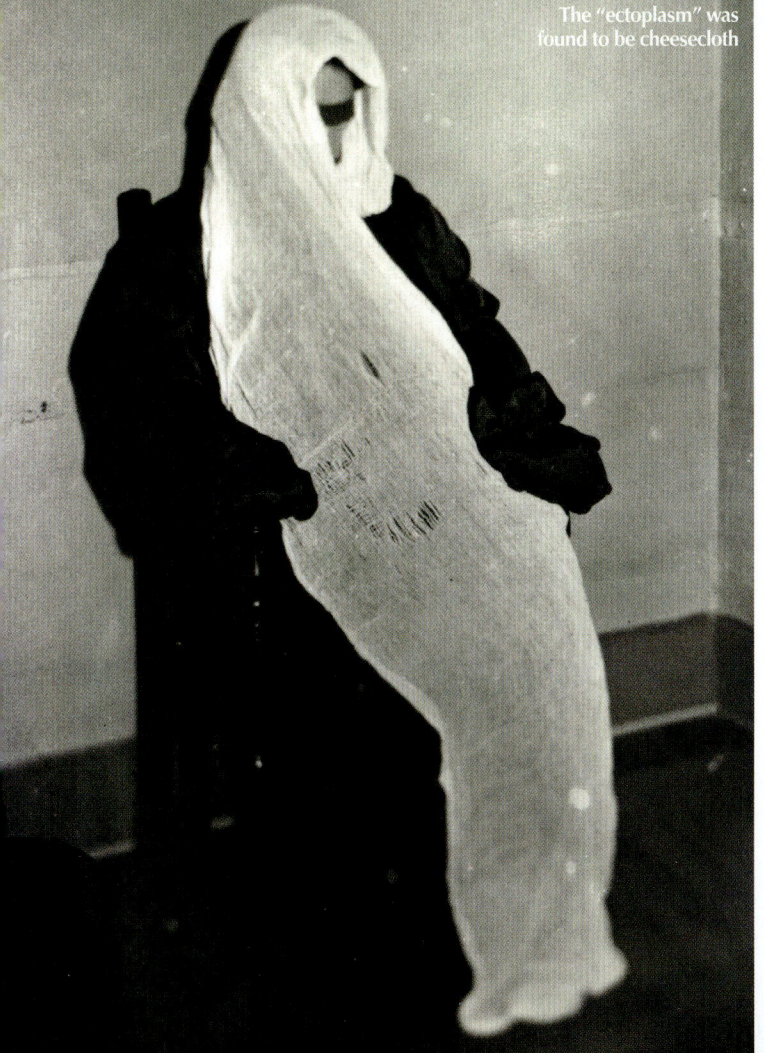

The "ectoplasm" was found to be cheesecloth

> "The mistakes of our past will never truly leave us"

Séances were popular during the war

Supernatural Scotland 59

Tales From The Vault

A few ghoulish east coast stories from the 19th-century archives...

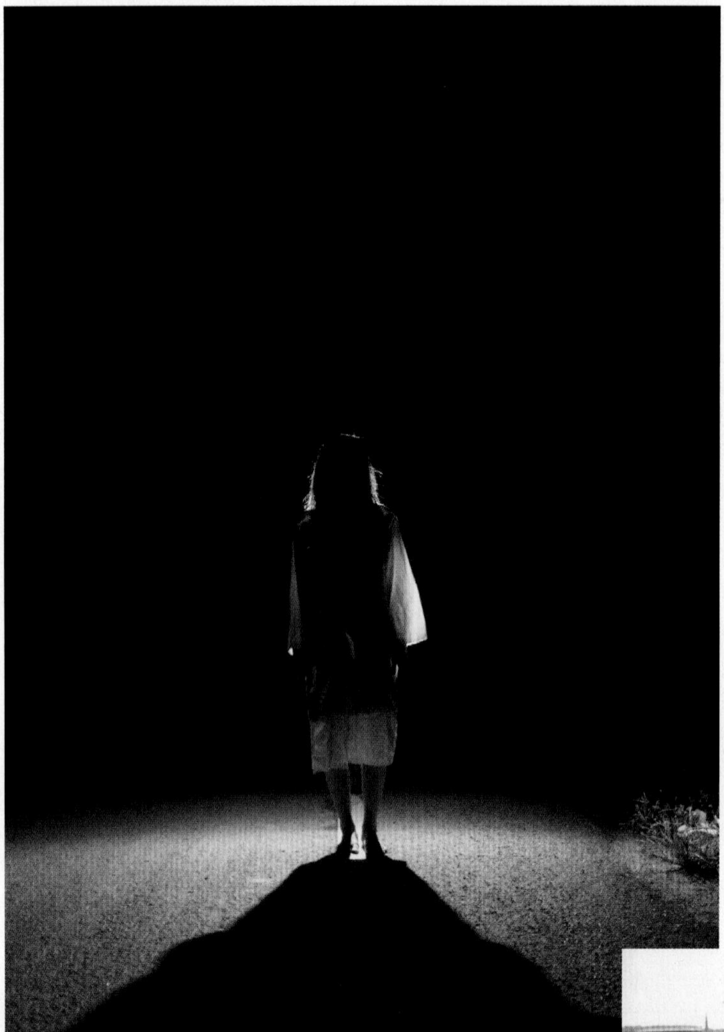
The gliding spectre dressed in white...

Words: CHRIS FERGUSON Images: SHUTTERSTOCK, DC THOMSON

GHOSTS were a dreadful scourge in the east of Scotland during the 19th century. They'd leap and glide, terrify residents and disappear into graveyards in blue flashes. Others banged on walls, frightened factory girls or appeared as illuminated, disembodied faces in trees on country roads.

In the cold, ghastly light of a May dawn in 1869, Dundee police officers encountered a gliding spectre with a face so awful they would not describe it.

The haunting began in Hilltown an hour before dawn while street lamps were unlit. In the gloom, a constable saw in the distance a tall, thin figure clad in white moving rapidly towards him.

The brave officer resolved to see what this awful thing could be and stood his ground.

He said, "This ghost did not even condescend to walk, as ghosts usually do – it did not touch the ground, as feet it appeared to have none."

The policeman's shriek was heard by his brother officers who witnessed the ghost on its journey down Murraygate, High Street and Reform Street.

A witness saw it disappear into the Howff Cemetery in a blue flash.

The spooks were at it in Fife, too. Factory

"The haunting began in Hilltown an hour before dawn"

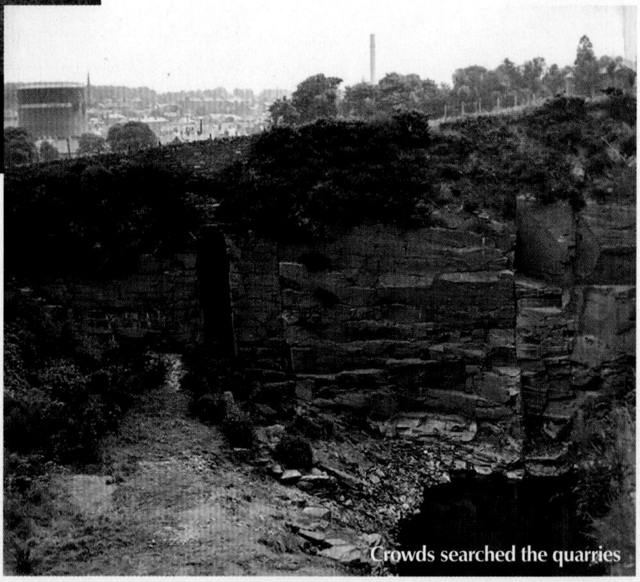
Crowds searched the quarries

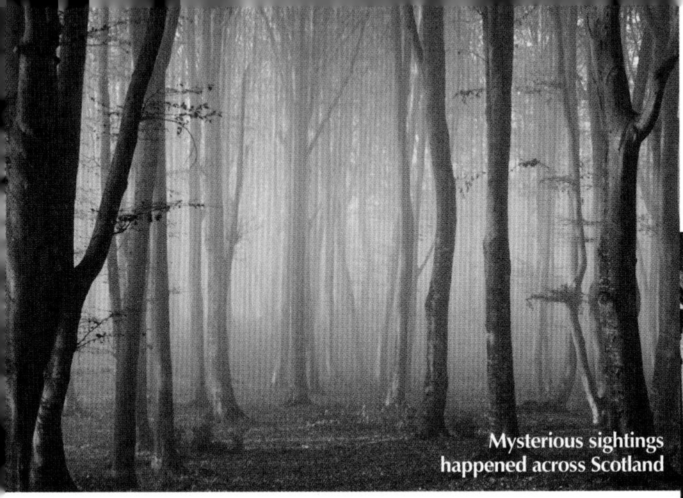

Mysterious sightings happened across Scotland

Below: Dundee's Hilltown

Bottom: The Hilltown clock

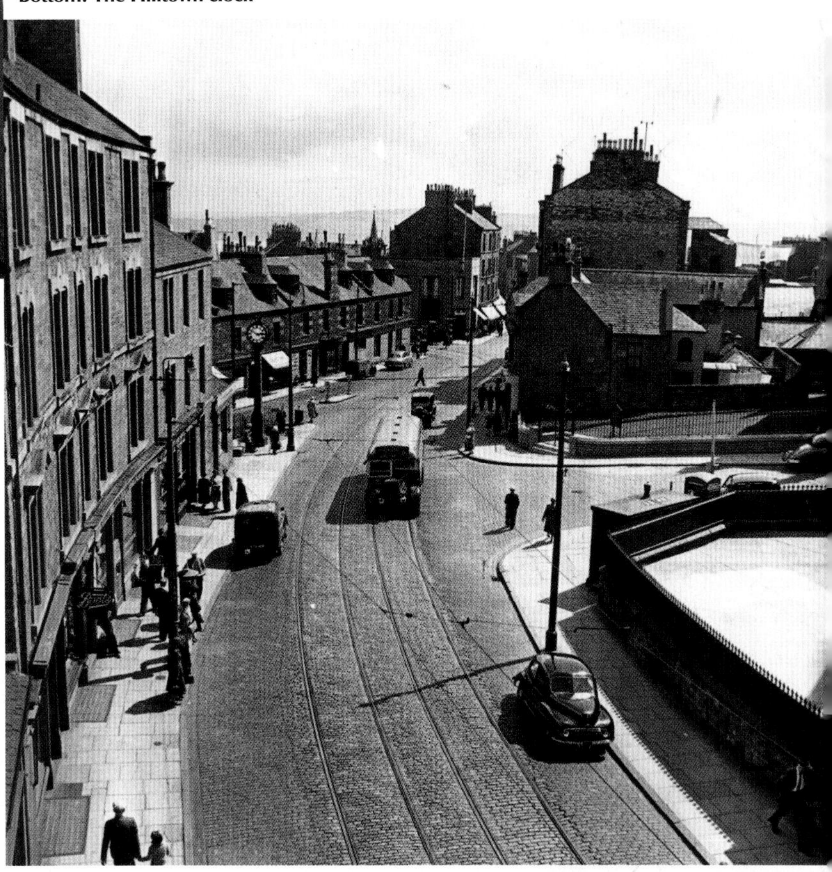

girls in Kirkcaldy were scared witless in 1875 by an eight-foot-tall ghost, dressed all in white, with an "ugly visage".

The ghost would apparently spring instead of walk.

In 1895, police investigated a spirit-rapping mystery in a grocer's shop in Market Street, Perth.

The owner put up with the phenomenon for a fortnight before calling the police. By this time, word had spread, and crowds gathered nightly to try to hear the spine-chilling knocking.

A force of police officers, the city's fire chief and a minister were drafted in. Holes were bored in the solid stone walls of the building, but nothing was found.

Inquiries moved to an internal cause and a 12-year-old girl in the house was found to be the culprit. She had used a knife handle to knock on the wall behind her bed.

In Arbroath, a violent ghost tried to interfere with the Royal Mail. In 1883, William Farquharson was driving the night mail-gig past Hercules Den on his way to Guthrie when a ghost, dressed in white, stood in his path.

Farquharson threatened the apparition, who replied by throwing a large stone at the driver. A few miles on, he encountered the ghost sitting on the road on Legaston Brae. This time, however, it leapt a dyke into a field.

It seems that the ghosts of today have stopped wearing white sheets...

When the locals reach for their pitchforks and torches, you know there will be trouble ahead. An angry mob gripped by mass hysteria strikes fear into even the bravest.

So imagine the terror of residents of Dalkeith Road in Dundee when a mob of 5,000 descended on their quiet street in 1927.

The peace of a late September Tuesday evening was shattered by the crowd armed with torches and a searchlight, determined to dish out justice to a ghost.

One or two ringleaders fired up the crowd with tales of the spook.

It had been seen riding a white pony in a field by a youth returning from church one evening.

Others had spotted it legging it through Craigie Quarries and down Dalkeith Road. The crowd raked around the quarries, streets and fields for about five hours but failed to catch the spectre.

Throughout the evening some left the crowd and others joined, so the total number chasing the ghost could have been closer to 10,000.

The Craigie ghost bore similarities to Dundee's gliding ghoul of 1869.

This thin figure with horrifying features was chased down Hilltown by police in dawn's cold light.

They tracked it along Murraygate, High Street and Reform Street but it disappeared into the Howff in a blue flash.

In Lochee, in 1906, residents were afraid to leave their homes because of a ghost.

A girl of 20 came across the awful vision on Perrie Street. It was dressed in white and its hat was ablaze with light. As the breeze blew the folds in its garments aside, it disclosed vestments of flaming red.

Across in Downfield that same week, residents called a council of war when a phosphorescent ghost got up to high jinks near the tennis courts.

It showed up just as they were getting ready for bed but they quickly formed a task force armed with sticks and bludgeons.

They tracked the ghost down to a field but as they closed in, it slipped into Camperdown Woods.

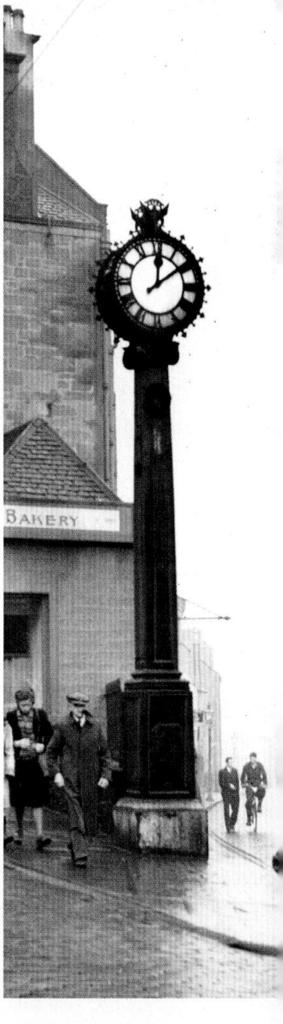
BAKERY

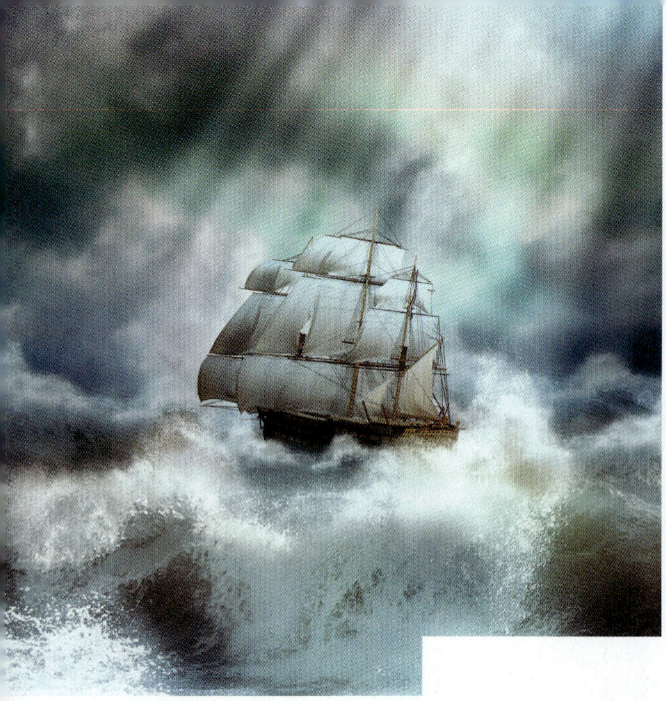

Seven Years

Breaking a mirror will result in seven years of bad luck. It is thought that this goes back to the belief that your reflection represented your soul, and shattering a mirror would shatter your soul.

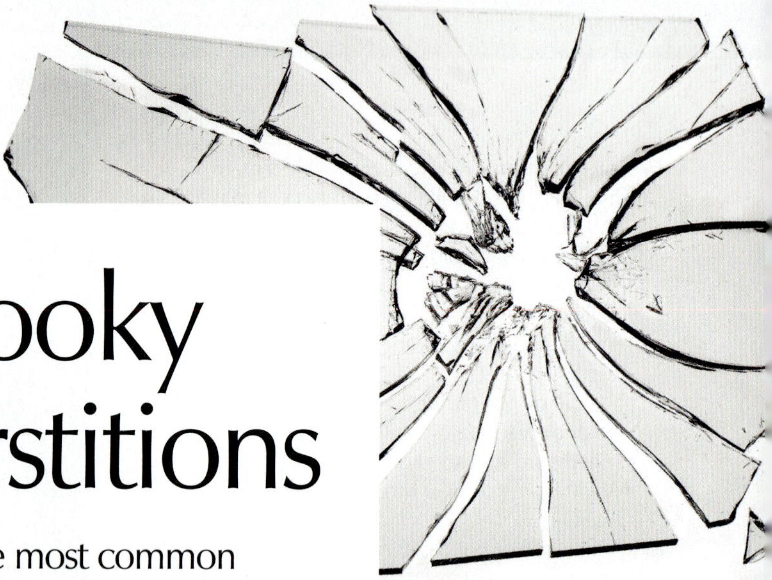

Spooky Superstitions

Some of the most common beliefs in Scotland

Women And Ships

Having a woman aboard was believed to bring storms down on the ship.

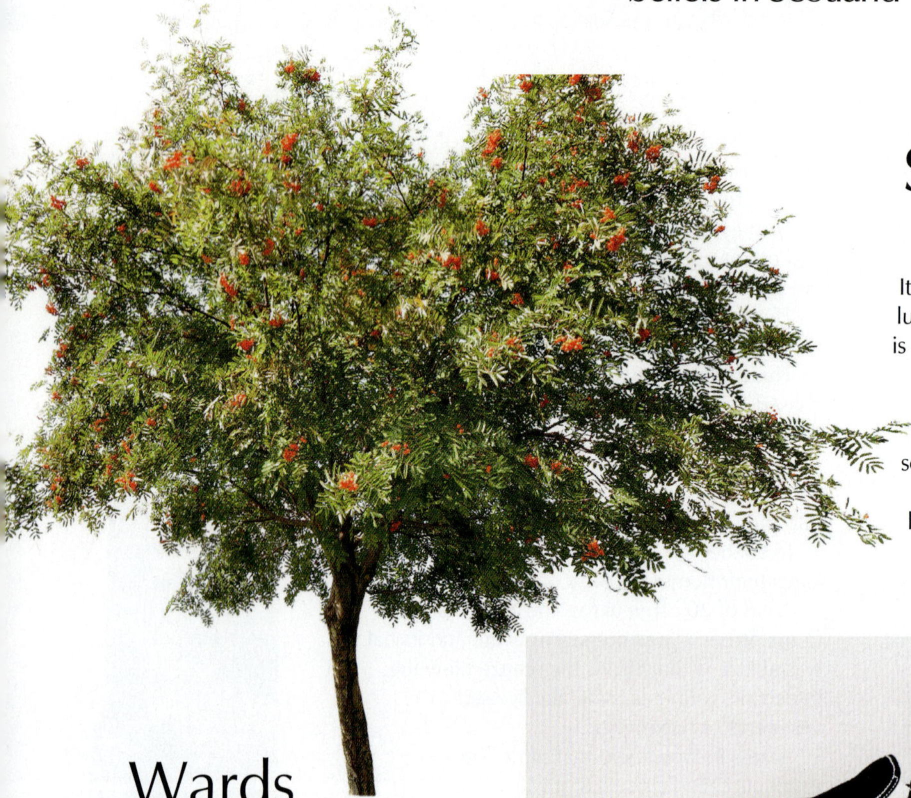

Spilling Salt

It is considered bad luck to spill salt as it is an invitation to let the devil in. To cancel the invite, however, throw some over your left shoulder. This will keep the devil and bad luck away.

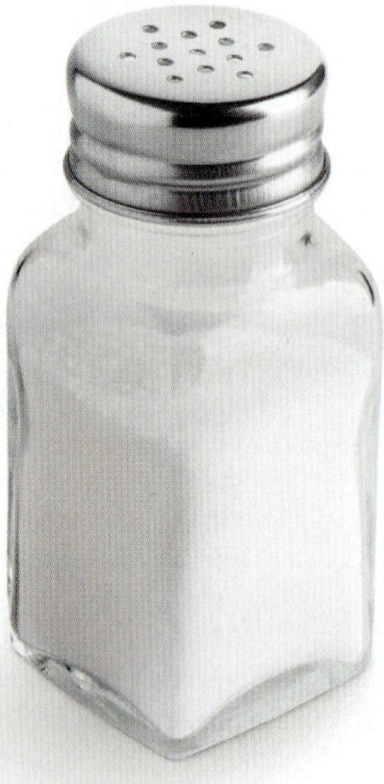

Wards Against Evil

There are many devices believed to ward off witches but the rowan tree is a particular favourite and planting one in your garden is believed to provide protection against witches.

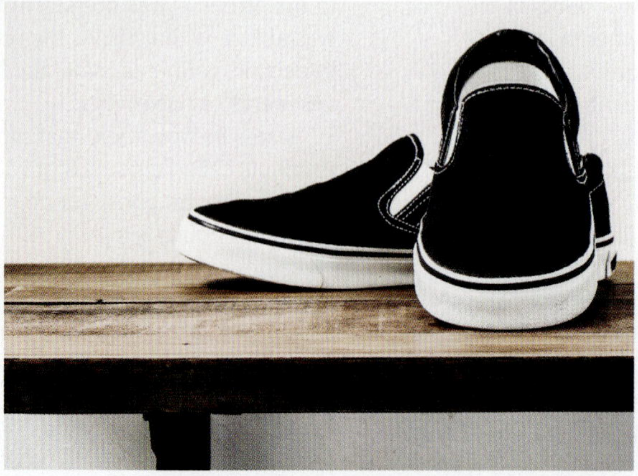

New Shoes

A pair of new shoes must never be placed on a table. This superstition is thought to come from mining communities – the shoes of a dead miner would be placed on the table in reverence.

Monsters & Creatures

Steel yourself for these terrifying tales of vampires and sea beasts, mountain marauders and UFOs...

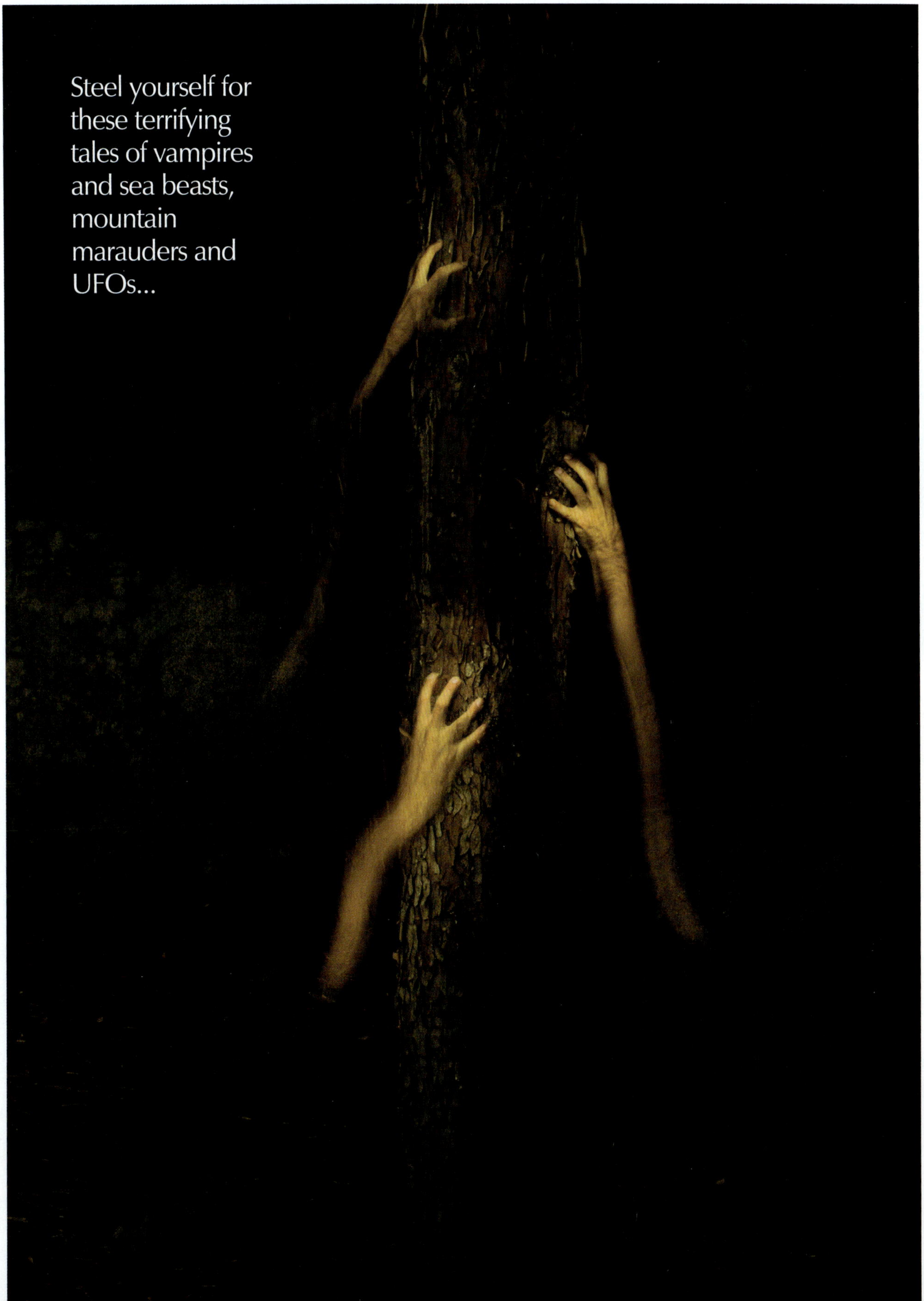

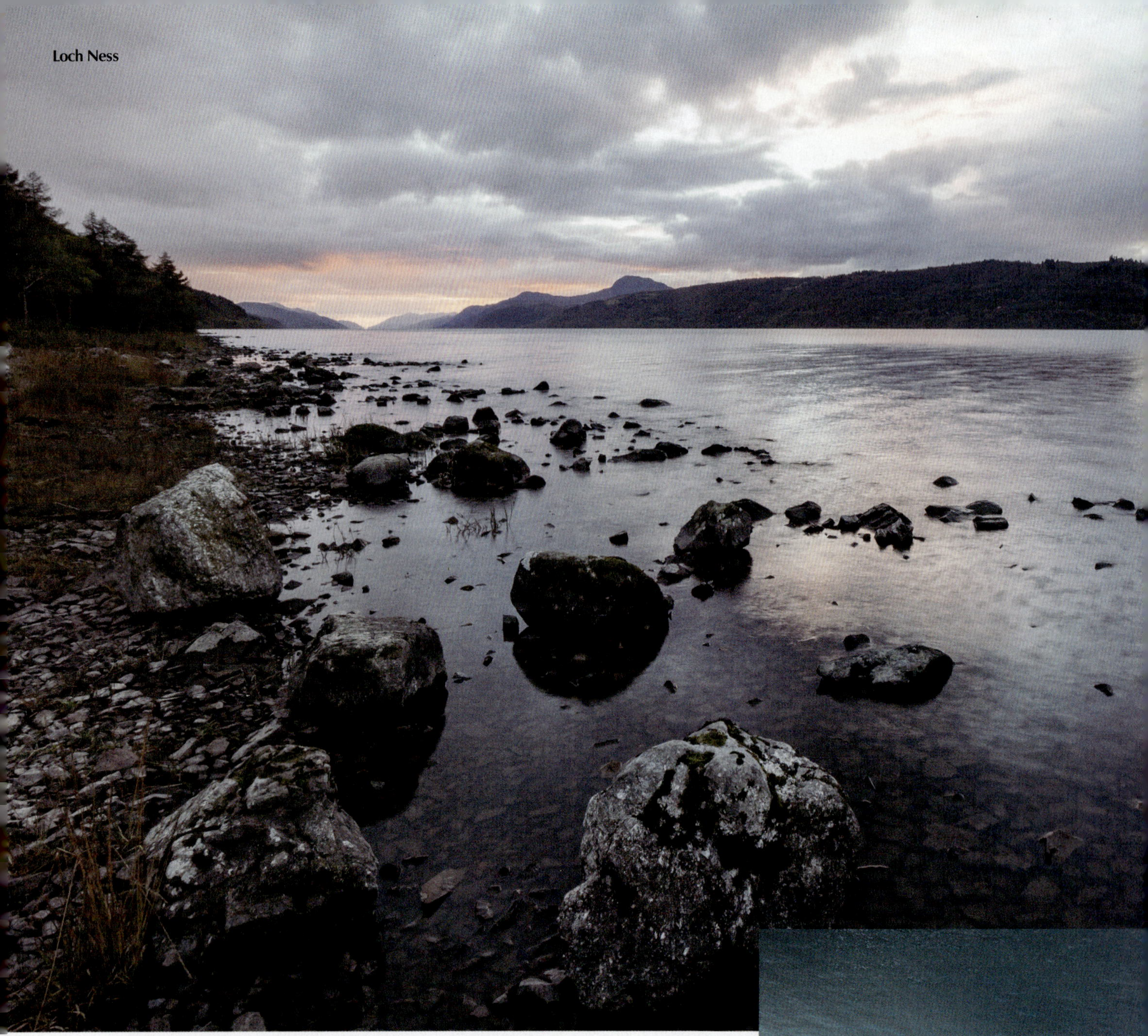

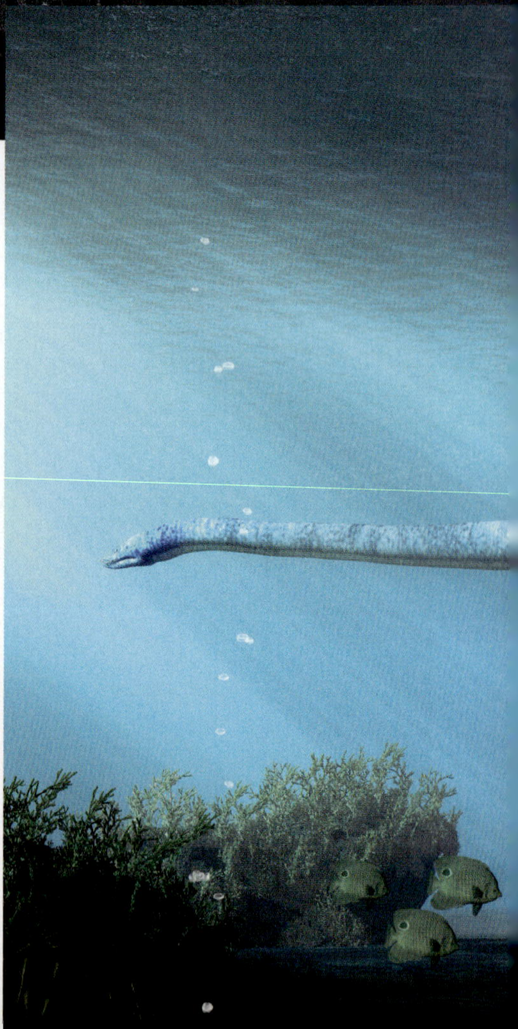

The Loch Ness Monster

Scotland's most famous monster still draws tourists from the world over

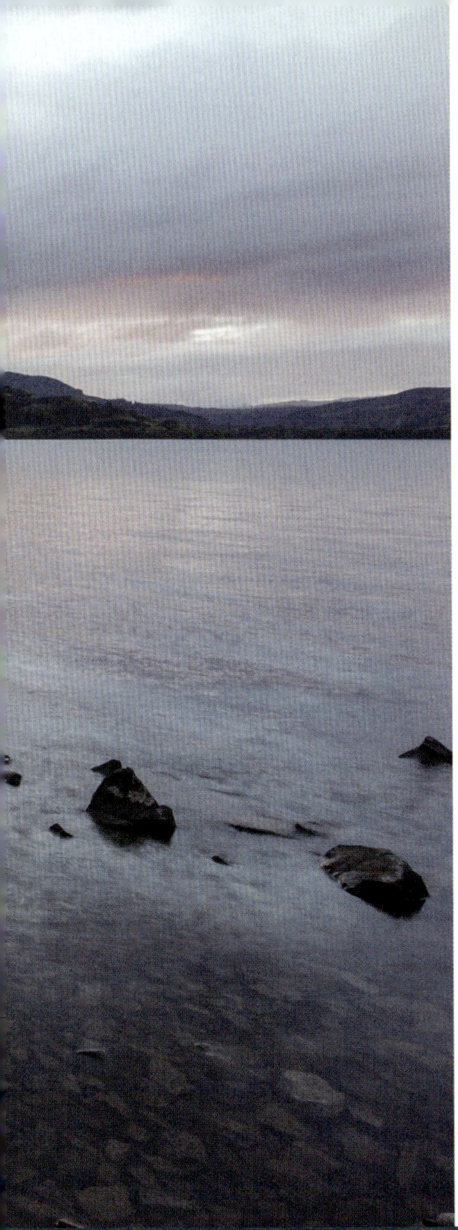

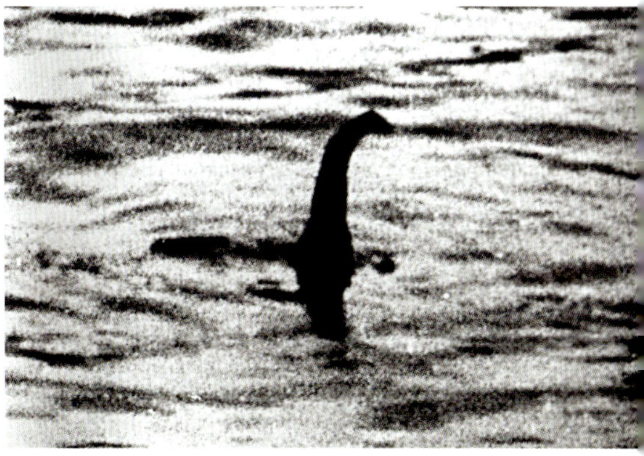

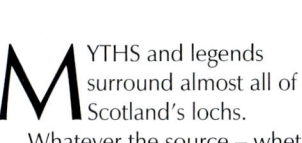

The famous 1934 photo

MYTHS and legends surround almost all of Scotland's lochs.

Whatever the source – whether it's the mist that clings to the glens and filled the imagination, ancient folklore passed down through generations, or real creatures lurking in the deeps – the tales make for fascinating reading.

Most popular of these myths, and most famous around the world, are the stories surrounding Scotland's largest loch, Loch Ness in the Highlands, and of Nessie, the monster who is said to inhabit it.

Rumours of sightings have been reported for centuries, all the way back to Adomnán's account of St Columba who is said to have seen the creature in AD 565.

Eye-witnesses often describe her – yes, the general consensus is that Nessie is a she – as large in size with a long neck and one or more humps protruding from the water, leading to popular theories that the creature is a lone survivor of the Jurassic era.

The evidence for Nessie isn't just from eye-witness testimony, however. In 1954, sonar readings from a fishing boat detected something large keeping pace with the vessel in the depths below.

There have been many photographs claiming to show Nessie, the most famous of which was taken in 1934 by Robert Kenneth Wilson. It appears to show a long reptilian neck and head emerging from the water.

This photo was circulated around the world, and Nessie-hunters flocked to Loch Ness, eager to see the creature for themselves.

In 1993, however, further analysis of the photograph proved it to be a »

Words: KATRINA PATRICK Images: SHUTTERSTOCK

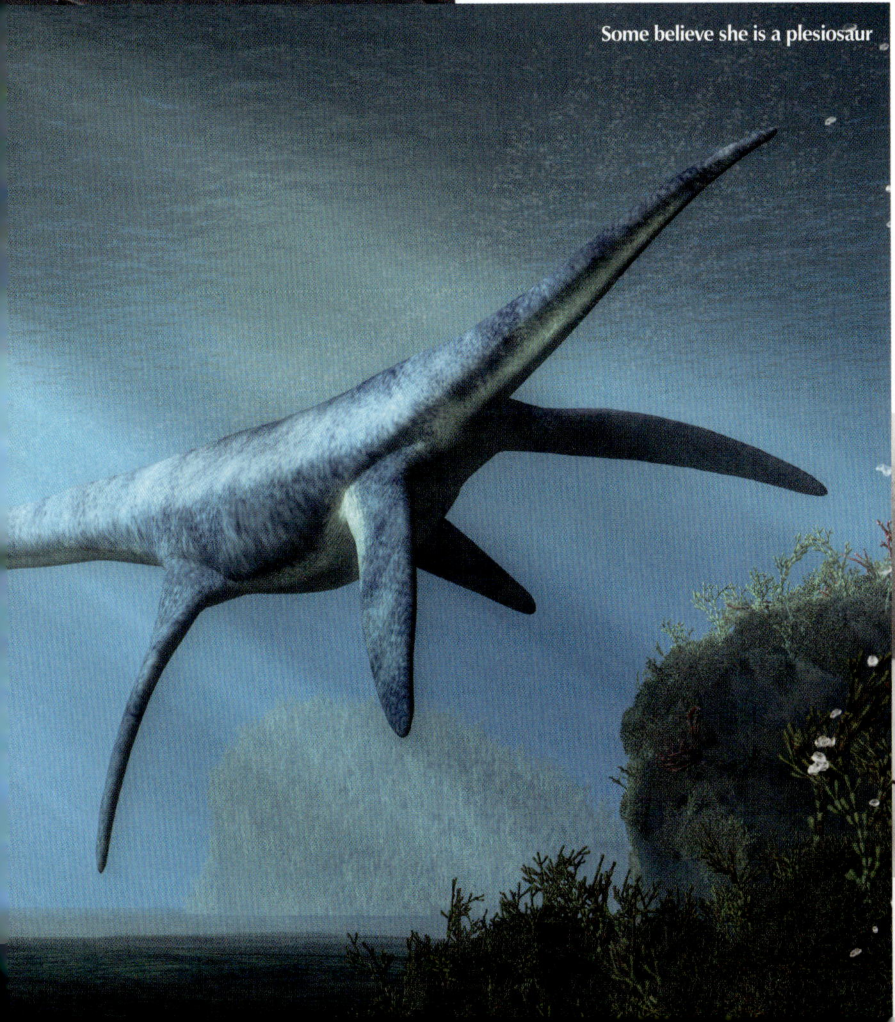

Some believe she is a plesiosaur

"Large in size with a long neck and one or more humps protruding"

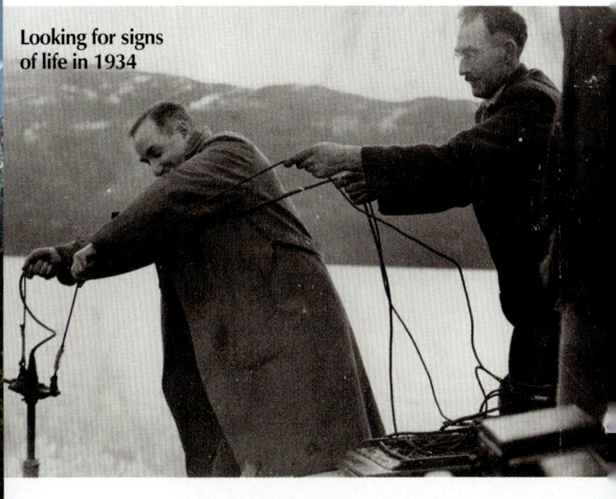

Looking for signs of life in 1934

“There are those who still believe Nessie is lurking in the loch”

fake, created with a man-made Nessie head towed behind the boat.

Many other photographs have been exposed as forgeries – or of large fish such as sturgeons or catfish – but there are still many who believe the Loch Ness Monster is real. She was even the subject of a film, *Loch Ness*, in 1996 starring Ted Danson as a sceptical zoologist who eventually becomes a believer.

There have been many expeditions to search for Nessie, including a BBC-sponsored search in 2013 involving 600 sonar beams, which scanned the loch and could not find any large creatures.

In 2018, DNA analysis of the loch's water to identify any mysterious species, came up blank too. Interestingly, however, the study failed to find DNA evidence of any sturgeons or catfish either.

Theories about where Nessie came from and if she's real have been widely debated. It has been said she could be a surviving plesiosaur – an aquatic dinosaur – but the argument against this is that Loch Ness it too small to sustain a breeding population of plesiosaurs for such a long time.

Many agree it's impossible for a monster of such size to survive in Loch Ness, but there are those who still believe that Nessie is lurking somewhere in the loch. Whatever the truth, many still spend hours scanning the loch for signs of life, with eight Nessie sightings reported in 2020.

Image ScreenShot002.png
100
189m
13.6°c
10.7kts
The 1954 sonar image

Could she be real?

Ted Danson in the film *Loch Ness*

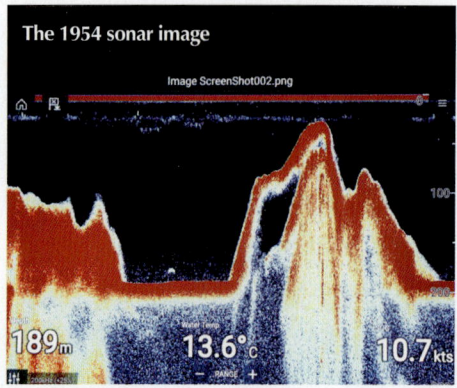

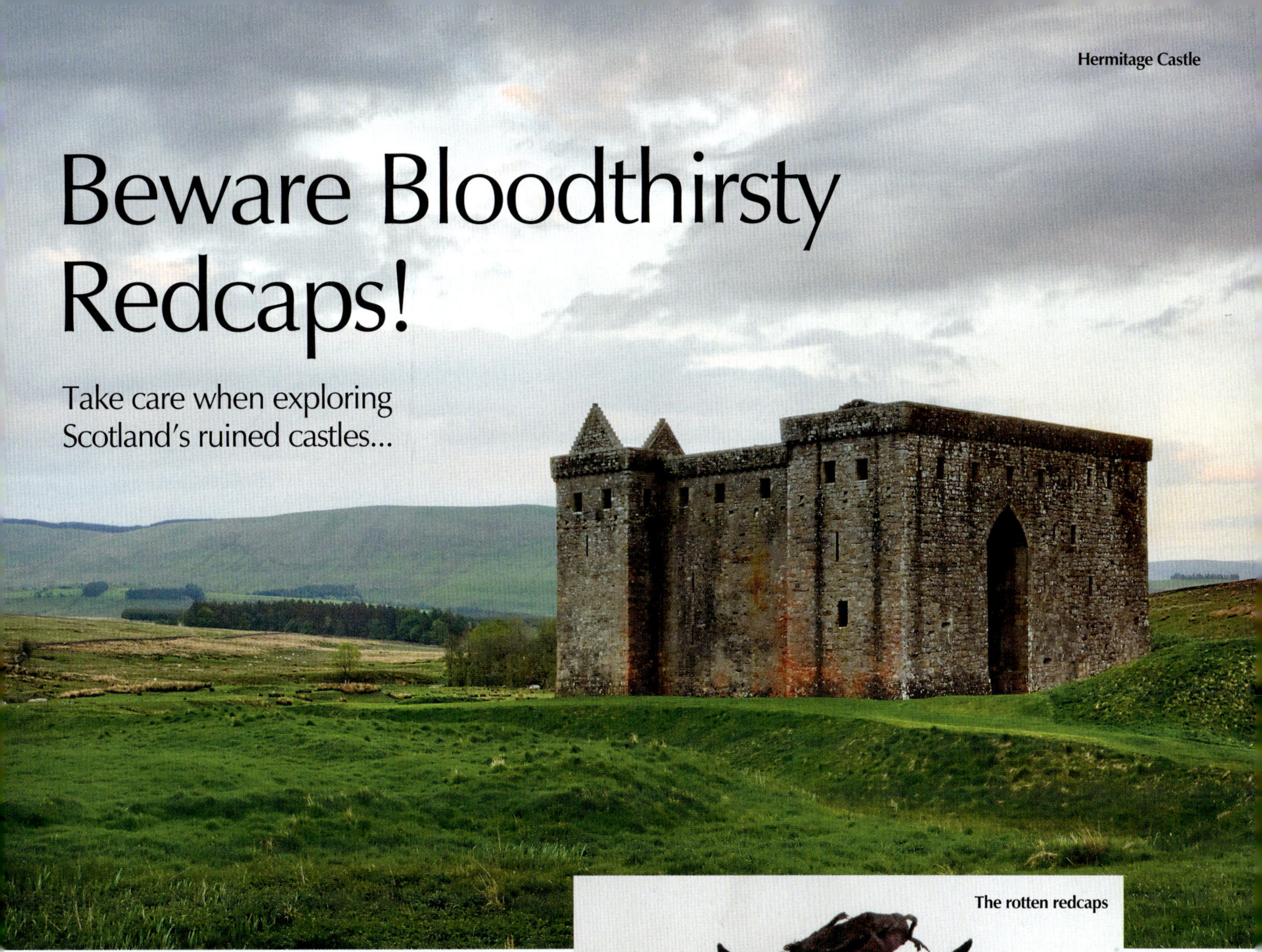

Hermitage Castle

Beware Bloodthirsty Redcaps!

Take care when exploring Scotland's ruined castles...

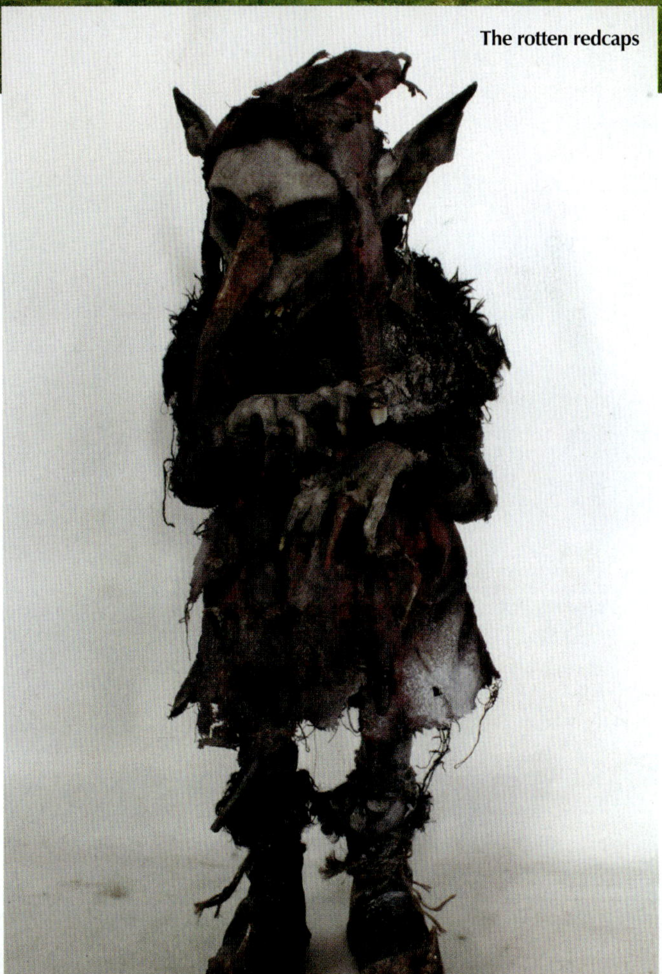

The rotten redcaps

MANY Scottish mythical beasts are mischievous, some are fairly benign, but others are downright malevolent.

Of all the supernatural stalkers or mythical creatures one could encounter while wandering a Scottish castle, the insatiable redcap demon is the most dreaded of all.

Redcaps are gremlin-like ghouls or goblins who allegedly live in the Scottish Borders and get their name from the distinctive red hats that they wear.

These are dyed with human blood, and if a redcap fails to keep his cap freshly drenched, his life force withers away. Not being the largest or burliest of demons, they have a distinct hunger for solo travellers, and lie in wait amid the nooks and crannies of ruined castles until suitable prey wanders innocently in.

One particularly bloodthirsty redcap is said to inhabit the already ominous ruins of Hermitage Castle, a brooding titan of a fortress set deep within Liddesdale in the Scottish Borders, a place known as the bloodiest valley in Britain. What better hunting grounds than that?

Many a lone reiver – the colloquial name for someone from the Scottish Borders – and romantic wanderer is said to have fallen prey to Hermitage Castle's ghoulish guardian over the centuries.

With an ever-increasing number of visitors exploring Scotland's castles the future for this redcap seems bright red, indeed.

Words: DAVID WEINCZOK Images: ©JACOB PETERSSON/CURIOMIRA

Morag Of Morar

Sightings and folklore attest to a creature in Scotland's deepest loch

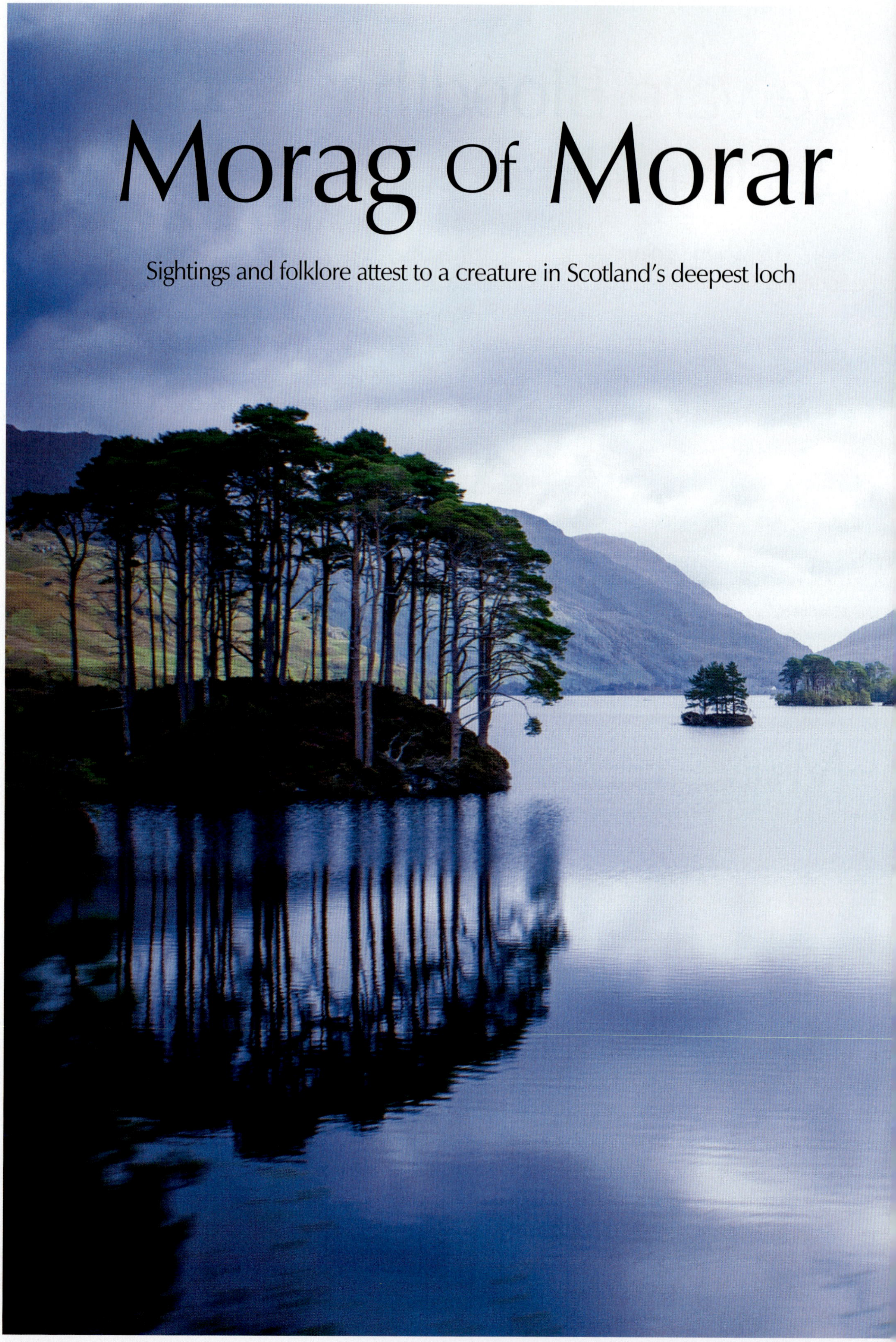

Words: KATRINA PATRICK Image: SHUTTERSTOCK

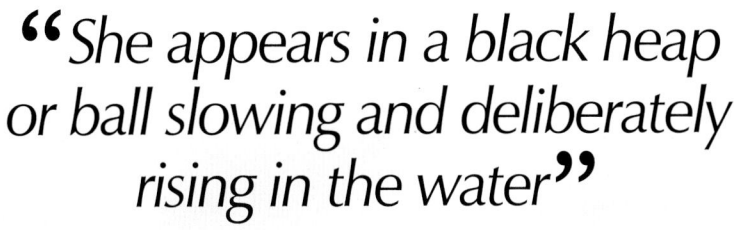

> "*She appears in a black heap or ball slowing and deliberately rising in the water*"

NESSIE isn't the only monster said to be lurking in Scotland's lochs. Loch Morar, in the Lochaber area of the Highlands, is home to Nessie's lesser-known cousin, Morag.

Morar is the deepest freshwater body in the British Isles, and is 310m (1017ft) at its deepest. The first recorded sighting of Morag was in 1887, and they have continued to the present day – though accounts differ. Some say the creature is a mermaid, some a plesiosaur-type creature like Nessie.

Alexander Carmichael, who collected local folklore at the turn of the 20th century, interviewed the inhabitants of the villages surrounding the loch, and wrote the following: "There is a creature in Loch Morar and she is called Morag. She is never seen save when one of the hereditary people of the place dies. The last time she was seen was when Aeneas Macdonnell died in 1898. The Morag is peculiar to Loch Morar. She is seen in broad daylight and by many persons, including church persons. She appears in a black heap or ball slowing and deliberately rising in the water and moving along like a boat waterlogged.

"The Morag is much disliked and is called by many uncomplimentary terms."

The sightings continued in the 20th century – in 1948 nine people in a boat claimed to have seen a creature measuring six metres (20ft).

Later, in 1969, two men claimed Morag had bumped into their boat, and only disappeared when they opened fire with a rifle and hit her with an oar. Things went quiet for a while and locals assumed Morag had succumbed to her wounds.

But a sighting in 2013 by holidaymakers, Doug and Charlotte Christie, confirmed the monster – or at least belief – was alive and well.

Beware the poetry-loving storm kelpies at the Minch

What Lurks Beneath...

Meet more mythical beings that inhabit our lochs, rivers and seas

Words: JUDY VICKERS Images: SHUTTERSTOCK, ALAMY

WITH a vast coastline, hundreds of islands, countless rivers, lochs and burns – not to mention a plentiful supply of water in the form of rain – it's little wonder that Scotland has a rich history of legendary water creatures… some of them more kindly disposed to humans than others.

The Blue Men Of The Minch

Also known as storm kelpies, these creatures are humanoid and blue in colour. They inhabit the treacherous waters of the Minch, between the Outer Hebrides and the mainland of Scotland. In fine weather they sleep on the water's surface but are capable of raising a storm.

Fond of poetry, they prey on ships and challenge captains to complete two lines of verse with two of their own. Sailors without a ready gift for rhyming have their ships capsized.

There are several theories as to where the stories originate. The blue men are said to swim with their torsos out of the water, and one theory suggests they derive from Picts, with their painted bodies, crossing the sea in kayak-like boats. Another theory is that they come from sightings of North African slaves taken by the Vikings overwintering by the Shiant Islands.

70 Supernatural Scotland

Kelpies

Kelpies or water horses appear in stories across the country. These shape-shifting sprites haunt rivers, lochs and shores, usually in the form of a horse so alluring that many cannot resist climbing on to its back. The demonic beast plunges into the water and the rider, spellbound to its back, is drowned. A kelpie can be tamed if a brave soul can get a bridle on it (or take the bridle off, depending on the story). Confusingly, in the old stories a kelpie can be a hairy man or a beautiful woman!

Their fame in Scotland has been helped by Andy Scott's 30m (100ft) sculptures at Falkirk – though they were originally based on two real life Clydesdale horses and were created to represent the lineage of Scotland's heavy horse of industry.

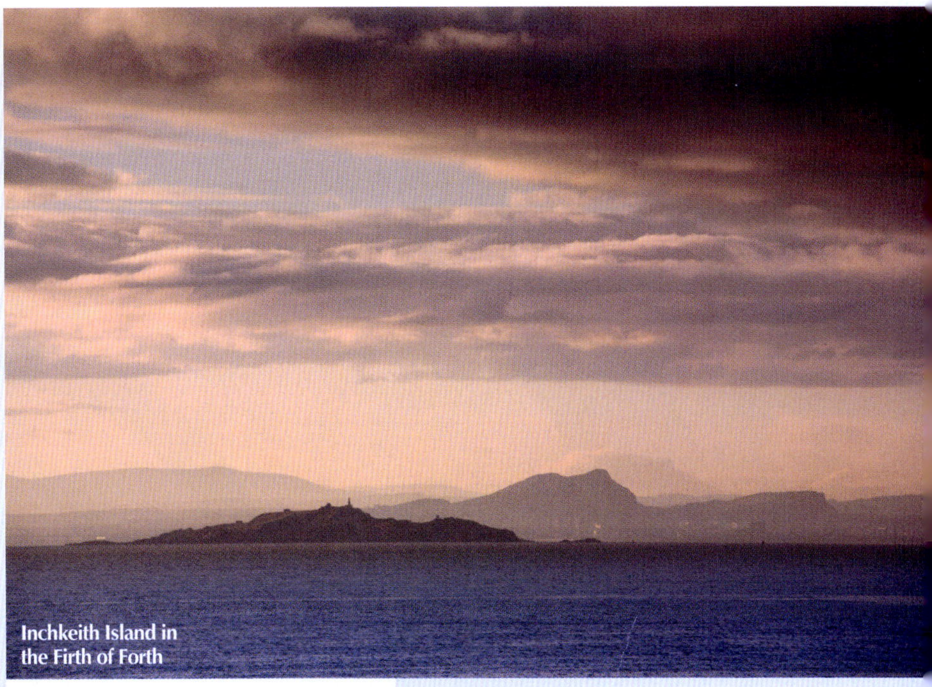

Inchkeith Island in the Firth of Forth

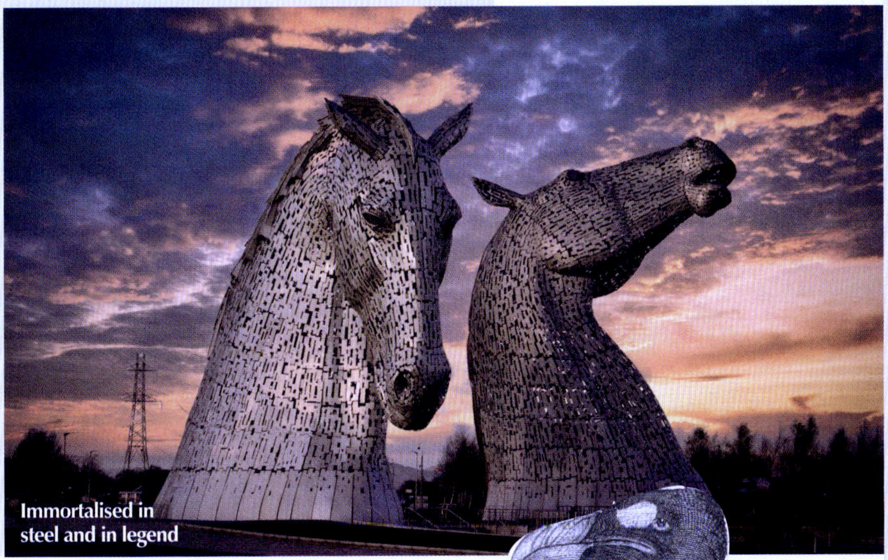

Immortalised in steel and in legend

Boobries

This west coast bogie is another shape-shifter. It is most commonly a large bird, but sometimes a water horse or a blood-sucking giant insect.

The bird, said to be as big as 17 eagles, snatched cattle from ships and took them to its watery lair clutched in claws as big as deer's horns. As an insect it sucked horses' blood and as a water horse it could gallop across the water.

Its cry was like a roaring bull, which some believe may be the call of a bittern, a bird rarely seen in Scotland. The great auk, a flightless bird extinct from the mid-19th century, matches some descriptions. Boobries also appeared in the 1980s fantasy game *Dungeons & Dragons*.

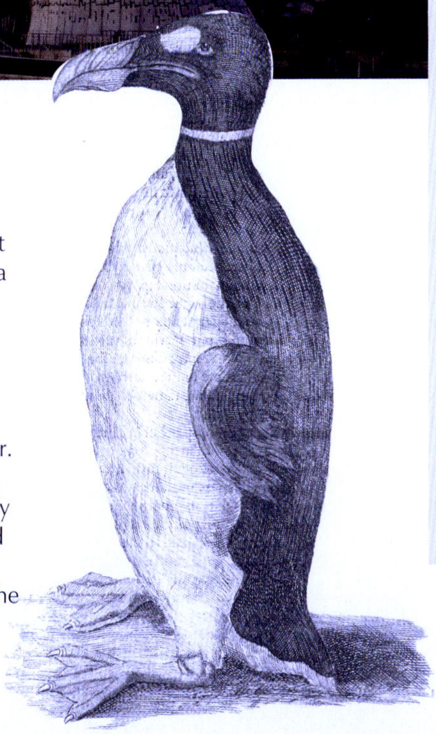

Shellycoats

The name refers to this water sprite's coat made out of shells that rattle as it moves through the rivers of its Borders and Lothian homes.

Sir Walter Scott once described the creature's favourite prank.

Two travellers by the River Ettrick hear the cry of a drowning man. Alarmed, they follow the sound throughout the night only to find, hours later, they have exhausted themselves for nothing – it was the shellycoat, now laughing himself silly.

A rather more vicious shellycoat lived at a stone on the shore at Leith. An English soldier was said, after a night in the pub, to be ready to defy the shellycoat. He set off to the stone. Found the next morning covered in bruises with both legs broken, he claimed the shellycoat had carried him to Inchkeith Island then hurled him repeatedly to the ground.

Other witnesses said that he had moved to another pub before attempting to climb the stone and falling off!

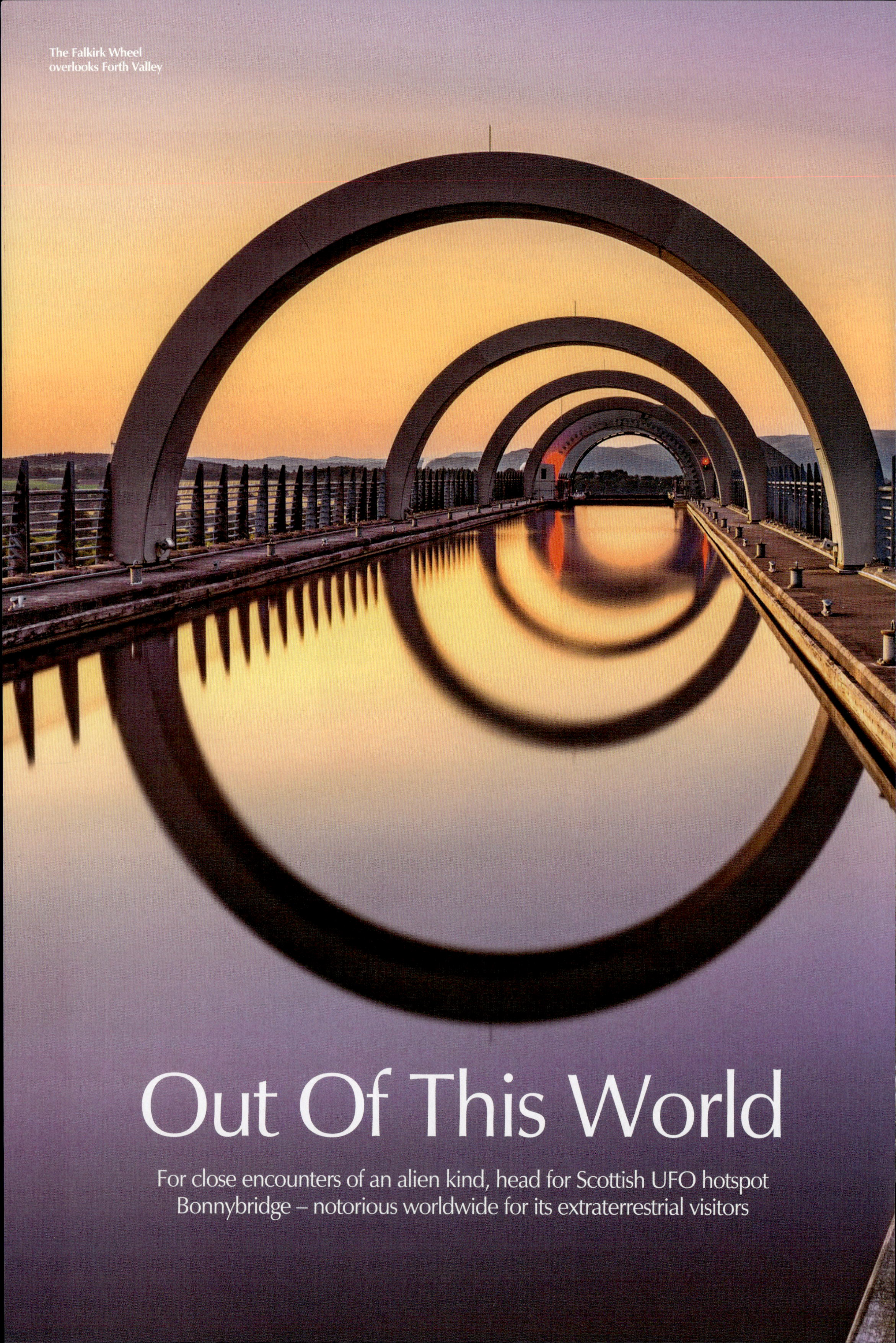

The Falkirk Wheel overlooks Forth Valley

Out Of This World

For close encounters of an alien kind, head for Scottish UFO hotspot Bonnybridge – notorious worldwide for its extraterrestrial visitors

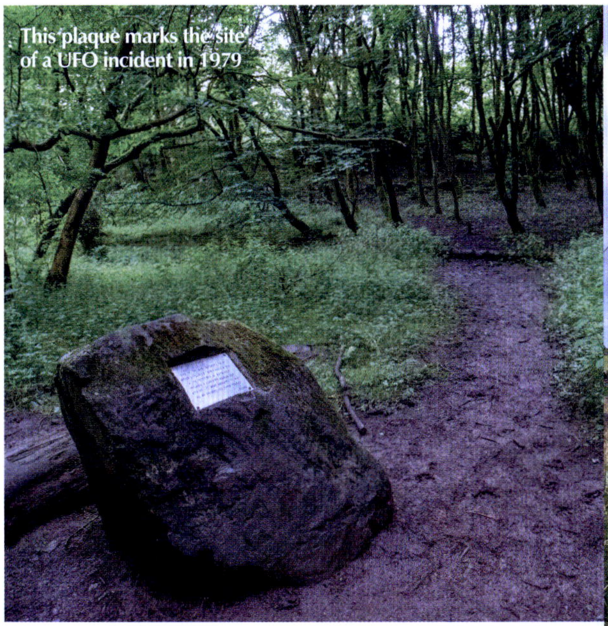

This plaque marks the site of a UFO incident in 1979

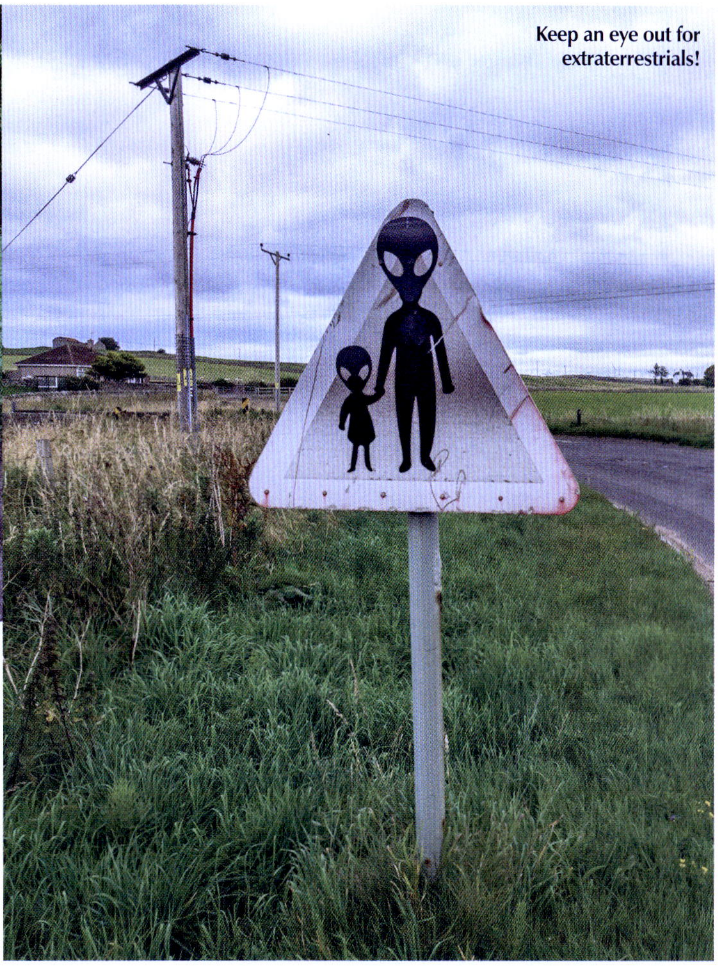

Keep an eye out for extraterrestrials!

SCOTLAND'S reputation for supernatural encounters isn't confined to traditional hauntings, monster-filled lochs and malicious spirits.

The country can also claim global notoriety in a much more modern "supernatural" concern – UFOs!

Despite its size, Scotland apparently has more sightings of Unidentified Flying Objects than almost any other country in the world, with a significant proportion from a Central Belt area referred to as the "Falkirk Triangle".

With Falkirk to the west, Edinburgh to the east and Stirling to the north, the area consists of rural farmland, rolling hills and small former mining villages.

It is a hotbed for UFO sightings, first coming to national prominence 30 years ago, although reports go back at least another decade.

According to the author and paranormal researcher Malcolm Robinson, founder of Strange Phenomena Investigations, the Triangle – and, in particular, the small town of Bonnybridge – is "probably the UK's main UFO hotspot. We call it a window – it generates a higher concentration of reports than any other place in the UK".

One of the earliest was back in March 1992, when a local family reported seeing a basketball-sized blue light hovering on the back road from Hallglen to Bonnybridge. They also described hearing a sound similar to an opening door, followed by a "howl".

Four years later, a video of an orange oval light floating above Falkirk, which changed shape to become the classic "flying saucer" white disc, went global.

Subsequent reports could be said to be as strange as they are varied, but in many respects they remain remarkably consistent – reports of orbs, lights, strange objects and even a spaceship landing on a local golf course – are all on record.

It is, of course, something of an intellectual leap »

"They described hearing a sound similar to an opening door, followed by a howl"

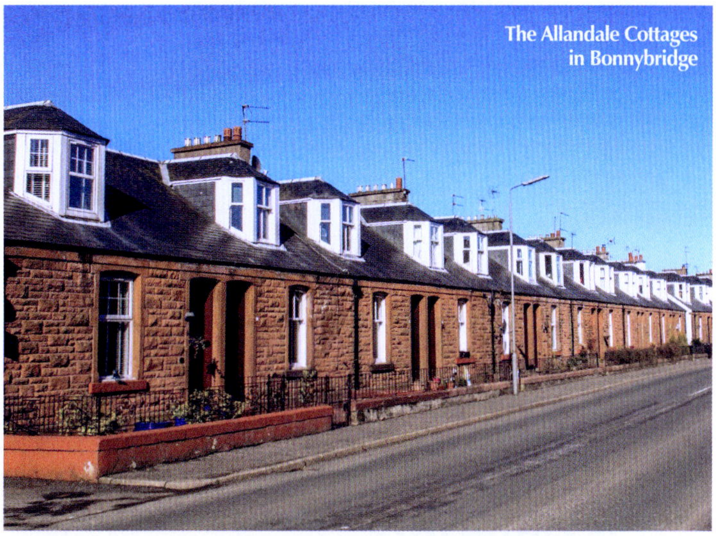

The Allandale Cottages in Bonnybridge

Words: PAUL COCKBURN Images: ALAMY, SHUTTERSTOCK, SWNS

Do aliens visit Forth Valley?

William Buchanan

"Being Scotland's UFO capital is unique"

to go from "mysterious lights in the sky" to "extra-terrestrial space craft" to "visiting aliens".

Perhaps aware of the somewhat negative reputation of certain UFOlogists, other investigators prefer to put the sightings down to a somewhat more human cause such as the testing of highly secret prototype military aircraft.

Others argue that some of the mysteries sighted in the area might be down to the existence of portals or weak spots in the fabric of reality, making the Falkirk Triangle an ideal "slipping point" between dimensional realms.

The area, after all, proved geographically amenable for the construction of the Forth and Clyde Canal in the 18th century, followed by railway lines in the 19th century and motorways during the 20th century – why not also some intergalactic route enabling somewhat more celestial travel through the Scottish Lowlands?

Malcolm, whose documentary on the Forth Valley town was broadcast on the Sky History Channel in 2021, accepts that many – even a majority – of UFO sightings in the area will have natural explanations or simply be the result of people's misperception. Many of the reported sightings, after all, took place at night.

Over the years, though, it's the small percentage of sightings which can't be easily explained that have made him less sceptical.

They are, as he once told journalists, "The fly in the ointment, and can be bona fide."

This doesn't stop some people remaining sceptical – it doesn't help that many of the sightings are not of unidentified flying objects at all, but simply misidentified aircraft. The area, after all, lies beneath the flightpaths of busy Glasgow, busy Edinburgh and slightly less busy Cumbernauld airports.

The UFOs are just as likely to be satellites, weather balloons, natural balls of gas or reflected luminance from nearby Grangemouth's petrochemical works.

But can these explanations be matched to every single sighting?

Not according to William Buchanan. In the 1990s, he was Falkirk's provost.

In various official capacities, he went on to lobby four British prime ministers – John Major, Tony Blair, Gordon Brown and David Cameron –

"The first recorded aliens to visit Scotland might have a criminal record"

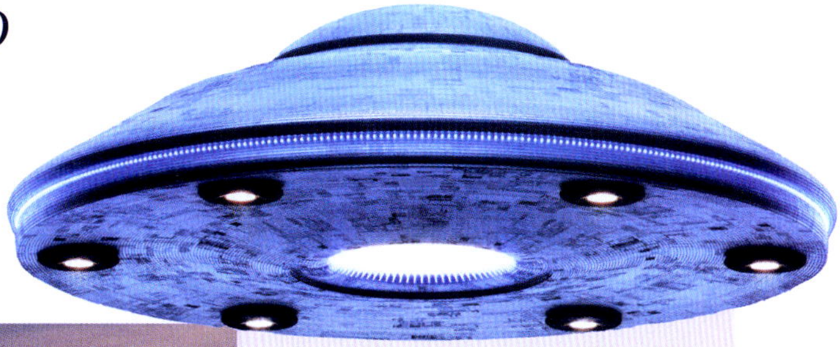

Bizarre sights fill the skies

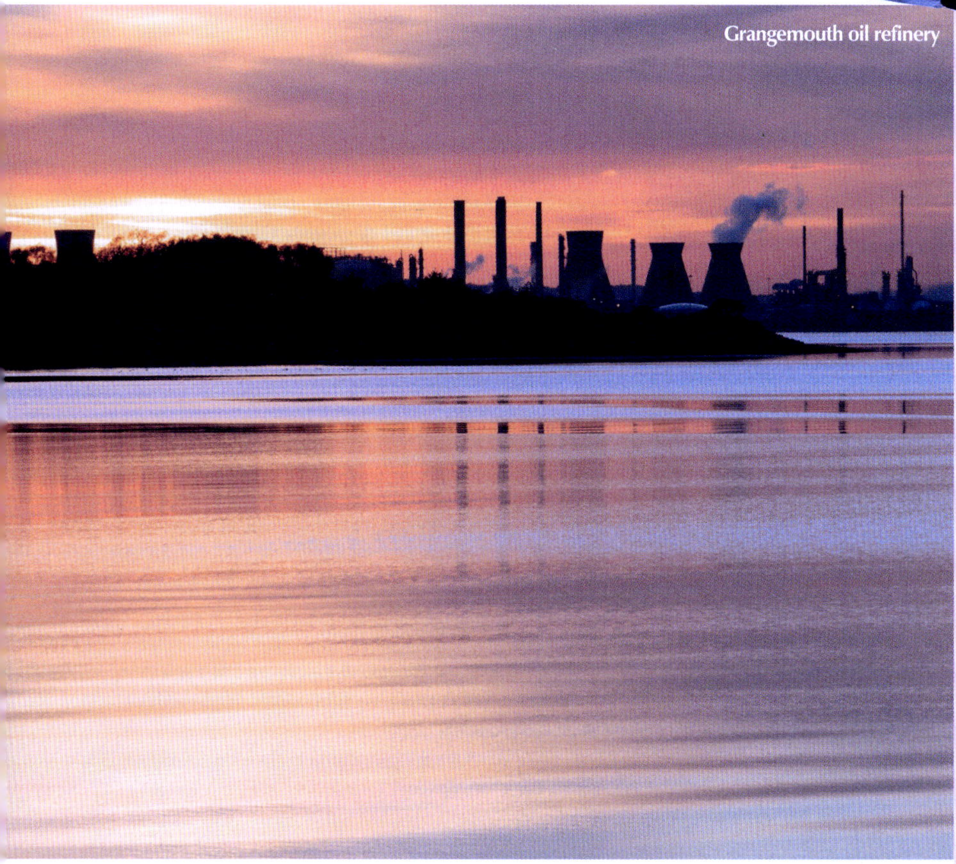

Grangemouth oil refinery

about the need for an official investigation.

In 1997 he said, "I have tried to get an answer for the people and have been ridiculed for it."

Yet, on each occasion, the Ministry of Defence responded that it was "satisfied that there is no evidence that the United Kingdom's airspace might have been compromised by hostile or unauthorised foreign military activity", and that it had "limited interest in UFOs".

That's not the case for the inhabitants of Bonnybridge – according to one recent survey, perhaps a third of the town's 6,900 inhabitants have either seen something strange in the skies, or have a family member or friend who has.

With an average of around 300 sightings a year, it is not surprising that "Scotland's Roswell" has twinned itself with the world-famous UFO location in the US state of New Mexico.

This is not without reason – alien hunters, whether serious or not, have spending power.

For a post-industrial town like Bonnybridge, being Scotland's "UFO capital" is a unique selling point the likes of Edinburgh and Glasgow cannot match.

It is understandable that walking tours around the area – in and around Bonnyfield Local Nature Reserve, along the Bonny Water riverbank or to Roughcastle Roman Fort and the Antonine Wall – are increasingly promoted notso much for their natural beauty, but as an opportunity "to see if you can spot anything strange"!

Notable Sightings

1979: Forestry worker Bob Taylor claims he found a large circular craft in woodland near Dechmont Law, near Livingston. As he approached, it dropped towards the ground and two smaller spheres with protruding spikes rolled towards him, ripping his trousers before beginning to drag him towards the craft. He blacked out for 20 minutes – when he came to, the UFO had vanished. As the case was investigated by Lothian and Borders Police as a potential assault, it's possible that the first recorded aliens to visit Scotland might have a criminal record.

1992: While driving home from Falkirk, local businessman James Walker claimed to have seen strange triangular lights in the sky following his car. When he stopped his car, the object took off at tremendous speed.

1992: Isabella Sloggett and her daughter Carole, heading towards Bonnybridge, saw a "circle of lights" ahead. These later landed in a field in front of them. Somewhat unnerved, they continued on their way until their path was blocked by a "football-sized blue light". Isabella later stated that a door opened on the craft in front of them, and they heard a "howl-like sound" – at which point they turned and ran away.

1994: An entire team of cleaners on their way to their shift at the Grangemouth oil refinery witnessed persistent and bizarre "flashing lights" and orange globes in the sky overhead.

The Grey Man of Ben Macdui

Scotland's very own yeti lurks around the Lairg Ghru pass

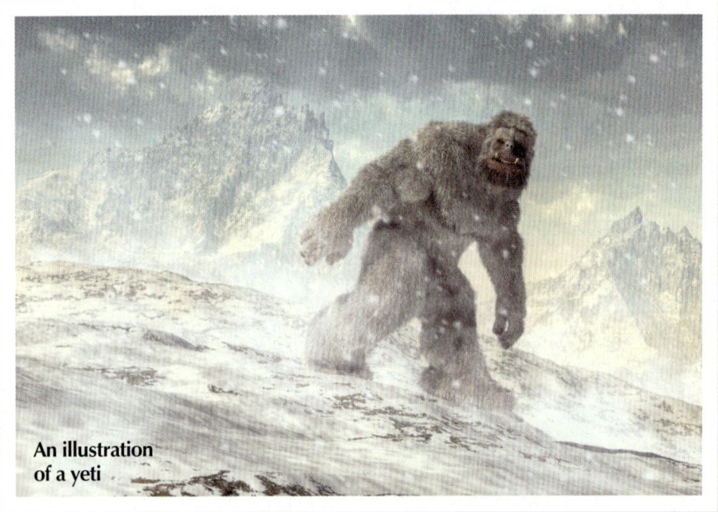

An illustration of a yeti

Words: CRISPIN ANDREWS Images: SHUTTERSTOCK

"Collie could see nothing, but the eerie crunching sound continued"

THE mountains of Tibet, the USA's Pacific North-West, the dense jungles of Sumatra – these are all places where, according to legend, an unlucky traveller might come across one of folklore's most fascinating creatures.

Bigfoot, yeti, orang pendek, yowie – people all over the world have given these creatures many names, but did you know that Scotland has its very own?

Am Fear Liath Mor, or The Big Grey Man of Ben Macdui, is no ordinary beast. It all started in 1891, when John Norman Collie, the famous mountaineer, scientist and explorer, believed he saw something strange lurking in the wilds near Ben Macdui, the highest mountain in the Cairngorm National Park.

Collie kept what he'd seen to himself for 35 years, before speaking of his encounter at the 1925 meeting of the Cairngorm Society. Collie was by the summit, on a misty day, when he heard footsteps.

"As if someone was walking after me but taking steps three or four times the length of my own," he said.

Collie could see nothing, but the eerie crunching sound continued. Finally, he was overcome with panic and terror and rushed down the mountainside, running until he dared stop. "Whatever you make of it I do not know,"

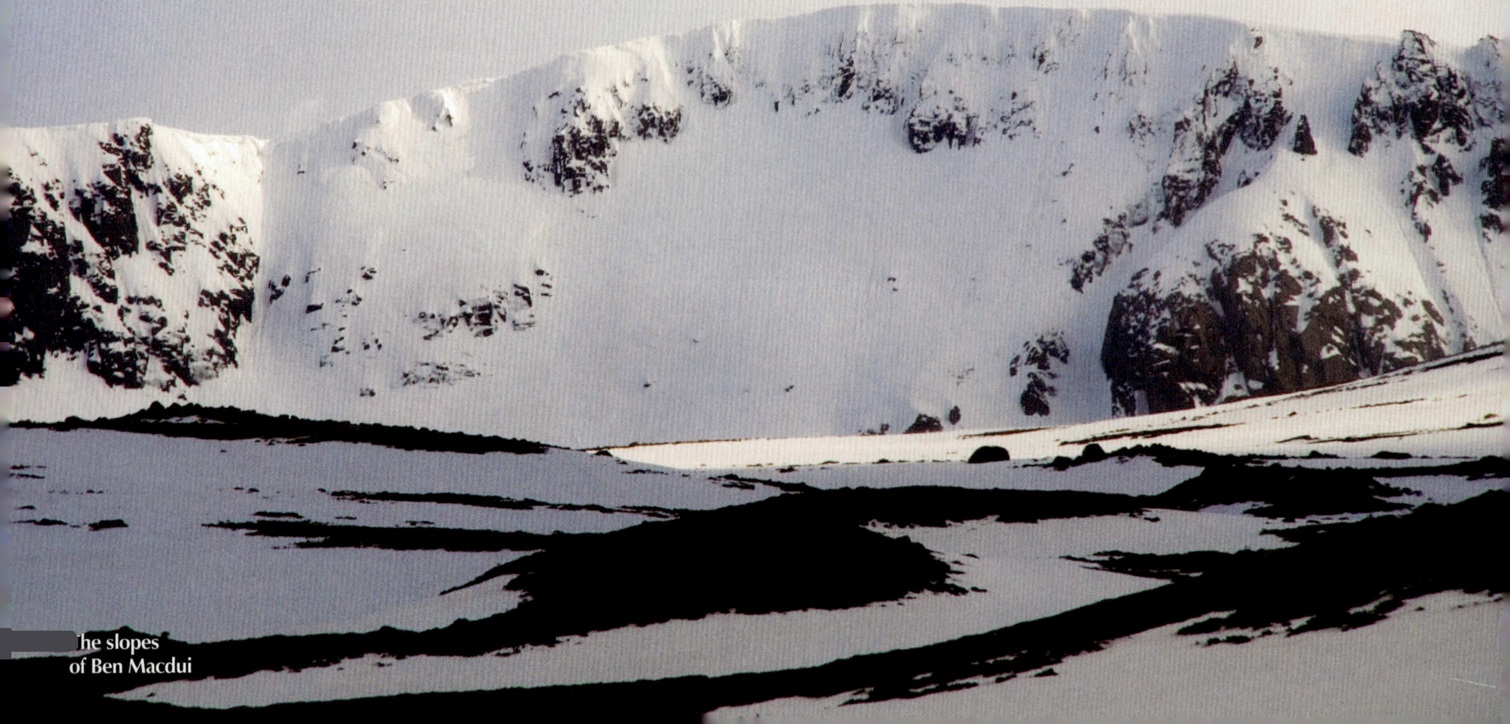

[redacted]he slopes of Ben Macdui

“People sense the presence of something threatening”

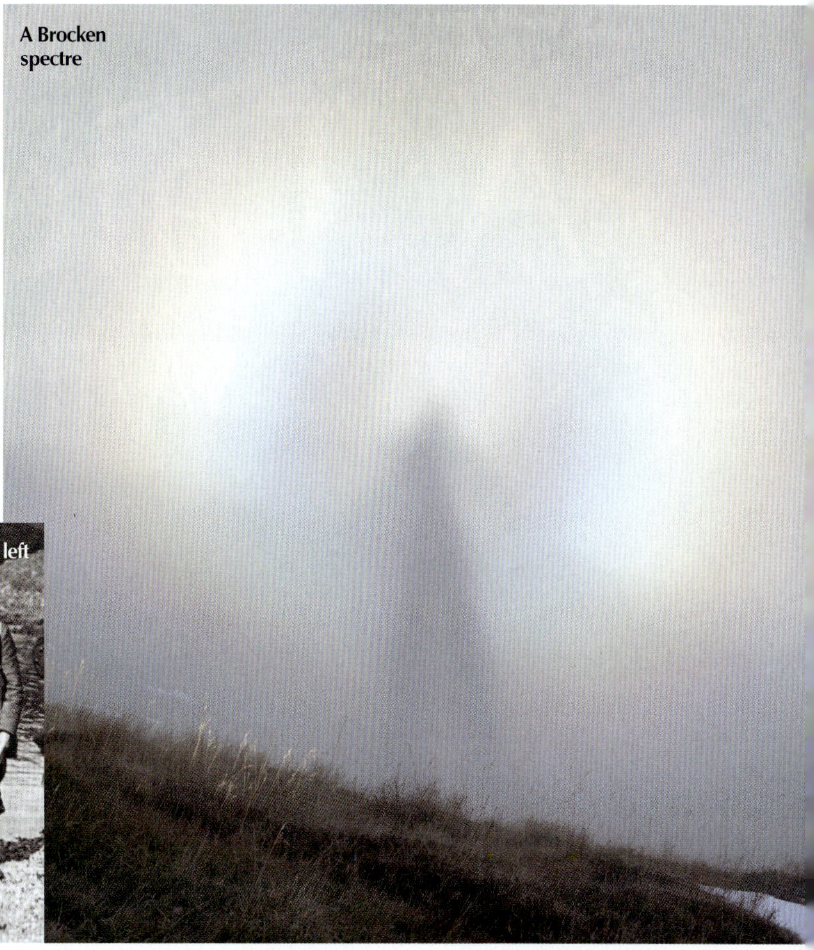
A Brocken spectre

Collie told the meeting. “But there is something very queer about the top of Ben Macdui and I will not go back there myself.”

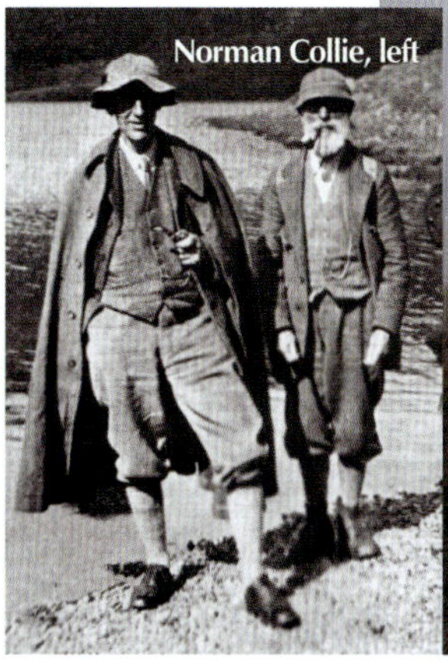
Norman Collie, left

Word of Collie’s encounter spread and, before long, he started receiving letters from other people who said that they too had seen something strange there – most often below the skyline near the Lairg Ghru pass.

Dr A.M. Kellas and his brother, Henry, spoke of a giant figure approaching them near the summit. Author, Richard Frere, told a story about a friend who’d seen a giant figure walking down the mountainside. Mountaineer, Alexander Tewnion, claimed to have actually shot a creature on Ben Macdui – 3m (10ft) tall, broad shouldered and covered in short hair, brown or olive, walking upright, with long arms. The descriptions seem to match other wildman sightings.

Mostly, however, the creature is not seen – people simply sense the presence of something threatening and malevolent and, overcome by uncontrollable fear, panic and despondency, they bolt down the mountainside to safety. Some report ghostly voices, and there are many accounts of ghostly footsteps and even eerie music. Others talk of being drawn, hypnotically, to the edge of dangerous ravines.

As to what, if anything, the Big Grey Man might be, opinions are divided.

An unknown creature that emits pheromones or low-frequency sounds that disorientate humans?

Similar feelings of despondency and panic have been in reports of sasquatch sightings in Canada. Or, could an ancient or even prehistoric species of ape or human be living in the Cairngorms? One interesting suggestion is that these creatures pass through an inter-dimensional portal, somewhere on the mountain, which apparently explains the shimmering and the fact that people hear but don’t see them.

There are more rational explanations, however. In 1791, poet and shepherd James Hogg was terrified when he saw a huge ghostly figure while out near Ben Macdui tending his sheep.

Hogg was doubly amazed when the figure started mimicking his movements. A wildman with a sense of humour, or an example of Brocken spectre? This scientific phenomena takes its name from the Brocken peak in the Harz Mountains, Germany. This optical illusion is seen when the observer’s apparently huge, magnified shadow is cast onto the mist or clouds by sunlight.

The observer over-estimates the size of the shadow because they compare it to faraway objects seen through gaps in the mist or clouds. Sometimes, when the cloud moves, the shadow appears to move with them.

Fortean investigator, Andy Roberts, believes the Big Grey Man sightings are symptoms of what he calls mountain panic – that is, fear and anxiety brought on by isolation and exhaustion.

Roberts spoke to mountaineers who’d experienced uncontrollable fits of panic while climbing elsewhere in Scotland, in Wales and in Papua New Guinea.

Roberts puts the appearance of the strange creatures down to folk tales about giants and other ghoulish creatures said to inhabit the Cairngorms.

The jury’s out, though – what’s your verdict?

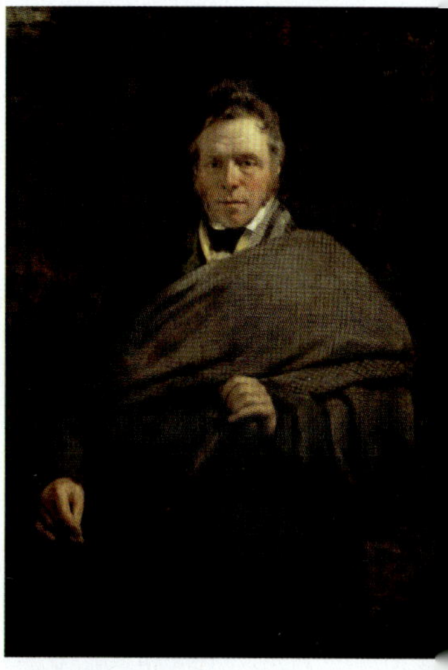
Above: Famous Scots author James Hogg

A Tale With Bite

The spine-tingling story of the Gorbals Vampire and the young Glasgow mob who set out to destroy it

IF you go down to Glasgow's Southern Necropolis after dark, you'd do well to pop some garlic in your pocket. The Gorbals Vampire, who was rumoured to have killed and eaten two boys in 1954, has never been caught.

On September 23 that year, hordes of angry schoolchildren – some as young as four years old – descended upon the cemetery. Many were armed with stakes and knives, others brought dogs or carried crucifixes.

Soon, there were hundreds of children patrolling the graves, all determined to find the two-metre (7ft) tall vampire with iron teeth that they believed had sacrificed the boys. It wasn't long before the police – who had no record of any missing boys in the area – were called to the scene, but even they couldn't calm the furious mob of tiny vigilantes.

"Even the police couldn't calm the furious mob"

Reliable west coast rain eventually forced the children indoors, but they weren't giving up that easily. The following evening, their monstrous mission resumed, and by the third night of vampire hunting, everyone from the local headmaster to Gorbals MP Alice Cullen had stepped in to call a halt to the frenzied search for this flesh-eating fiend.

Alice issued an urgent plea to mums and dads in the area. She advised them to keep their outraged offspring at home for a while, and to tell them it was all "a lot of hooey". It seemed to do the trick, and interest in the vampire waned, but just as the children's hysteria died down, it was reaching fever pitch among the concerned grown-ups.

Unsurprisingly, the incredible story was making headlines, not only across the country, but across the seas, too. Speculation was rife – what exactly had sparked the schoolyard gossip that had spread like wildfire?

The finger of blame was firmly pointed at American comic books – in particular one entitled *The Vampire With The Iron Teeth*. There were calls for them to be banned, lest they corrupted more young minds.

In stark contrast to that theory, some people reckoned the children might have actually been inspired by the Bible (a passage in Daniel 7:7 references a beast with iron teeth).

Others wondered if Jenny wi' the Airn Teeth – a legend about a ghoulish woman who was said to roam around Glasgow Green – could be the culprit.

The young people quickly moved on from the eerie goings-on in the Southern Necropolis, but the case wasn't yet closed. It ended up in parliament, and in 1955, the Children and Young Persons (Harmful Publications) Act was passed, prohibiting the sale of gory comics to under-18s.

A Glaswegian playground whisper had unexpectedly changed the law, and the Gorbals Vampire had earned his place in the horror history books.

Words: LAURA BROWN Images: SHUTTERSTOCK, ALAMY

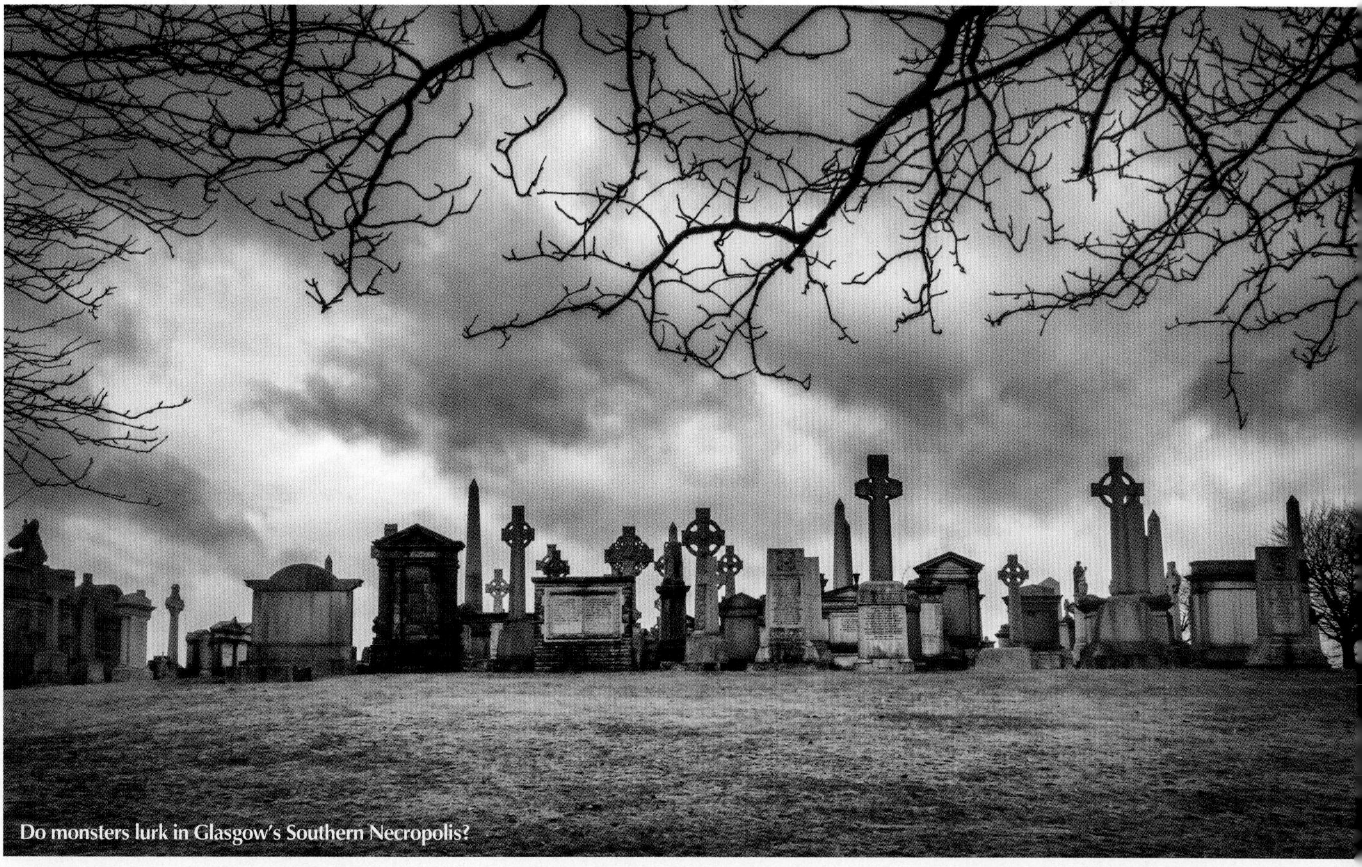

Do monsters lurk in Glasgow's Southern Necropolis?

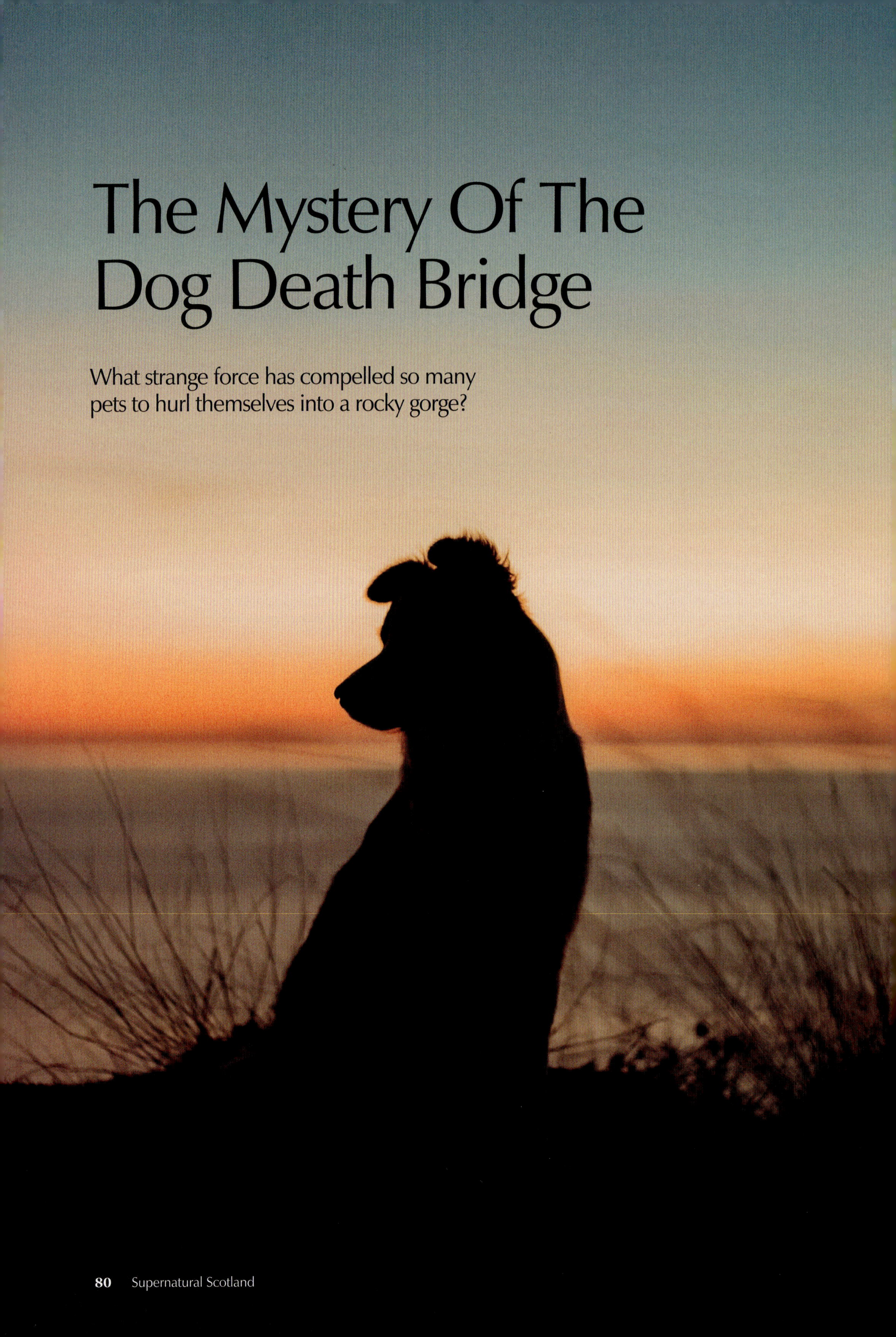

The Mystery Of The Dog Death Bridge

What strange force has compelled so many pets to hurl themselves into a rocky gorge?

IN rural Dunbartonshire, the Overtoun Burn flows peacefully near historic Overtoun House. The B-listed Overtoun Bridge crosses the water – and opens a portal to the spirit world for unwary canines…

Since the 1950s, it seems more than 600 dogs have taken a leap into the unknown over its sloping parapet. Some say there have been more than 50 fatalities.

Reports claim dog walkers froze in terror as pets hurled themselves to the rocky gorge 15 metres (50ft) below. Owners believed an uncanny compulsion took hold of their pets moments before they leaped.

Experts agree that dogs have neither a concept of nor an inclination towards suicide. What hidden forces, then, could have lured those hounds to their fate?

Members of the Scottish Society for Psychical Research visited the site after a spate of incidents in the early 2000s. They told newspapers at the time that they experienced "negative feelings". Some sensed a woman in a grey shawl, while others described the feeling of children "grasping" at them.

Yet no sudden chill or wraith-like mist had indicated a paranormal presence. The sun had been shining each time a dog launched itself into the abyss.

A 2005 television documentary asked animal behaviour expert Dr David Sands to investigate. He was able to disprove several popular theories, such as the mesmerising effect of water, optical illusions, or sonic effects from the nearby Faslane Naval base.

However, Dr Sands noticed that, from a dog's perspective, the solid stone walls of the bridge masked the sight and sound of the gorge below. He predicted that this would heighten dogs' sense of smell. Detecting a strong scent from nearby wildlife could excite a dog into sudden pursuit, leaping towards its quarry and anticipating a landing on level ground.

He tested the idea with Hendrix, a 19-year-old golden retriever, a lucky survivor of a leap years before. Secure on her lead, Hendrix was nevertheless drawn to the exact spot and tensed as if preparing to jump.

> *"What hidden forces could have lured those hounds to their fate?"*

Wildlife expert David Sexton checked the site below and found evidence of mice, mink and squirrel habitats. Mink have bred in large numbers in Scotland only since the 1950s, which fits the timeline of incidents. They give off a scent irresistible to dogs. Significantly, that scent would carry further in fine, dry weather.

Has the mystery of the death bridge been solved?

Not according to local teacher and author Paul Owens. His 11-year research convinced him that the area is a centre of supernatural activity. Dogs are said to be particularly sensitive to the other world. Paul interviewed some of the owners whose dogs had leapt from the bridge. Some told him of "a grey shadowy figure" or a force "like a poltergeist" that assailed their pets.

His book *The Baron of Rainbow Bridge: Overtoun's Death Leaping Dog Mystery Unravelled* contends that the "White Lady of Overtoun" may provide the key.

When Lord Overtoun opened the bridge he'd commissioned in 1895, the dedication was performed by his wife. He died in 1905, his widow living alone for 30 years. Speaking to the press, Paul described how she paced the bridge in her grief. Her ghost is reputed to roam the estate. Could that lonely spirit now be seeking companions in the afterlife?

Perhaps the truth will never be known, but if you take your furry friends for a walk across the bridge, do keep them on a lead – just in case.

Words: MARION MCGIVERN Images: ALAMY

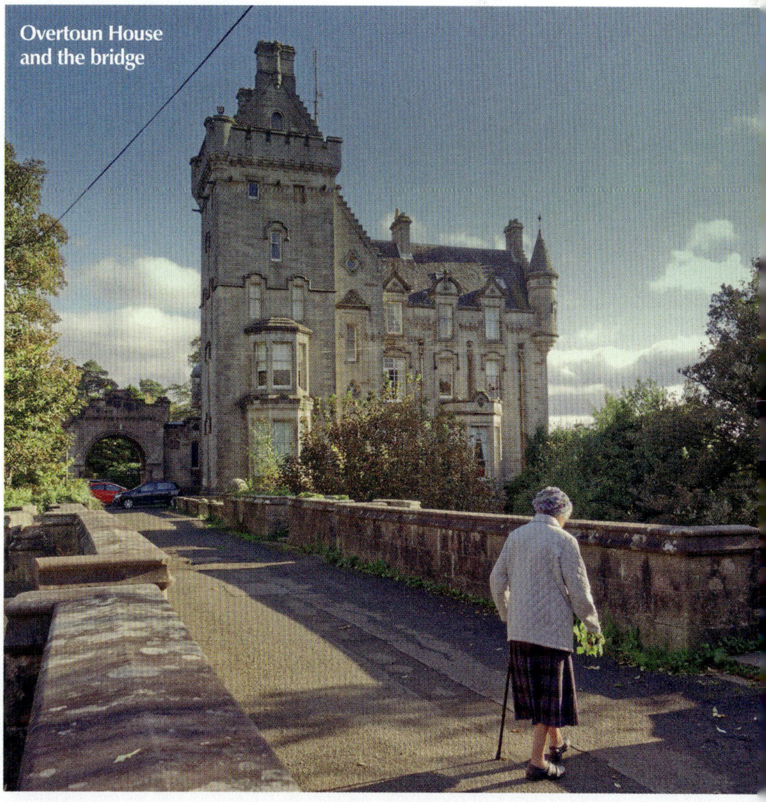
Overtoun House and the bridge

Strange Tales

Mystifying myths and legends from Scottish folkore

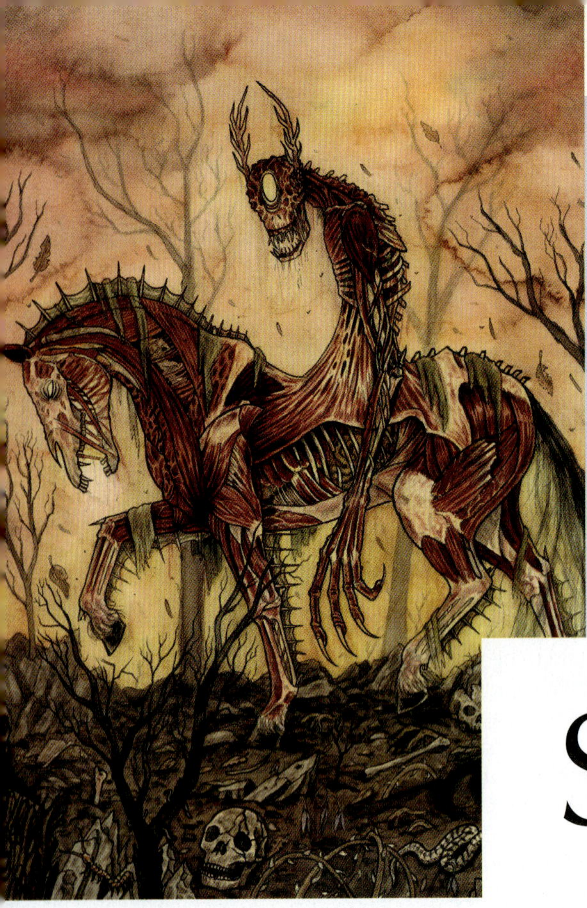

Nuckelavee

One of the most terrifying creatures in Scottish mythology is a demon from Orkney. He is part-horse and part-devil, with no skin to cover his yellow veins of black blood. His breath withers crops and infects livestock, and if you speak his name you better say a prayer quickly in case he hears you. He can't cross running water, though, so if you see Nuckelavee – run for the nearest stream.

Words: KATRINA PATRICK Images: ©JOAN LLOPIS DOMENÉCH ILLUSTRATIONS, SHUTTERSTOCK, ALAMY

Wulver

This werewolf is unique to the Shetland Islands and, according to folklorist Jessie Saxby, is unlike the werewolves of other legends, in that it is not aggressive but is instead a benevolent creature who helps those in need. It is often depicted as a man with a wolf's head, and is known for its solitary lifestyle and fishing skills.

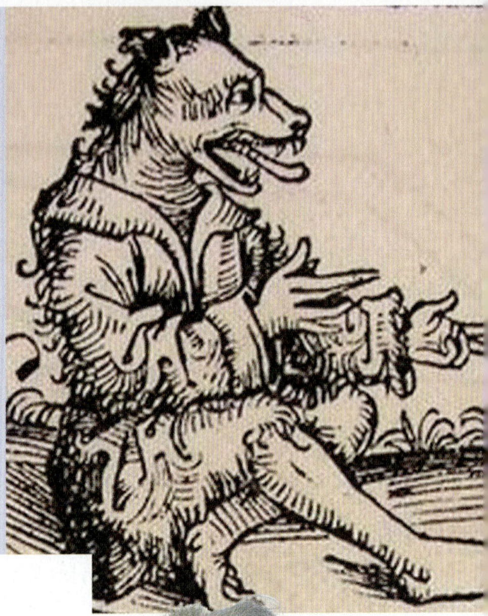

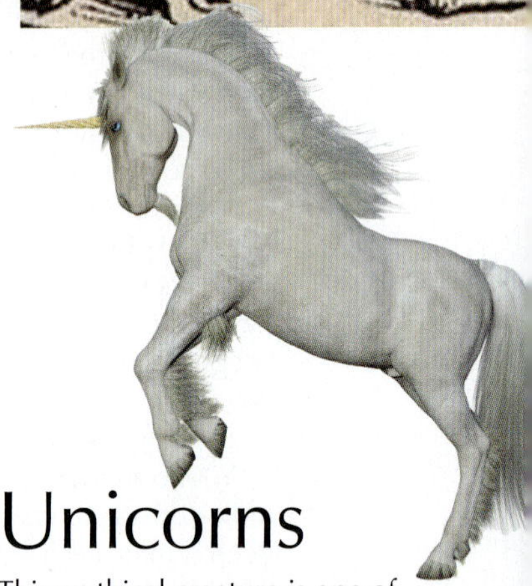

Unicorns

This mythical creature is one of the most universally believed world-wide, and nowhere more so than in Scotland. It is even the country's national animal, and appears on the Royal Coat of Arms for the United Kingdom. In Celtic mythology unicorns are synonymous with purity and unrivalled strength.

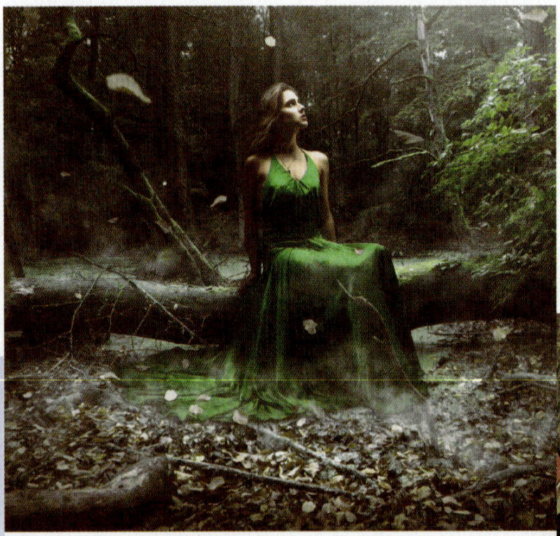

Highland Vampire

The baobhan sith is also known as the vampire of the Highlands. She appears as a beautiful young woman in a long green dress – but with deer hooves instead of feet. She is drawn to the scent of blood and preys on male hunters. She dances with them until they are exhausted, then drains their blood.

House Elves

Brownies are small, nocturnal spirits who sneak into human houses and do chores while the occupants are asleep. They're also known as brùnaidh or gruagach in Scottish Gaelic. English versions sleep in the house, but Scottish brownies prefer to live near burns – small streams – out of sight behind waterfalls or under the heather.

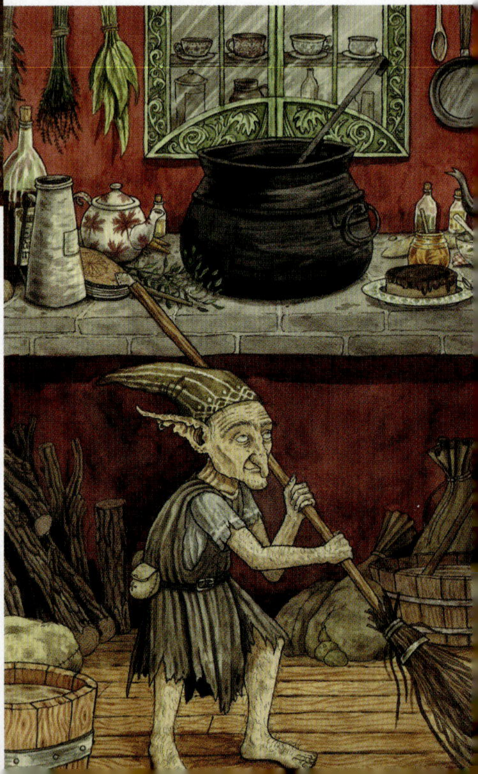

Creepy Castles

Scotland's frightening fortresses harbour more than their fair share of spectral sightings and hidden remains...

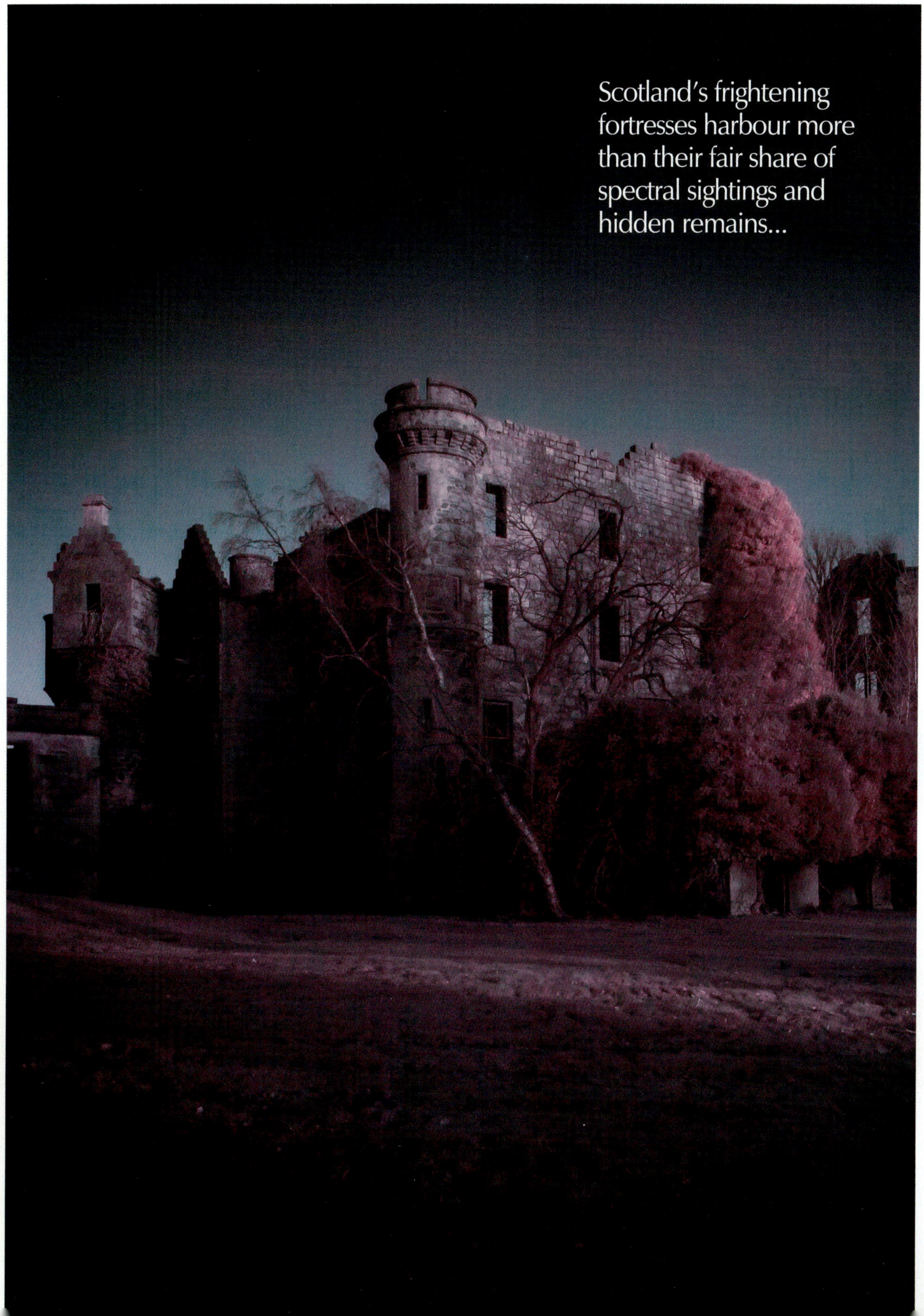

Terror of TANTALLON

This 14th century coastal ruin has experienced its fair share of drama and intrigue, from brutal sieges to ghostly goings-on

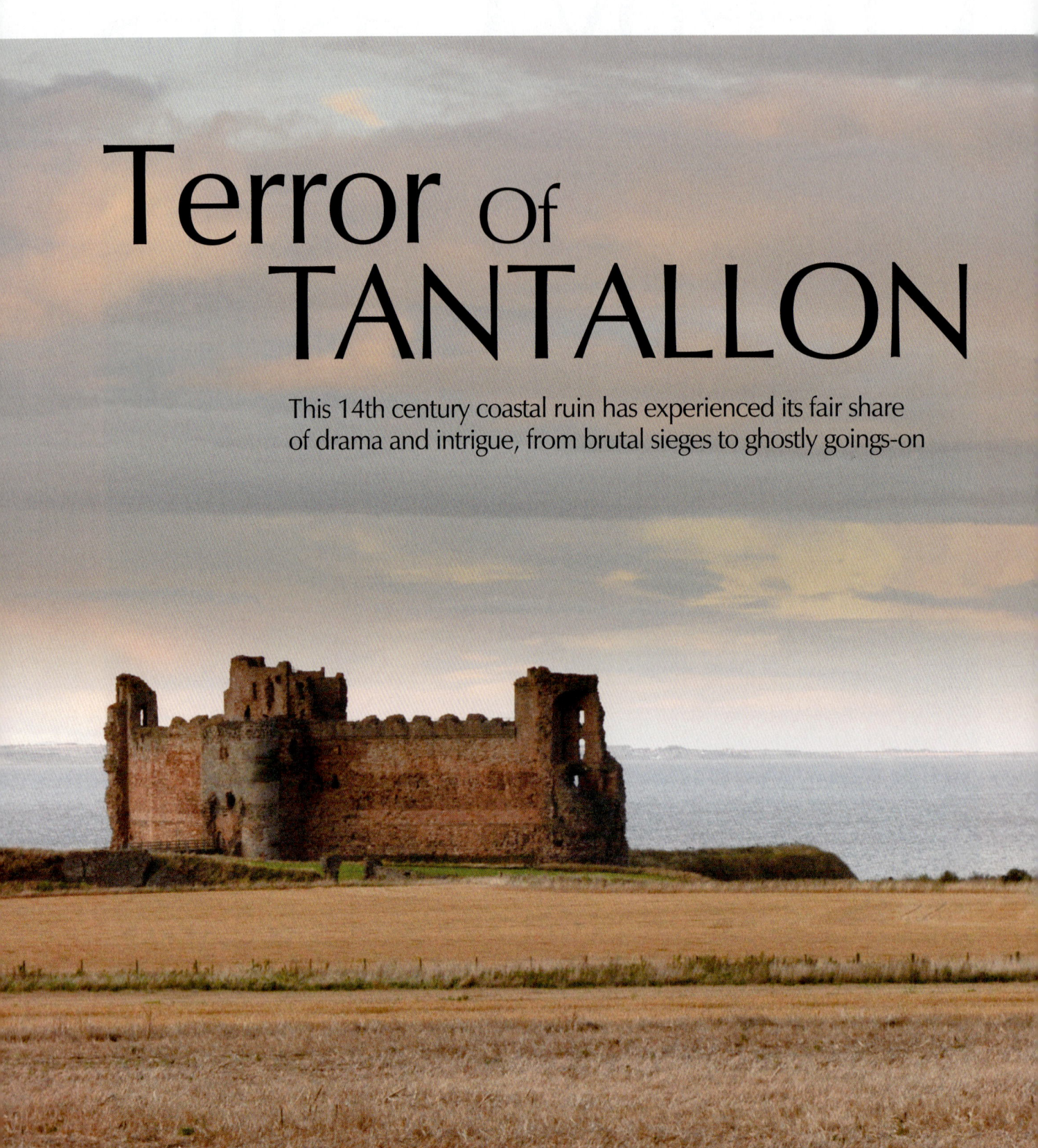

Tantallon, built by nobleman William Douglas, was attacked by Oliver Cromwell in 1671, and was subsequently abandoned

Tantallon is less than an hour's drive from Edinburgh

> "The castle's long and turbulent history has contributed to its reputation as a haunted site"

LOCATED on the east coast, near North Berwick, Tantallon Castle is steeped in history and folklore, with tales of hauntings adding to its mystique.

The castle's long and turbulent history has contributed to its reputation as a haunted site.

One of the most famous ghostly encounters associated with Tantallon Castle is the apparition of the Green Lady. Legend has it that she is the ghost of a woman who died at the castle.

Some stories say she was a member of the Douglas family, while others claim she was a servant who threw herself to her death from the cliffs nearby after falling in love with the master of the castle.

Witnesses have reported sightings of a spectral figure dressed in green roaming the castle grounds, and some even claim to have photos of her.

Visitors often report feeling an eerie sense of being watched, or unexplained strange sounds while exploring the castle's crumbling walls and echoing chambers.

Words: RACHEL MCCONACHIE Pictures: SHUTTERSTOCK, ALAMY

The coastal wall provided perfect defence from the sea

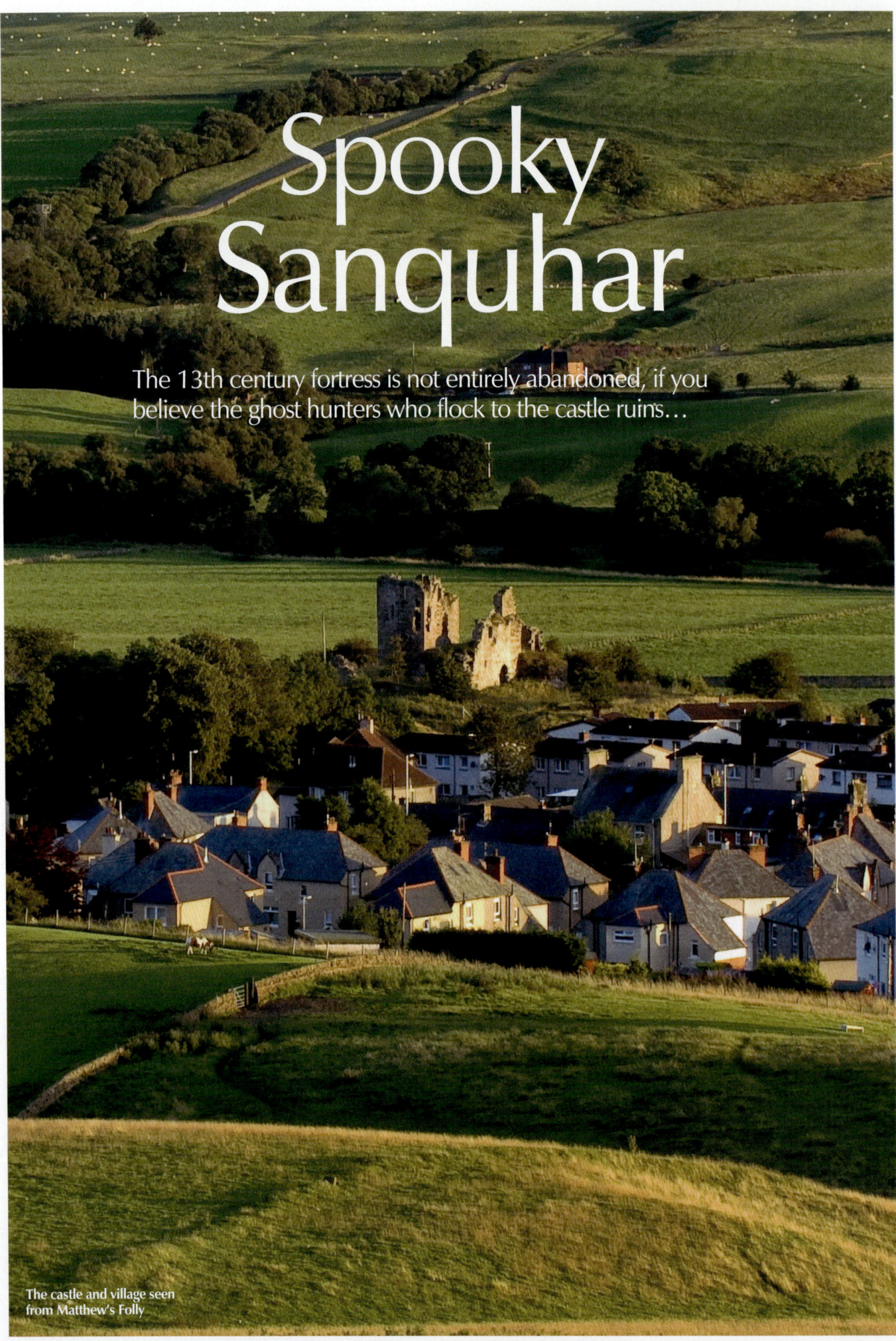

Spooky Sanquhar

The 13th century fortress is not entirely abandoned, if you believe the ghost hunters who flock to the castle ruins…

The castle and village seen from Matthew's Folly

“A woman’s skeleton was discovered in a pit in the 1870s”

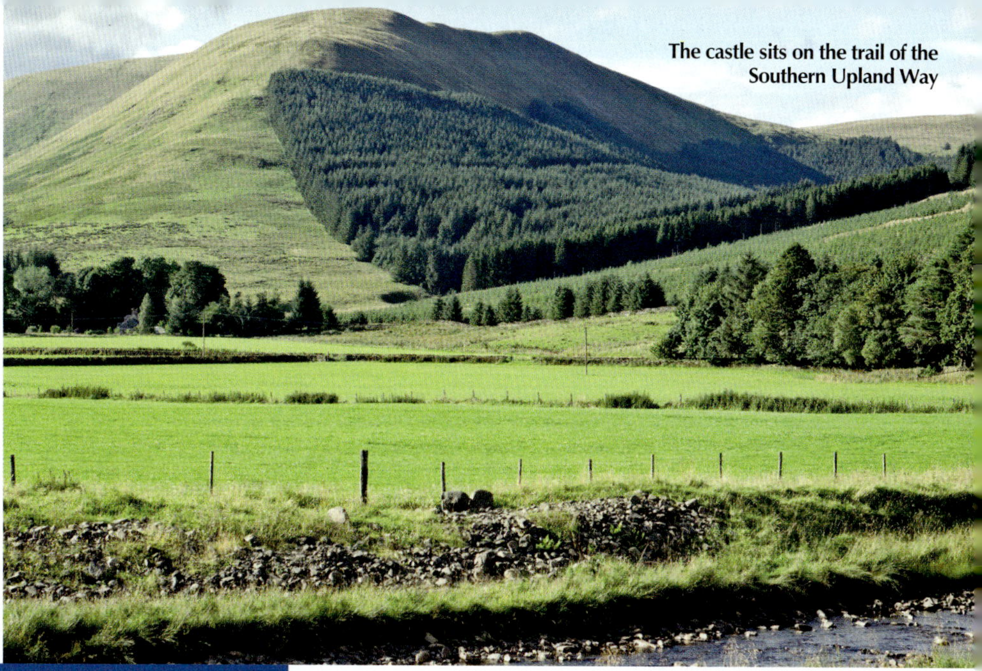

The castle sits on the trail of the Southern Upland Way

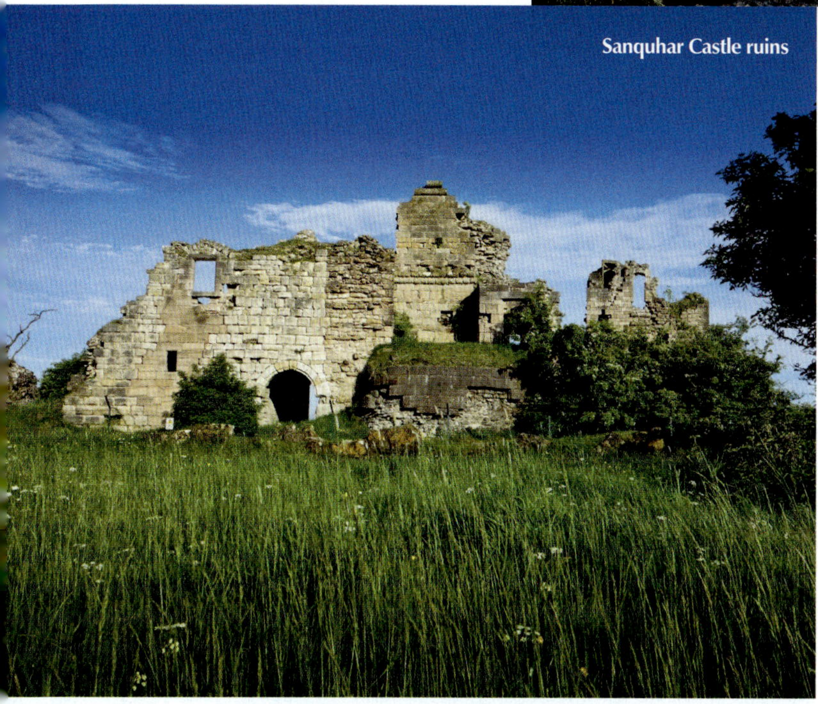

Sanquhar Castle ruins

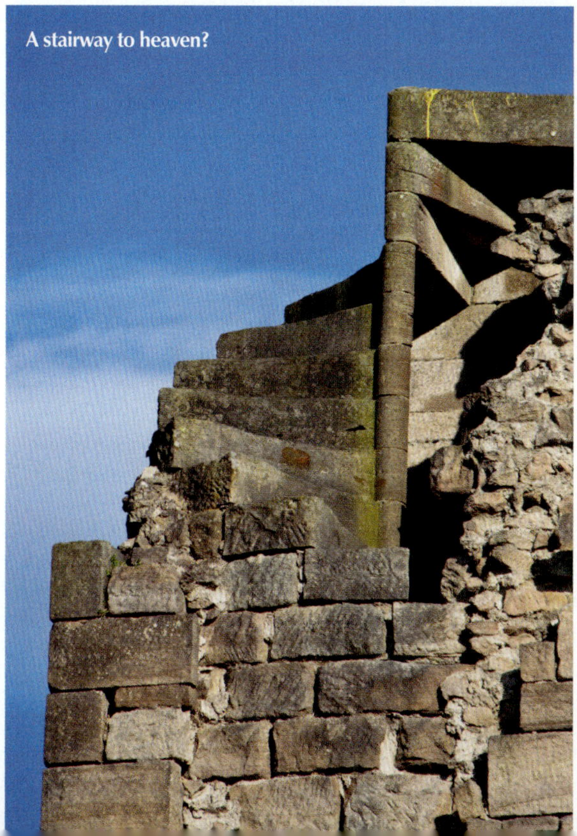

A stairway to heaven?

ONCE an intimidating fortress, the ruins of Sanquhar Castle still stand in the heart of Dumfries and Galloway dominated by a crumbling four-storey tower alongside remnants of a hall block, gateway passage and semi-circular tower.

Constructed in the mid-13th century, the castle served as a stronghold during the turbulent years of the Wars of Scottish Independence. Its strategic location made it a significant military site.

The Crichtons, a prominent Scottish family, came into possession of the castle in the late 14th century and during the 16th century, it saw various renovations and expansions.

However, by the late 17th century, the family's fortunes had declined, and the castle began to fall into disrepair.

By the 18th century, it was largely abandoned and left to decay.

In recent times, efforts have been made to preserve the ruins.

It remains an important architectural site, drawing interest from historians, tourists and most significantly to ghost hunters who are familiar with its haunted history.

Visitors to Sanquhar have reported chilling experiences, including inexplicable cold spots, strange whispers, and shadowy figures drifting through the ruins.

The castle is said to be haunted by a mysterious “White Lady”. She is believed to be Marion of Dalpeddar, who disappeared under suspicious circumstances in the 1590s possibly having been murdered by Lord Robert Crichton.

A woman's skeleton was discovered in a pit during excavations in the 1870s which might support this story.

Another ghost is thought to be that of John Wilson, who was unjustly accused and hanged, who apparently rattles chains and moans while stalking the castle as a reminder of its previous owner's cruelty.

Words: RACHEL MCCONACHIE Images: ALAMY

Deathly DUNTRUNE

Severed hands, ghostly bagpipes, strange bumps in the night... this Argyll stronghold is steeped in centuries of horrible history

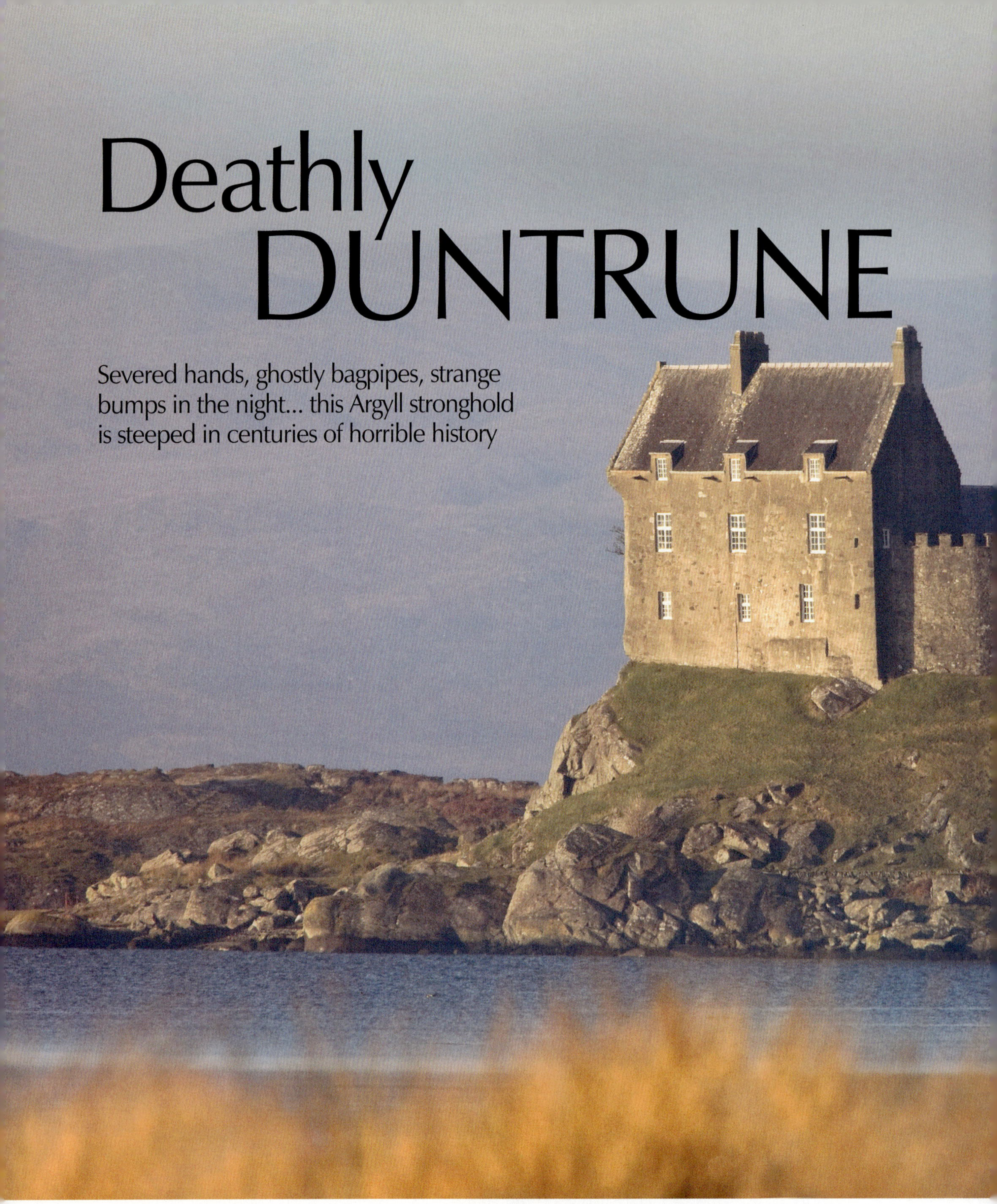

“Dating back over 700 years, tales of eerie phenomena have surrounded the castle”

Originally built by the MacDougall clan in the 13th century

DUNTRUNE CASTLE, nestled in the picturesque landscapes of Argyll and Bute, has earned a reputation as one of the country's most haunted locations.

Dating back over 700 years, tales of eerie phenomena have surrounded the castle, with phantom footsteps, shadowy figures and the mysterious sound of bagpipes playing.

Legend has it that the unearthly pipes are played by the ghost of a brave MacDonald piper who warned his clansmen that their castle had been taken by the Campbell clan by playing the wrong notes in a well known tune.

When his action was discovered the Campbell's chopped his hands off, leaving the poor man to bleed to death.

Although some have dismissed this tale as myth, a renovation project in the late 1800s uncovered skeletal remains, complete save for the hands, buried within the castle walls.

Shockingly, subsequent excavations revealed the isolated bones of two hands, buried separately beneath a castle room.

There have also been numerous reports of poltergeist activity within the castle. Objects have been said to move on their own, strange noises are often heard, and doors reportedly open and close by themselves.

Meanwhile visitors and residents have experienced feelings of being watched or followed, and cold spots and sudden drops in temperature are common too.

Words: RACHEL MCCONACHIE Pictures: SHUTTERSTOCK, ALAMY

Located on the north side of Loch Crinan in Argyll

A Cursed Castle

Haunting follows Lord Fyvie's deadly quest for an heir

Fyvie Ca

Words: KATRINA PATRICK Images: SHUTTERSTOCK

ACCORDING to legend, 13th-century bard and seer Thomas the Rhymer appeared at Fyvie Castle's door requesting shelter. When this was denied him, he placed a curse on the castle that it would never pass in direct line between more than two generations.

Fast forward a few centuries to 1599 when Lord Fyvie, Alexander Seton, was frustrated that his marriage to Lillias Drummond was producing no sons, only daughters. Women could not inherit property at that time, so it seemed Thomas's curse was still active.

Unfortunately, Lord Fyvie blamed his wife, rather than the curse for the lack of male heirs, and promptly began an affair with Lillias's cousin.

Lillias died soon after, but stories differ on how this came about. Some say that Lillias learned of the affair and died of a broken heart, but many say her husband starved her to death in the castle's tower for failing to produce a male heir for him.

Lord Fyvie then married Lillias's cousin, Grizel, but on their wedding night, ghostly wails were heard outside the bedchamber window. In the morning servants found the name D. LILLIAS DRUMMOND etched into the stone windowsill, which can still be seen to this day.

Lord Fyvie's second marriage didn't last long either after two daughters and a son who died in infancy. Grizel died in 1606, again under suspicious circumstances, and Lord Fyvie married again, and finally raised a son who would inherit

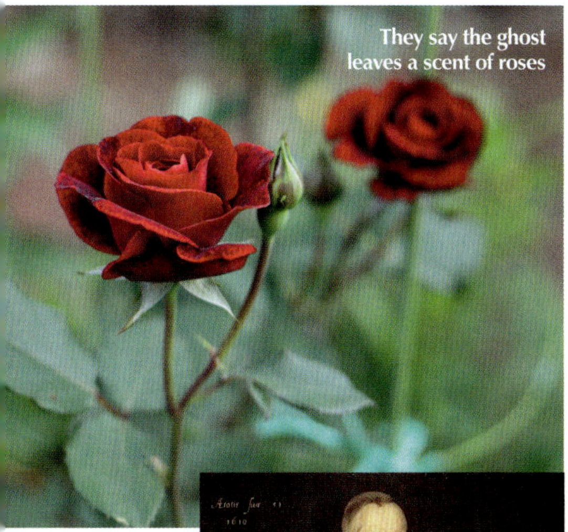

They say the ghost leaves a scent of roses

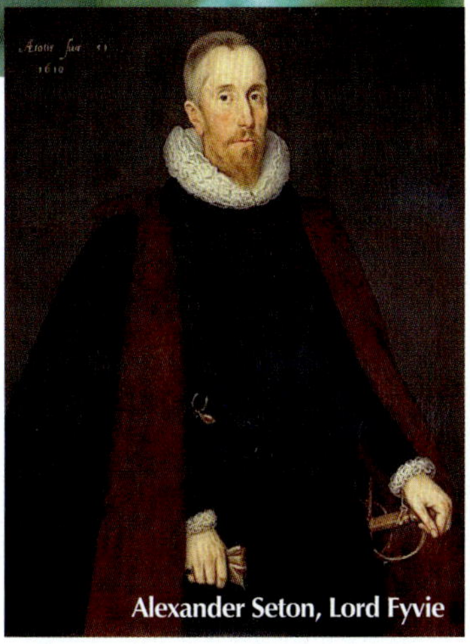

Alexander Seton, Lord Fyvie

"Ghostly wails were heard outside the bedchamber"

his estate. But what happened to Grizel?

A story is also told that in 1920 during renovation work, a skeletal woman was discovered behind a bedroom wall. On the day her remains were laid to rest in Fyvie cemetery, the castle residents started to be plagued by strange noises and unexplained occurrences.

Fearing he had offended the deceased woman, this castle's Laird had the skeleton exhumed and replaced behind the bedroom wall, at which point the haunting ceased.

Was this the body of Lillias, starved to death in the tower? Or that of her cousin, Grizel?

We may never know, but to this day a grey lady is said to walk the halls of Fyvie Castle, leaving behind the scent of roses.

Ghostly Goings-On

Leith Hall in Aberdeenshire definitely makes the rankings for one of Scotland's creepiest castles. Behind its foreboding entrance lie large rooms that visitors say feel inexplicably claustrophobic, with sudden drops in temperature, strange smells and presences.

Several ghosts of the Leith family have been sighted over the years, but the one most frequently reported is that of John Leith III.

After a drunken brawl in Archie Campbell's Tavern in Aberdeen in 1763, John was shot in the head. He was brought home, but died three days later on Christmas Day. It is said his spirit lingers, moaning in pain with a bloodied bandage around his eyes.

Guests have reported seeing him in their bed chambers, and several reported nightmares about a face bending over them while they slept.

But he's not the only ghost that walks the eerie grounds of Leith Hall.

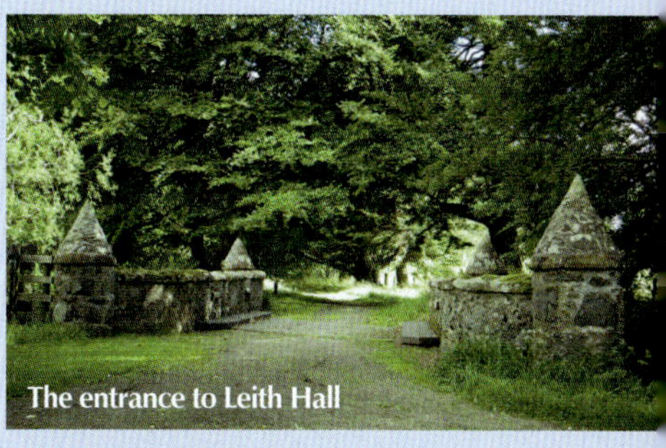

The entrance to Leith Hall

An episode of TV show *Most Haunted* was filmed here in 2003, and researchers discovered that a strange-looking tree in the garden was used by the lairds for executions – the scars left by the hanging rope are still visible on its branches.

During the First World War, Leith Hall became a temporary hospital for more than 500 wounded soldiers shipped back from France and Belgium.

The smell of camphor still lingers in some of the rooms – despite a century of cleaning – and the ghosts of men in military uniforms are still seen by visitors.

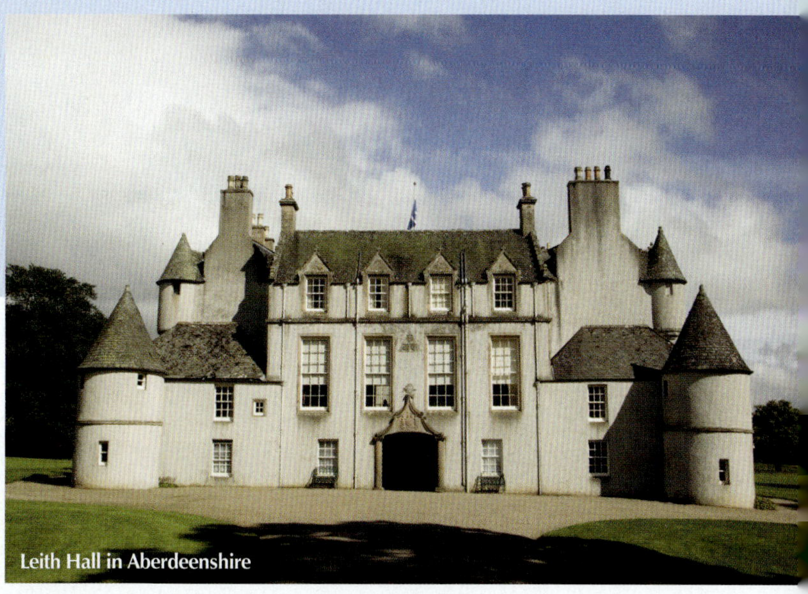

Leith Hall in Aberdeenshire

Fairytale Castle Of Phantoms

Beautiful Crathes Castle hosts at least two spooky spirits from a haunted history

> "Workers found skeletal remains"

CONSIDERING the battles, murders, conspiracies, and tragedies that unfolded within the walls of Scotland's castles, it is no wonder that so many are believed to be haunted.

One of the most beloved and well-documented of these ghosts is the Green Lady of Crathes Castle in Aberdeenshire.

At first glance Crathes does not seem a particularly spooky place. Its resplendent gardens and pink hue would be better suited to a Disney fable than a tale of terror.

Yet Crathes' fairytale facade hides a sinister past. A ghostly lady has been seen floating through the castle, often holding a baby, and with a distinctly green tinge.

The castle dates from the 16th century, and the Burnett family, who are still in residence, were granted the land by Robert the Bruce in 1323. The land was boggy, yet the Burnetts were determined to build a castle there. Many generations of Burnetts attempted to drain the loch and alter their surroundings, and some speculate that nature itself rose up in retaliation.

During renovations in the 19th century, workers were shocked to find the skeletal remains of a young woman and infant. They were buried beneath the hearthstone of the fireplace in what would become known as the Green Lady's Room. While no one knows the identity of the child – or the spectral woman in green – the story seems to have a pedigree dating to at least the 18th century.

In around 1746, the year of the Battle of Culloden, Alexander Burnett, 4th Baronet of Crathes, attempted to drain the loch surrounding his ancient home of Leys several miles from Crathes Castle.

His son was killed in the attempt and

Crathes Castle

family records state the Green Lady began to appear to him shortly after this loss. The Baronet developed an obsessive fear of ghosts – was she trying to confide in another who had felt the pain of losing a child?

It is notable that the Green Lady has never acted maliciously or brought harm to any who see her. She is an echo of a tragedy, not of terror.

Still, that does not prevent the castle's staff from being spooked. Sudden drops in temperature, a feeling of being watched, and strange noises of someone walking around after opening hours are frequently reported by its caretakers.

Queen Victoria stayed at Crathes on several occasions, and was among those who witnessed the Green Lady pacing back and forth in front of the fireplace.

Much more recently, during a family visit to Crathes in 2016, Bill Andrew snapped a photograph of his daughter, granddaughter, and great-grandson posing in front of the tower. Later, when he was looking at the photograph, he discovered that his family were not alone.

An unusual tangible figure can be seen standing behind them in the castle's entrance, wearing a simple, wide dress typical of the 17th and 18th centuries with what appears to be a hood or veil, almost as though she were in mourning.

The Green Lady's sorrow, it seems, shall be a part of Crathes Castle's story for many years to come.

Murderer Or Victim?

There is another female ghost said to frequent Crathes Castle, but the jury is out on whether she was the murderer or the victim in this tragic tale.

In the 16th century, Baronet Alexander Burnett – there were many Alexanders in this family – married the ambitious Agnes Lechtoun. The story goes that he died suddenly and suspiciously leaving Agnes to run the estate in guardianship for their young son, who was called – you've guessed it – Alexander.

When the son came of age Agnes made plans for his marriage that would heighten their power. The young Alexander, however, had fallen for another woman, Bertha.

Bertha didn't fit with Agnes's plans and she poisoned her in the tower room of Crathes Castle, but died suddenly herself on the anniversary of the murder – just as suspicion was beginning to turn on her.

Over the years visitors have reported a female ghost in the tower, now named the White Lady. Whether she is Agnes or Bertha we will never know, but she reappears on the anniversary of the murder.

The tower

Words: DAVID WEINCZOK Images: SHUTTERSTOCK

The castle's walled garden

The Mystery Of The Phantom Pipers

Ghostly notes of trapped pipers echo through Scotland's castles

Dunskey Castle

> "His pipes below the cobbles went silent"

RUMOURS of mysterious tunnels running beneath Scottish castles are as common as midges in June. Not all are nefarious though. One, for instance, is said to simply provide swift and secret passage between Blackness Castle and the House of the Binns.

But then, there is the tunnel beneath Yester Castle in East Lothian, blocked up by terrified locals convinced that it led to a "Hell Mouth".

There is one story that appears again and again in Scotland – that of the trapped phantom bagpiper.

The most famous version is at Edinburgh Castle. Tunnels were apparently discovered leading from the castle towards Holyrood Palace, and a young piper was sent into them to discover their extent. He walked into the tunnel, playing his pipes, with the rest of the group following safely above ground.

Halfway along the Royal Mile the sound of his pipes below the cobbles went silent, and for fear of what took him the tunnel entrance was sealed.

A variation on the ghostly piper tale has the doomed soul bring a canine companion with them, only for the man to vanish and the dog to reappear with all its hair plucked or singed away. The meaning of this would not have been lost on the deeply superstitious Scots of the 18th century – the pair had encountered the devil himself.

“Workers found a large, cavernous space in the sea cliffs where an eerie tune plays”

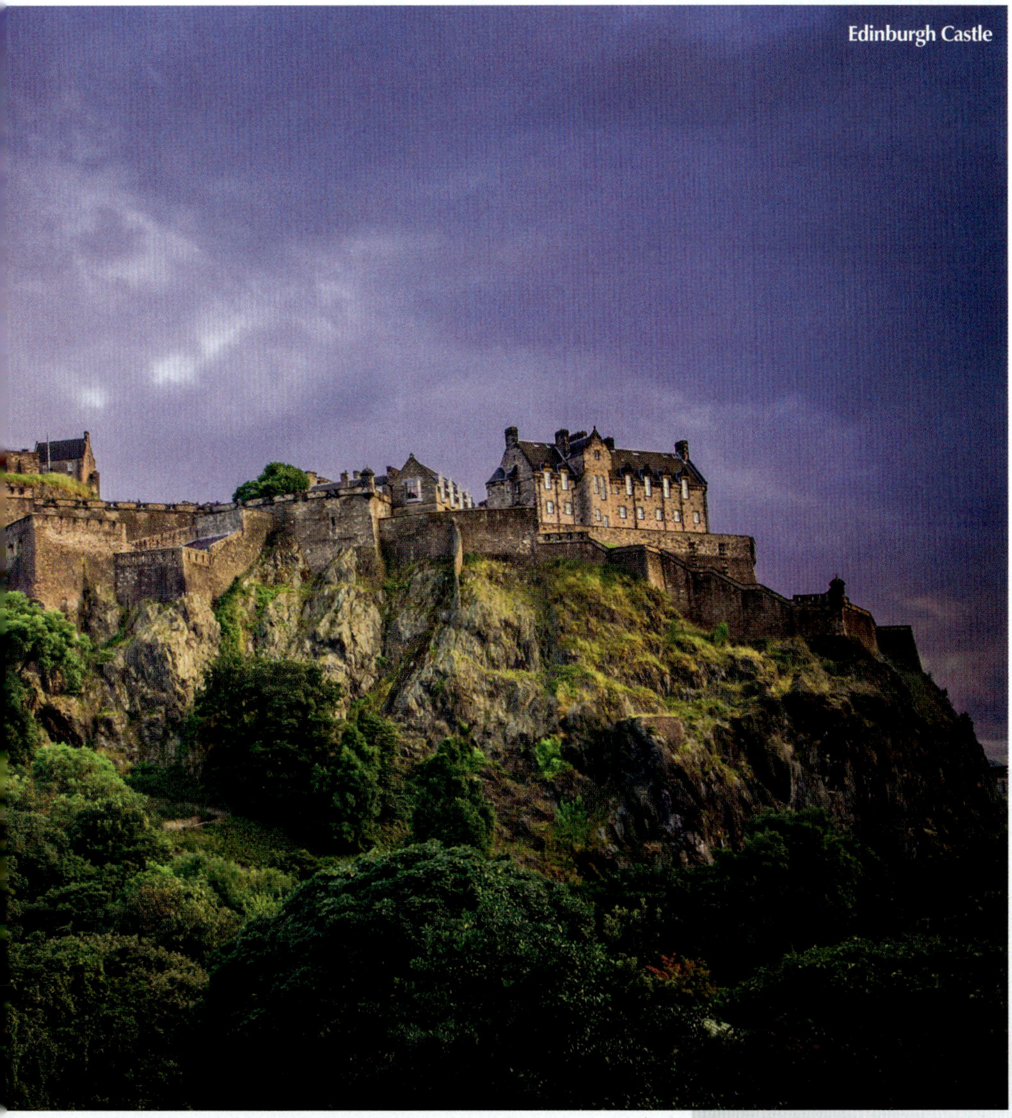

Edinburgh Castle

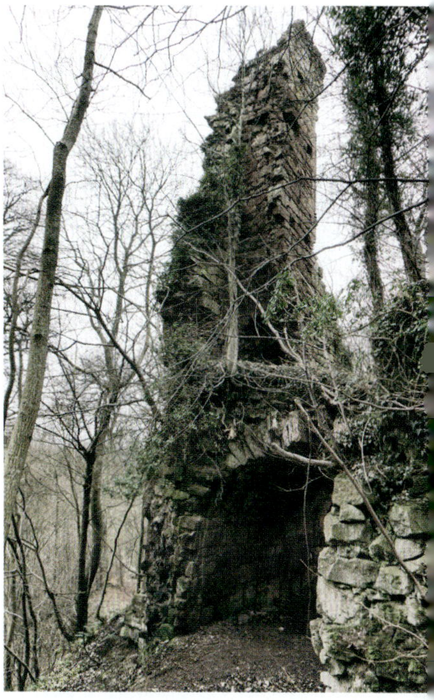

Above: Yester Castle ruins

Below: Scotland is haunted by many phantom pipers

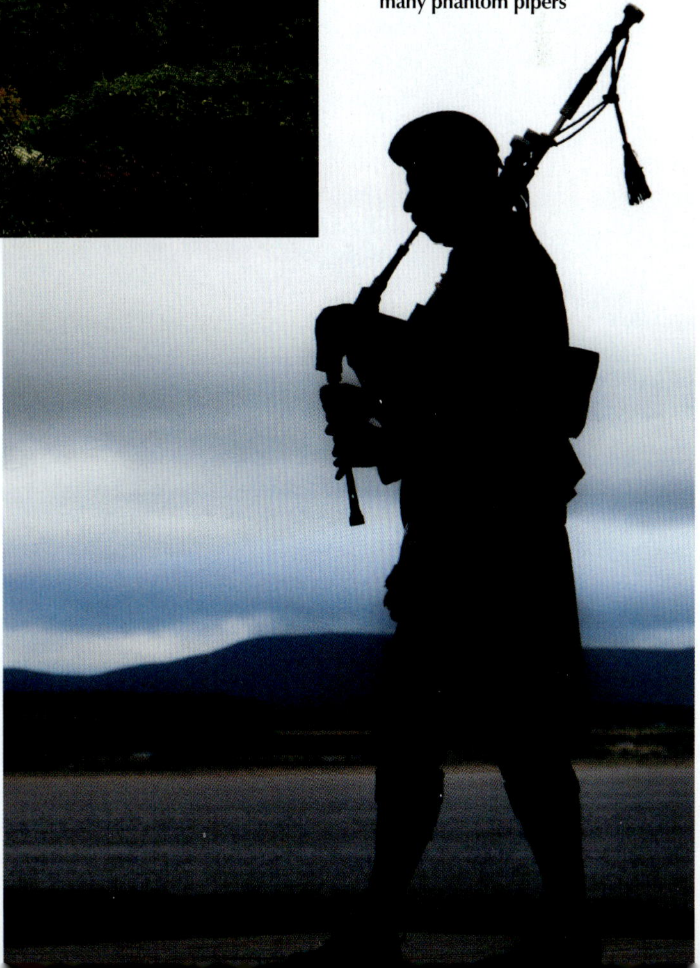

Another phantom piper can be heard beneath Dunskey Castle near Stranraer. Its 14th-century laird Walter de Curry, described as a “sea rover”, captured a rival piper and humiliated the man by forcing him to serve as his jester. The piper didn’t suffer this indignity quietly and was sentenced to starve in the dungeons for his outspokenness, with only his pipes for company. Desperate for freedom he followed a tunnel that seemed to lead to a seaside cave, but never emerged.

Intriguingly, workers in 1911 found a large, cavernous space in the sea cliffs where an eerie tune plays. Whether it’s a whistle of the wind or the forlorn tune of the proud piper is for you to decide.

Words: DAVID WEINCZOK Images: SHUTTERSTOCK

ONWARD, VOYAGER

to Orkney and Shetland

Discovering the Northern Isles has never been easier with NorthLink Ferries.

The comfortable and reliable service offers sailings to Orkney's port of Stromness from Caithness, just off the North Coast 500 route. This 90 minute journey on MV Hamnavoe is the only sailing to Orkney which passes the iconic sea stack, the Old Man of Hoy.

Alternatively travel from Aberdeen to Shetland's port of Lerwick. This convenient service calls regularly into Orkney's capital of Kirkwall.

northlinkferries.co.uk

Operated by serco

NorthLink FERRIES

Chilling Culture

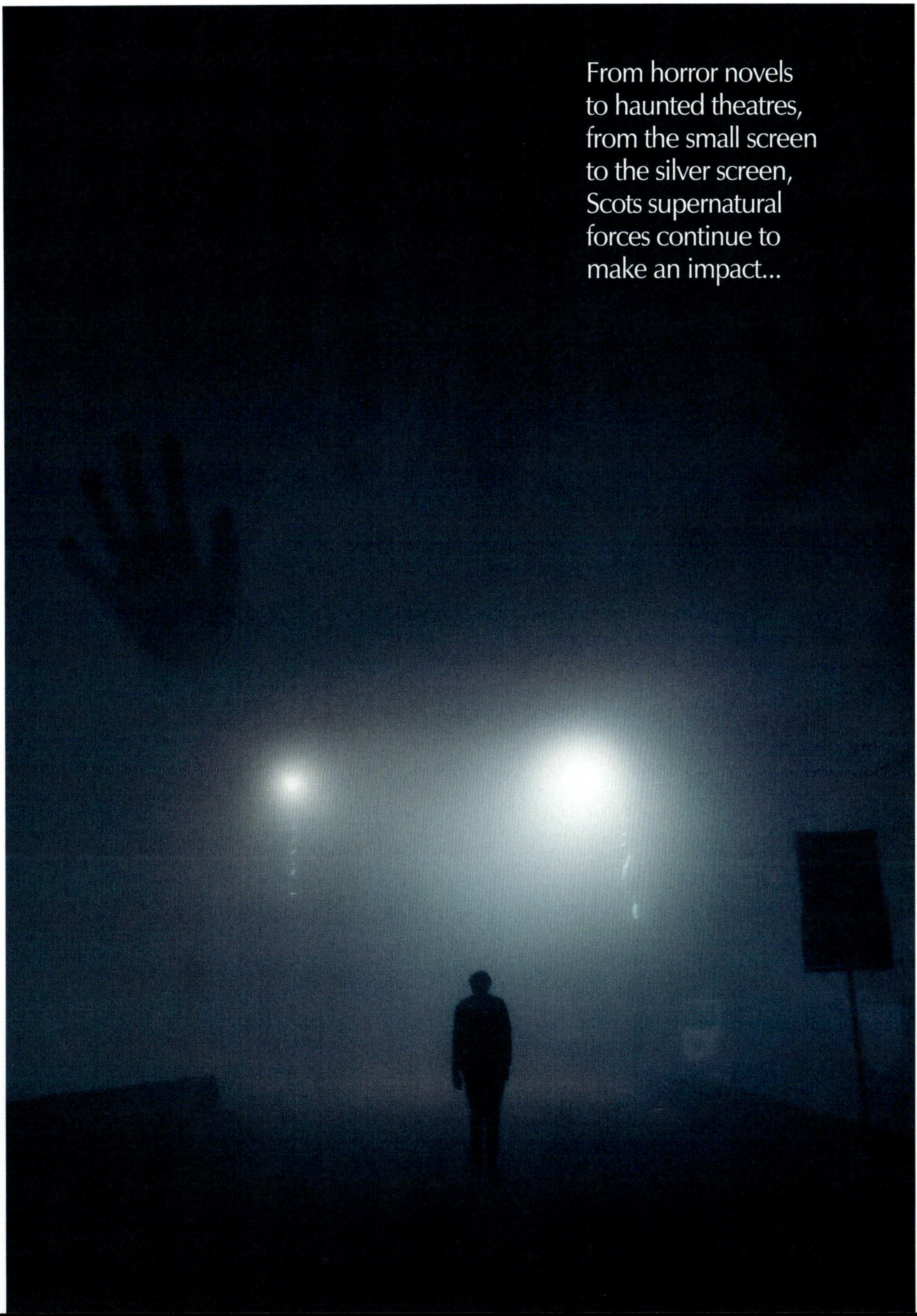

From horror novels to haunted theatres, from the small screen to the silver screen, Scots supernatural forces continue to make an impact...

Outlander Legends

Delving into the strange Scottish folklore and spooky encounters explored in hit TV show

ONE franchise successfully tapping into the gold mine that is Scotland's spooky past is the hit US TV show *Outlander*.

The series follows Second World War nurse Claire, who accidentally travels back in time to 18th-century Scotland.

It's a period of superstition and political turmoil, and Claire encounters more than a few strange goings-on as she comes to terms with her new life in the Highlands.

Indeed, in the first episode Claire's husband Frank says, "There's no place on earth with more magic and more superstition mixed into its daily life than the Scottish Highlands."

Here are just some of the spooky encounters and strange Scottish legends explored in the series...

Outlander protagonists Jamie and Claire Fraser

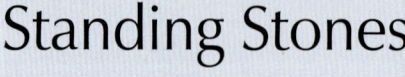

Callanish stones, Isle of Lewis

Standing Stones

The mystical stone circle, Craigh na Dun – which, in the series, transports character Claire 200 years into the past – was inspired by the hundreds of stone circles built in Scotland during the Bronze Age. This includes Callanish on the Isle of Lewis, set up between 2900 and 2600 BC – predating Stonehenge. The purpose of these impressive structures, some built with stones weighing several tonnes, still baffle archaeologists to this day. Theories include primitive calendars, lunar-tracking systems or – in the case of *Outlander* – portals to the past.

Ghosts Of Culloden

In the very first episode of *Outlander*, set in Inverness after the Second World War, we see a ghostly figure watching Claire. Later it is revealed that this is the ghost of Jamie Fraser, whom she meets and falls in love with after travelling back in time to the 18th century. His ghost is wearing Highland battle dress, and it is presumed that Jamie dies at the bloody, real-life Battle of Culloden in 1746. While lying gravely wounded on the battlefield, Jamie also sees Claire's spirit. It is said that Culloden, the site of the last pitched battle fought on British soil, is haunted in real life – ghosts of fallen soldiers are said to rise again on the anniversary of April 16, and the cries of the wounded are heard echoing across the moor.

Samhain

The Gaelic festival marks the end of the harvest season and the beginning of winter, on the eve of November 1. It was believed to be a liminal day, where the boundary between this world and the "otherworld" was thinned – meaning spirits and fairies could cross over. At Samhain, food and drink were offered and bonfires lit to keep the spirits at bay, and it is believed that this festival has merged with the Christian All Saints' Day to become what we know today as Hallowe'en. It is on Samhain in *Outlander* that the time portals are open, enabling the characters to cross through the standing stones to another place in history.

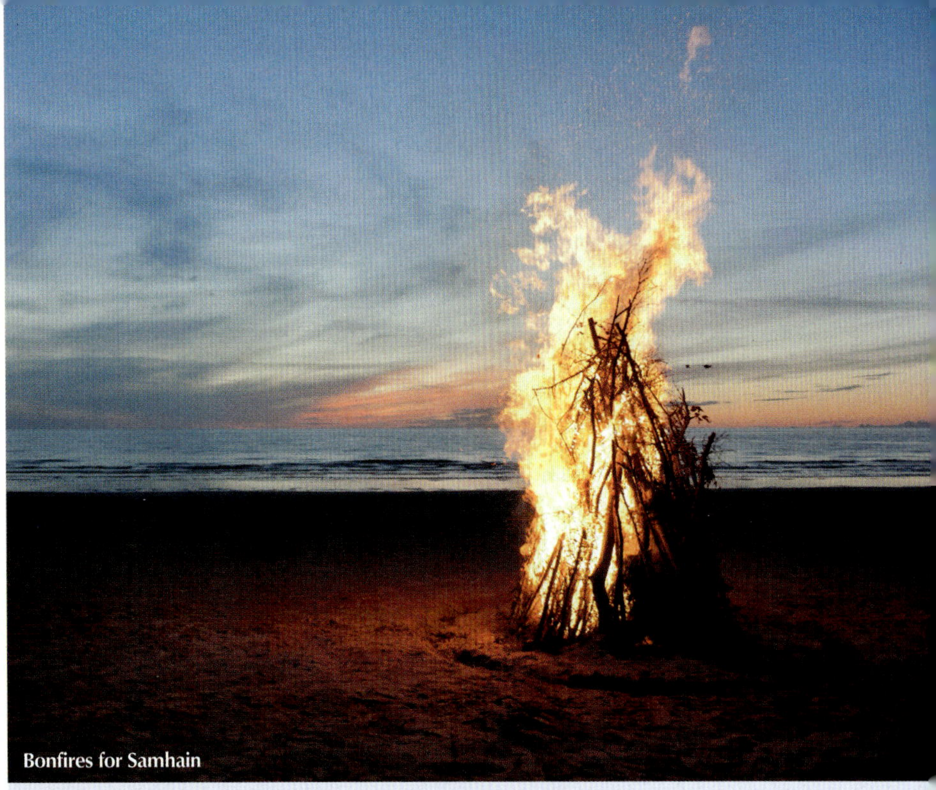
Bonfires for Samhain

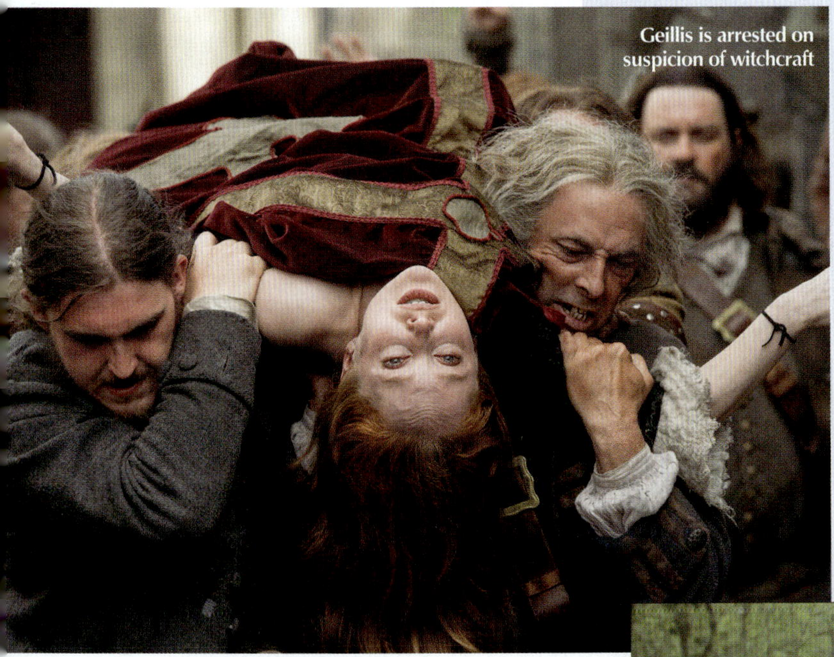
Geillis is arrested on suspicion of witchcraft

Geillis Duncan

The *Outlander* character Geillis is a time-traveller like Claire, who came back from the 1960s to aid the Jacobite cause, aiming to put Charles Stuart on the throne. In the series she is arrested on suspicion of witchcraft, and confesses to poisoning her husband and selling a magical charm called an "ill-wish". She is sentenced to burn at the stake – just like her real-life namesake. The real Geillis Duncan was an unfortunate teenage maid who was tried as a witch during the North Berwick trials in 1591. Under brutal torture, she confessed, and was later burned at the stake for her alleged crimes.

Changelings

In Scottish folklore, if an infant suffered a prolonged sickness, it was believed that the fairies had taken the healthy baby and swapped it for a changeling. The advice to parents was to leave the changeling out on a fairy hill overnight. If it was found alive in the morning, it meant the fairies had swapped them back – but, if not, the parents could be consoled with the fact that their baby was living forever elsewhere.

In *Outlander*, Claire is naturally horrified when she comes across a crying infant left alone in the woods – she can't help but go to it, though it sadly dies.

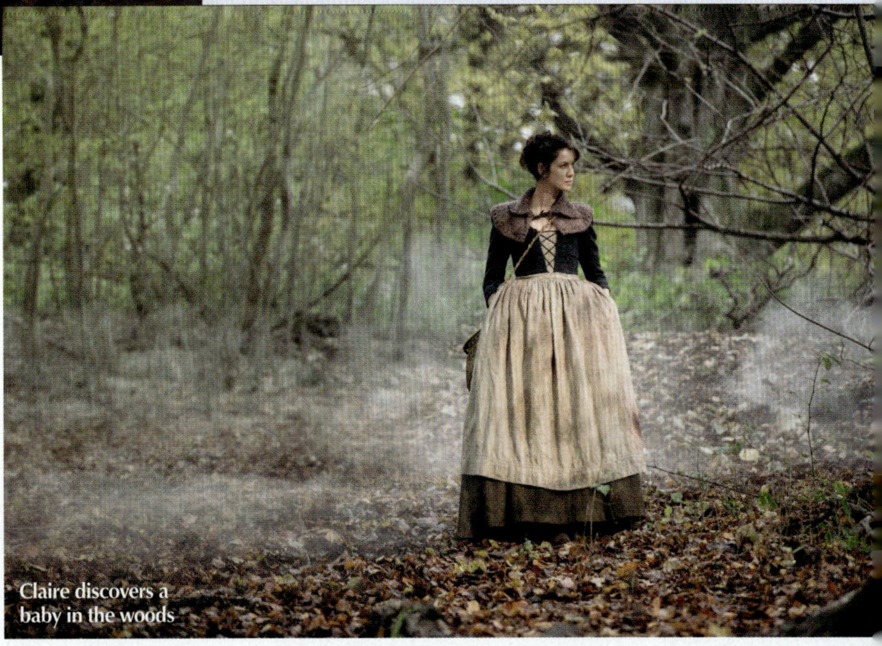
Claire discovers a baby in the woods

Stoker's DARK DAYS

The brooding Dracula author included a nod to an eerie Aberdeenshire castle in his iconic vampire story

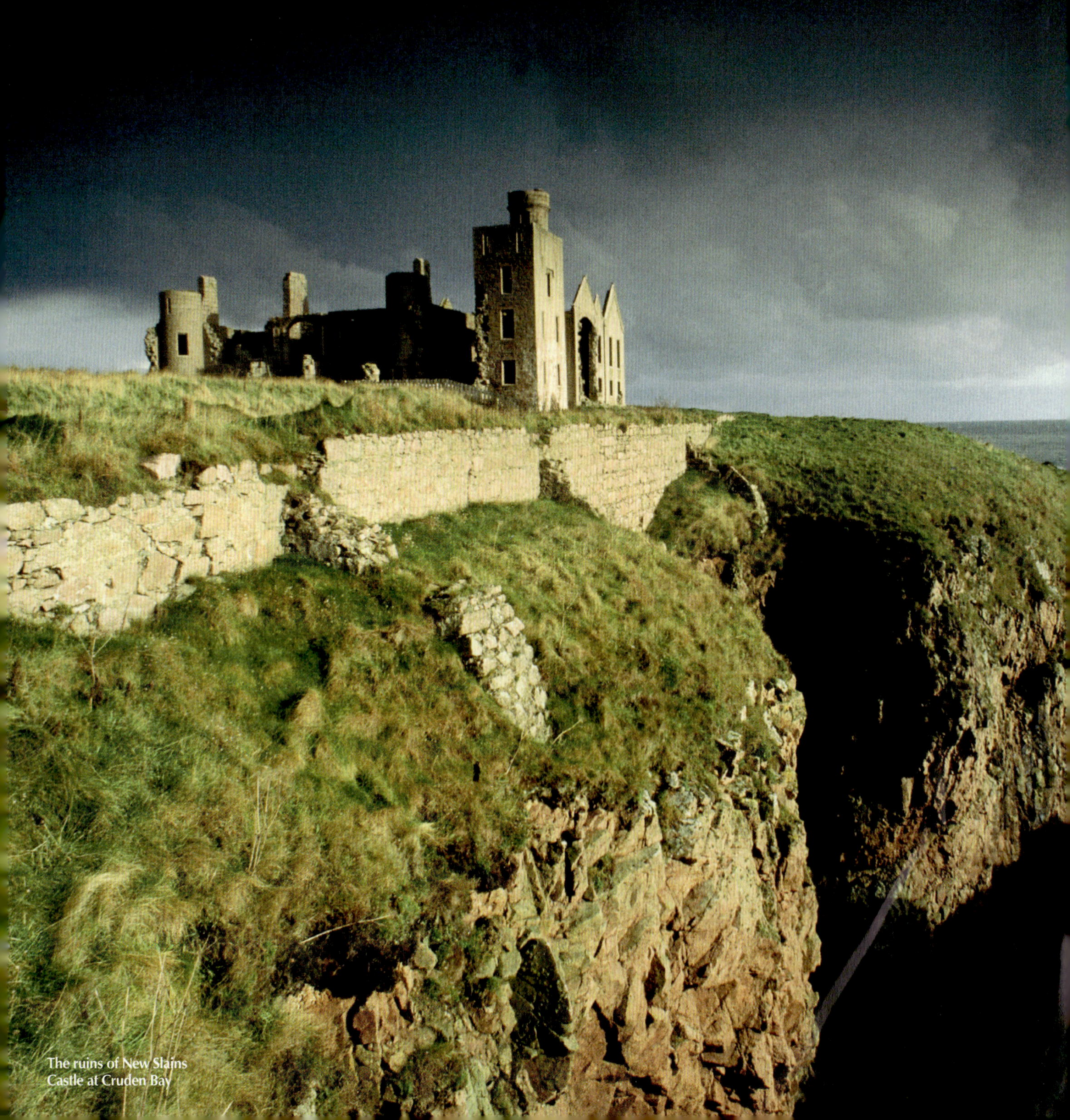

The ruins of New Slains Castle at Cruden Bay

PICTURE a small fishing village on the north-east coast of Scotland in August towards the end of the 19th century. A man is walking up and down the bay, seemingly lost in dark thoughts.

Every so often, he stops to perch on some rocks "like a giant bat", as author Mike Shepherd puts it.

The year is 1895, the location is Cruden Bay – then known as Port Erroll – and the man is the usually witty, urbane and good-humoured author Bram Stoker.

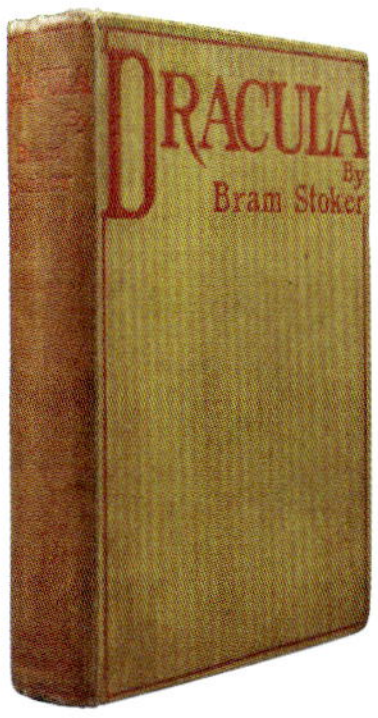
DRACULA
By
Bram Stoker

He is, however, none of these things at this point – despite the fact that the month of August is the only time off from his job as theatre manager of the high-class Lyceum Theatre in London and from his rather demanding boss, the famous actor Henry Irving.

Nor was he unhappy with his holiday location. This was the first year he had visited – getting off the train at Peterhead and walking along the coast until he found somewhere he liked, then telegramming his family to join him.

But he quickly became passionate about the village and returned almost every summer until his death in 1912, setting two of his books there – one including a description of the fang-like rocks of the bay.

That first summer he was working on his latest novel, the plot of which he had created five years previously but had never managed to get on paper.

"When he was writing *Dracula* in Cruden Bay, his family described his behaviour as extremely odd," says Mike, author of *When Brave Men Shudder: The Scottish Origins Of Dracula* and co-author of *Slains Castle's Secret History* with Stoker's descendant Dacre Stoker.

"He was usually full of jokes, but his family found his personality had changed and he became quite dark. He would march up and down Cruden Bay or perch like a giant bat on the rocks on the shore."

The year 2022 was the 125th anniversary of the publication of *Dracula*, and it was marked with the unveiling of a plaque at the Kilmarnock Arms Hotel where the author and his family – wife Florence and son Noel – stayed on their first few visits.

The iconic vampire story is set in Transylvania in Romania – where Stoker had never been – the English village of Whitby, which he had visited once, and London, not Cruden Bay.

Yet it was here that Stoker's muse was finally let loose and he wrote the first chapters of the book – and quite possibly finished it the following summer.

And while there are no named Cruden Bay locations in the novel, there is more than a distinct possibility that the brooding cliff-top castle just around the headland from the village puts in an appearance.

When the novel's hero Jonathan Harker arrives at Castle Dracula, he is guided along a corridor to an octagonal room with no windows, lit by a single lamp hanging from the ceiling – exactly the same as New Slains Castle. "A picture of the room at the time matches the description in *Dracula*," says Mike.

Photographs of the castle at the time also show there was no bell or door knocker, so Stoker – if he had visited – would have had the same dilemma that Harker did on his arrival as to whether his knock would be heard.

And Mike believes it is likely Stoker, with his connections to London society, would have been invited by the owner, the Earl of Erroll.

The castle is now in ruins, although the octagonal room still exists.

Stoker never made much money from writing – *Dracula* only became a best-seller after the 1920s film version was released – and his dream of buying a holiday home in the village never materialised.

But Mike discovered that he was held in great affection by the villagers. "They were very proud he came to write here," he says.

Shortly before Stoker died, his wife Florence was asked to contribute a recipe to a booklet Cruden Parish Church were creating to raise funds. She sent a recipe for "Dracula Salad" – made with red plums and tomatoes!

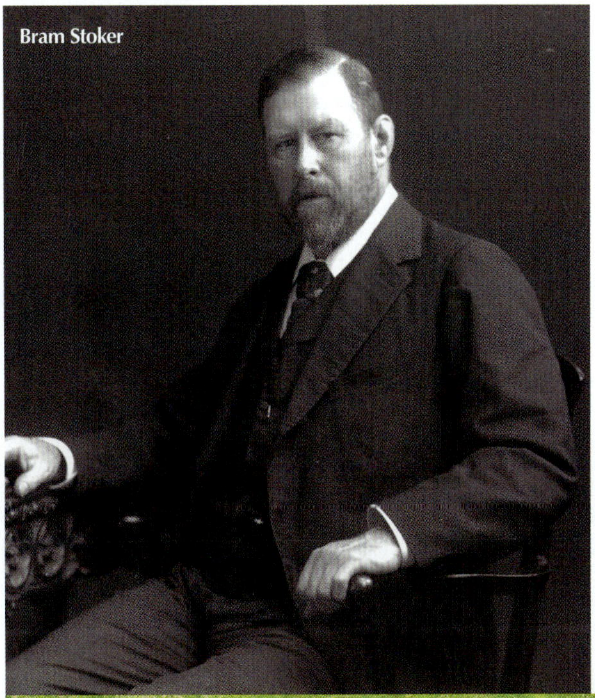
Bram Stoker

Words: JUDY VICKERS Pictures: SHUTTERSTOCK, ALAMY

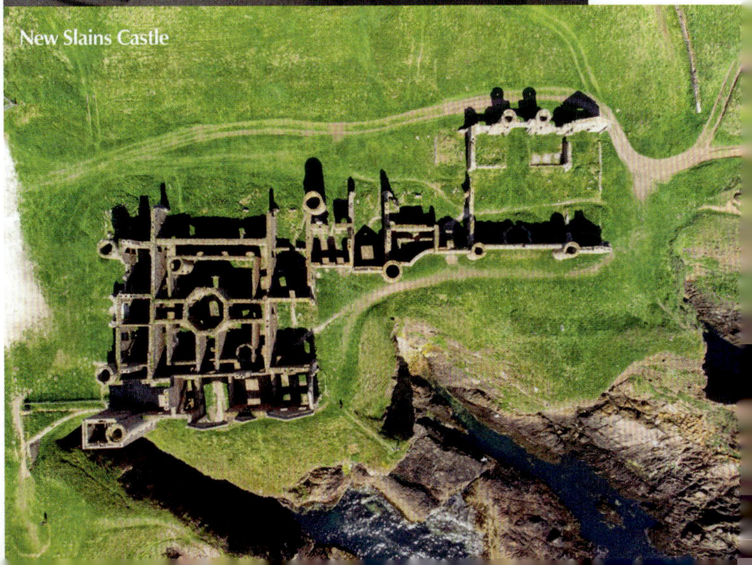
New Slains Castle

"Stoker would march up and down Cruden Bay"

Gripping Plots

The spooky Scottish locations featured in famous works of fiction

Orkney

Words: JUDY VICKERS Images: SHUTTERSTOCK, ALAMY

In Mary Shelley's 1818 novel *Frankenstein; Or, The Modern Prometheus* – which tells the story of a young scientist who creates a living creature – Victor Frankenstein heads to an unnamed island in Orkney "hardly more than a rock, whose high sides were continually beaten upon by the waves" to work on creating a mate for his creation, closely pursued by the "monster". The isolation, wild weather and fog were the main reasons for Shelley's selection of the location – she had never visited.

Orkney

Buckie Thistle

Not a location, but the Highland football team was given a name check in horror maestro Stephen King's 2020 novel *If It Bleeds*. And *The Shining* and *Carrie* author followed this up by appearing in one of the Moray team's shirts at a Zoom appearance at a Bloody Scotland crime book festival event the following year.

> *"The isolation, wild weather and fog were the main reasons for Shelley's selection of Orkney"*

Isle Of Barra

Zombie writer Max Brooks's novel *World War Z* might be best-known in Scotland for the Glasgow locations used in the 2013 film version starring Brad Pitt. But the book itself has another Scottish connection – the island stronghold of Kisimul Castle on the Isle of Barra is named as the perfect place to hide from the zombie plague which has devastated the world.

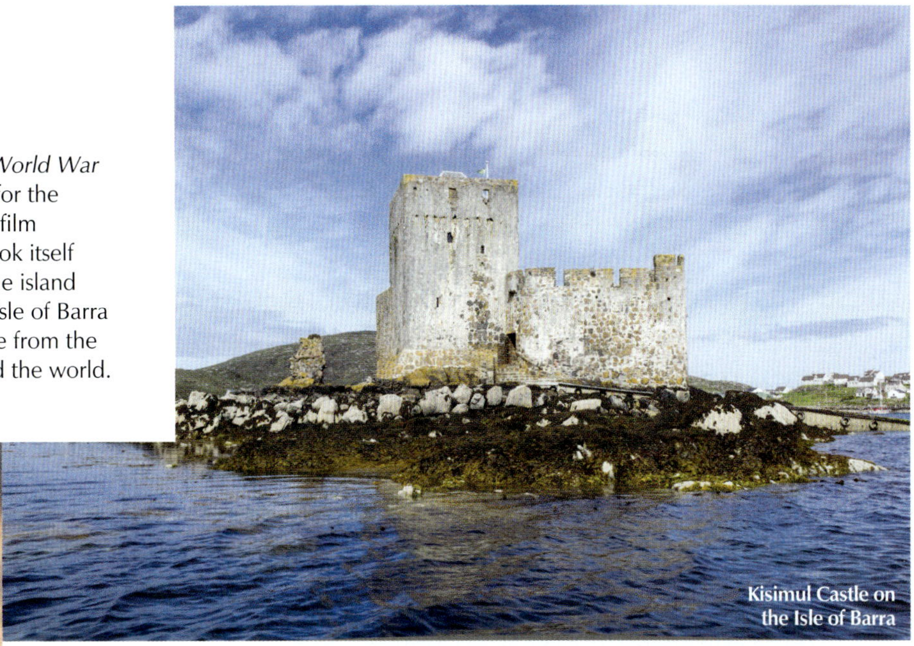

Kisimul Castle on the Isle of Barra

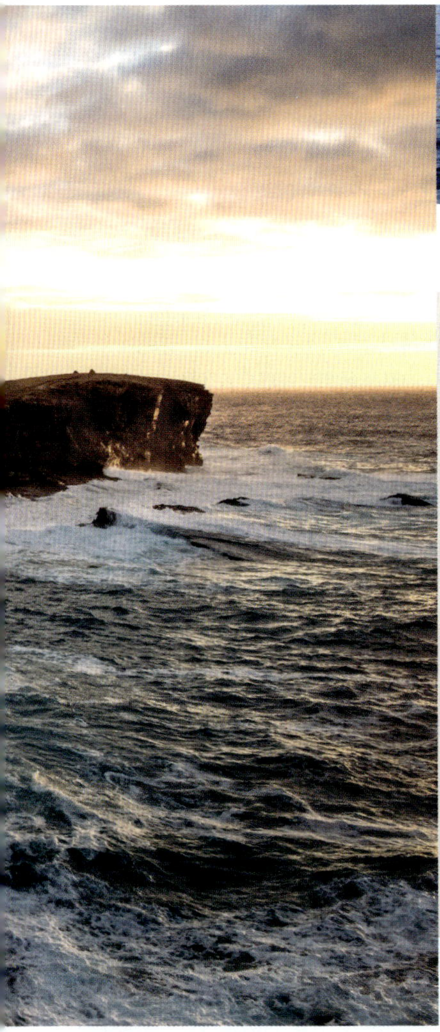

Edinburgh

In Robert Louis Stevenson's *Strange Case Of Dr Jekyll And Mr Hyde*, it's the foggy streets of London that provide the eerie setting for the Scottish author's tale of a man with two very different sides. However, Stevenson was inspired not just by Edinburgh characters such as Deacon Brodie for the novella but by the seedy closes of Edinburgh, such as Fleshmarket Close where Brodie – by day a respected councillor – met his unsavoury friends in a disreputable tavern.

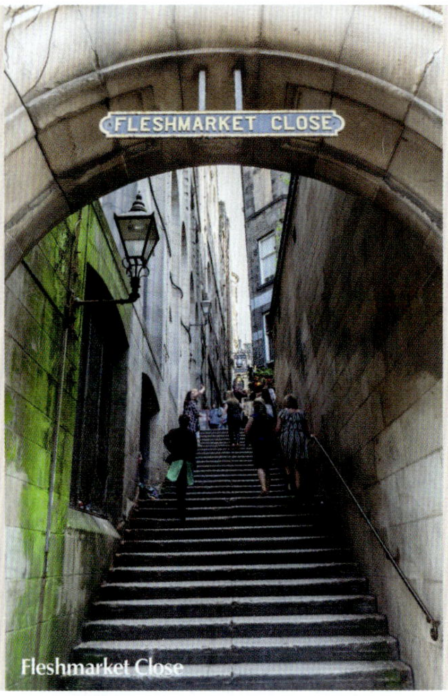
FLESHMARKET CLOSE

Fleshmarket Close

Ayrshire

Ayrshire is the location of haunted Alloway Kirk, where *Tam O'Shanter* sees witches dance and the Devil playing the bagpipes in Robert Burns's 1790 poem. American writer Edgar Allan Poe, famous for his macabre short stories and poems, lived for a time in Irvine after he was orphaned at the age of two. He was adopted and brought to Scotland by a tobacco merchant. His poem *To The Lake* is said to be inspired by the Lady's Walk at Kilmarnock House, haunted by the spirit of Lord Kilmarnock.

Alloway Kirk

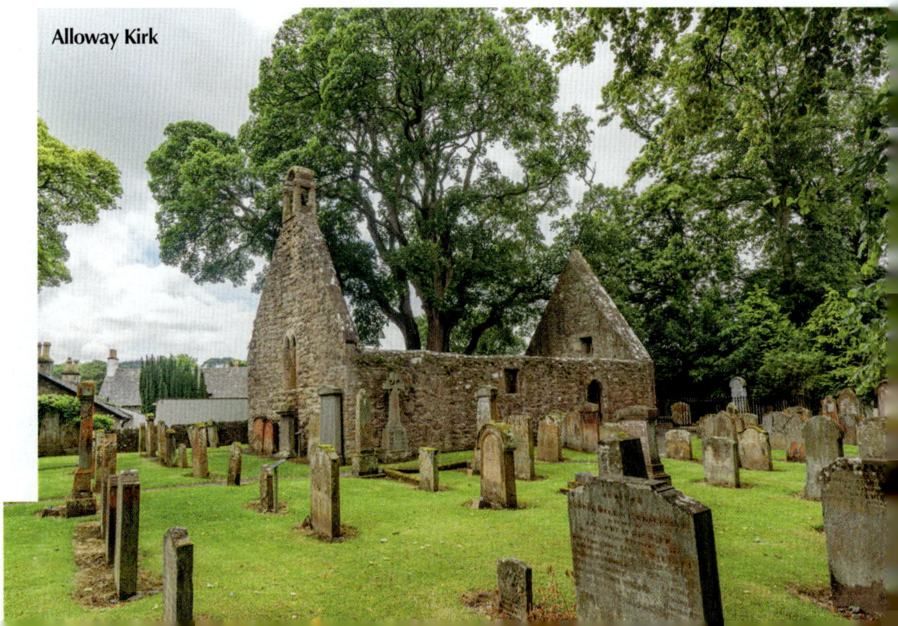

Screen Screams

These frightening films set in Scotland are sure to make you scatter your popcorn!

THANDIE NEWTON CILLIAN MURPHY AND JAMIE BELL
RETREAT
NO NEIGHBOURS. NO HELP. NO ESCAPE.

Let Us Prey
(2014)

For anyone of the opinion that the gorier the horror film, the better – this is the movie for you. Filmed between western Scotland and Ireland, it is set in a small, rural Scottish town – a town that is seemingly entirely populated by society's most undesirable residents. New on the job, PC Rachel Long soon makes her first arrest, but the victim – played by *Game Of Thrones'* Liam Cunningham – seems to bring more problems than the accused. With the arrival of this mysterious bearded man, secrets – and a lot of blood – begin to be spilled.

LIAM CUNNINGHAM POLLYANNA McINTOSH
LET US PREY
DARKNESS SHALL RISE
www.letuspreymovie.com

Retreat
(2011)

A film with an air of prophecy about it. This star-studded flick is set on a remote island of the Outer Hebrides.

A couple – played by Peaky Blinders' Cillian Murphy and *Line Of Duty's* Thandiwe Newton – move to the island to rebuild their lives. On their first night, a storm wipes out connection with the mainland and a stranger appears washed up on the island. The stranger comes claiming terrible news, a deadly airborne virus is sweeping Europe and their only option is to seal themselves in the once seemingly idyllic cottage – where things quickly descend into horror.

Words: GEORGINA MACKENZIE-SMITH Images: SHUTTERSTOCK

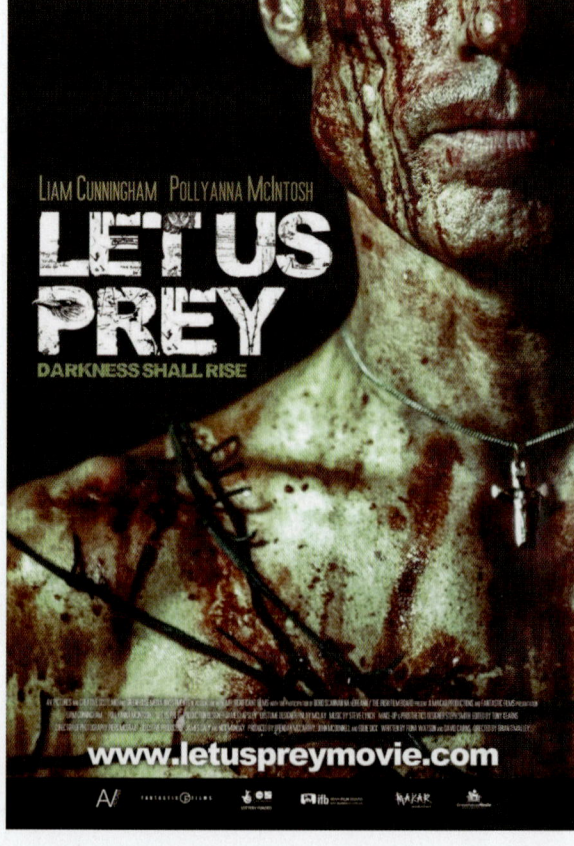

White Settlers
(2014)

This film was coincidentally released just a month before the Scottish independence referendum, but its status as political commentary has never been confirmed by the director. English couple Ed and Sarah choose to abandon their busy London lives in favour of a slow-paced existence in the Scottish Borders. Their strained marriage takes a turn for the better with the move and on their first night they decide to take a romantic walk in the nearby woods. But what starts as a peaceful stroll soon descends into chaos, terror and bloodshed.

THE THRILLER THAT FUELLED THE SCOTTISH INDEPENDENCE DEBATE
"TENSE AND BRUTAL"
"INTENSE AND TERRIFYING"
"NAILBITINGLY TENSE"
WHITE SETTLERS
CROSS THE BORDER INTO FEAR

Scarlett Johansson
UNDER THE SKIN
A FILM BY Jonathan Glazer
"A GENESIS MOMENT OF SCI-FI FABLE."
LOS ANGELES TIMES
"UNIQUE, ORIGINAL AND MINDBLOWING."
THE PLAYLIST

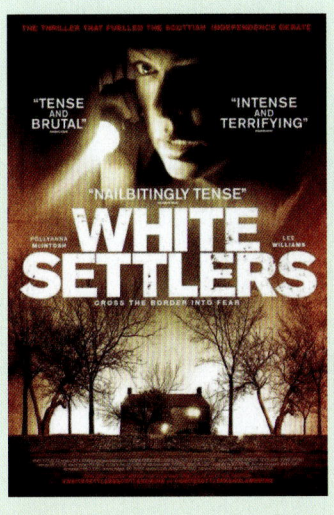

Under The Skin
(2013)

Based on the novel by Scotland-based author Michel Faber, this sci-fi horror was filmed all across the country – from Glasgow city centre to the beach in Arbroath. Featuring Hollywood star Scarlett Johansson as a flesh-eating alien, the film follows her journey along Scotland's roads to find, seduce and consume her unsuspecting male victims. But the film isn't just a spooky alien thriller – as her character learns more about humans she begins to doubt her alien identity and finds herself connecting more and more with her victims, leading to tragic and terrifying consequences.

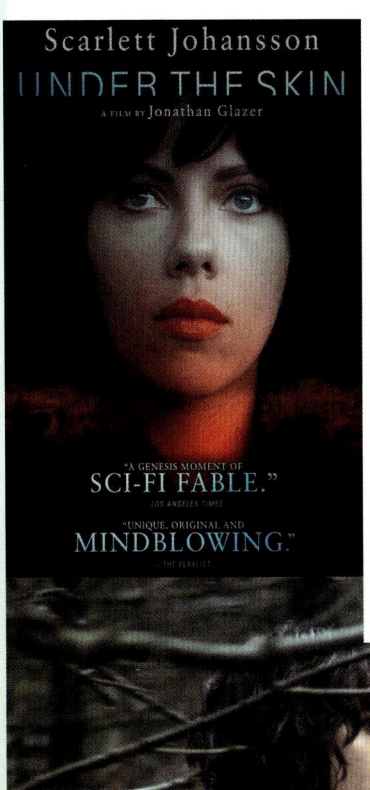

The Unkindness Of Ravens
(2016)

This film follows the story of homeless war veteran Andrew as he roams the Highlands, documenting his mental decline. Surprisingly, given the subject matter, the film uses a mixture of dark humour and jump scares and to paint a picture of the ex-soldier's mental state as he begins to hallucinate and talk to himself. Filmed between Fife, Edinburgh and Perthshire, but set largely against the dramatic backdrop of the Highlands, the depth of the protagonist's mental anguish and loneliness is amplified by his barren surroundings.

The Unkindness of RAVENS
'WHEN THE WAR ENDS, THE BATTLE BEGINS'

"The protagonist's mental anguish and loneliness is amplified by his barren surroundings"

Phantoms Of The Opera

Scotland's theatres are a hotbed of paranormal activity, according to visitors and experts alike

WHAT is it about theatres that attracts spooks and spectres? Is it because these places – like pubs, where large numbers of people gather over the years – have a higher than usual level of ectoplasm, or spiritual energy? It might well be.

Building up over time, this energy allegedly enables spirits to materialise by giving them a link to the corporeal world, so that they can be seen or heard occasionally.

Read on – if you dare...

Tron Theatre
Glasgow

The Tron, in Glasgow's Merchant City, has served as a theatre since 1981. Before then it was a church, which is said to have burnt down in 1793.

In its time, it was also used as a meeting place by members of Glasgow's Hellfire Club. These clubs' supposedly satanic deeds are shrouded in secrecy, but it's little wonder that reports of paranormal happenings in this theatre are many and scary.

Staff have reported uncomfortable feelings of being watched, while two phantom children and a man dressed in horse-riding apparel have apparently been encountered.

The most paranormally active site here is centred on the two back rows of the auditorium.

Investigators have contacted a swathe of spirits here, including a child thought to be around eight years old, as well as a teenage girl.

Words: GILLY PICKUP Images: SHUTTERSTOCK

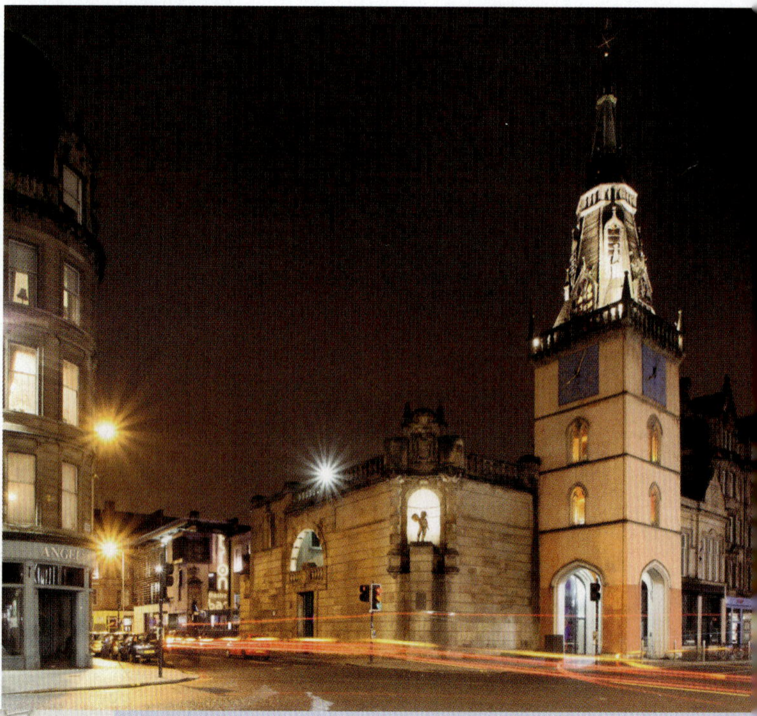

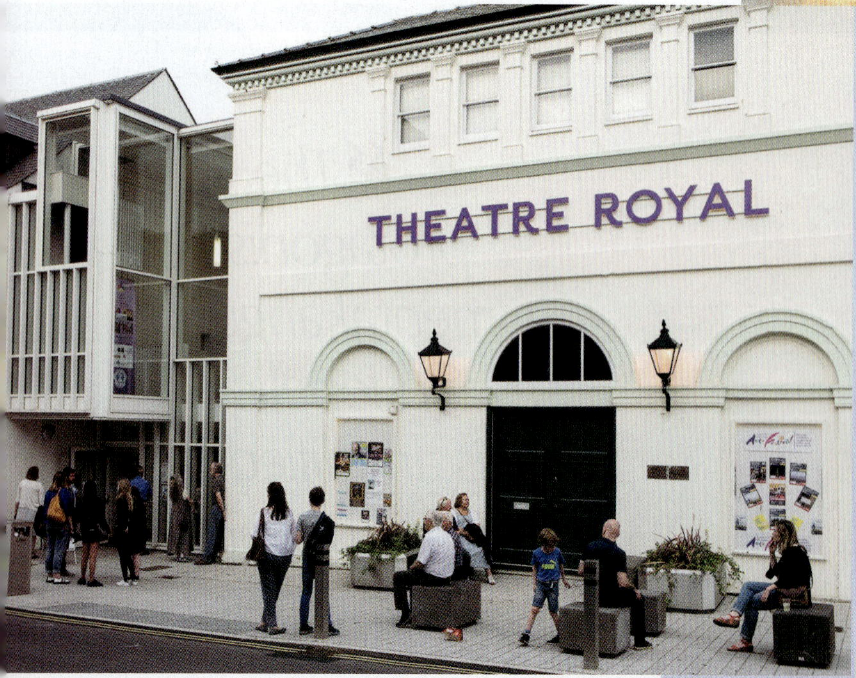
THEATRE ROYAL

Theatre Royal
Dumfries

Paranormal occurrences are rife in the Theatre Royal, which is Scotland's oldest working theatre.

Scotland's bard Robert Burns and JM Barrie, of Peter Pan fame, are among those who have thrilled audiences here.

Many unexplained episodes seem to occur in the theatre's green room, where a ghostly female makes her presence felt to unsuspecting guests by blowing on their necks. At other times, opera singing has been heard – though no one is there.

There is a particularly unnerving staircase in this theatre, too. People who use it have said they are sure a presence is walking right alongside them.

And ghost hunters who held a vigil there reported hearing unexplained sounds and objects being moved.

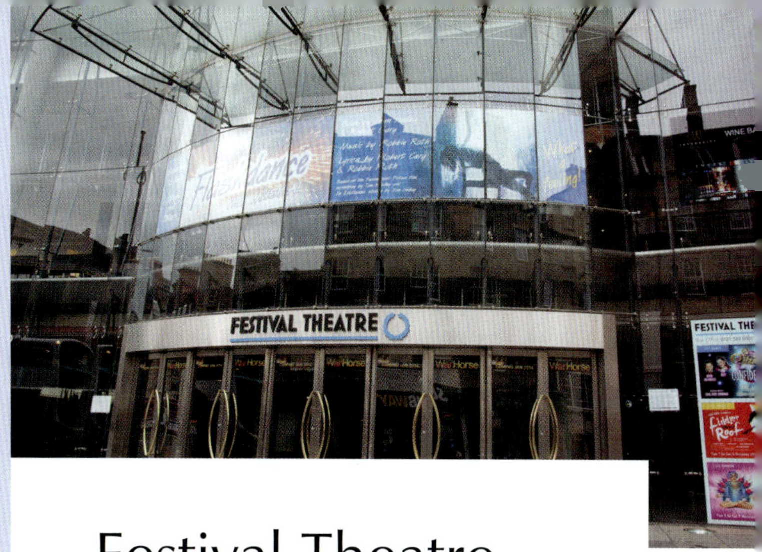
FESTIVAL THEATRE

Playhouse
Edinburgh

Albert the ghost sometimes appears at the Playhouse, the UK's largest all-seated theatre, and his arrival is usually accompanied by a chill in the air.

The building was once a cinema and before that a tabernacle, a religious meeting site. It even served as an insane asylum run by nuns – quite a history.

One day, after a reported break-in, the police arrived. An officer said he'd met a man in grey overalls who introduced himself as Albert the doorman. The manager said no one else was in the building and there was definitely no Albert the doorman.

Staff have reported hearing footsteps when no one is around, while others have spotted a shadowy grey figure lurking on level six.

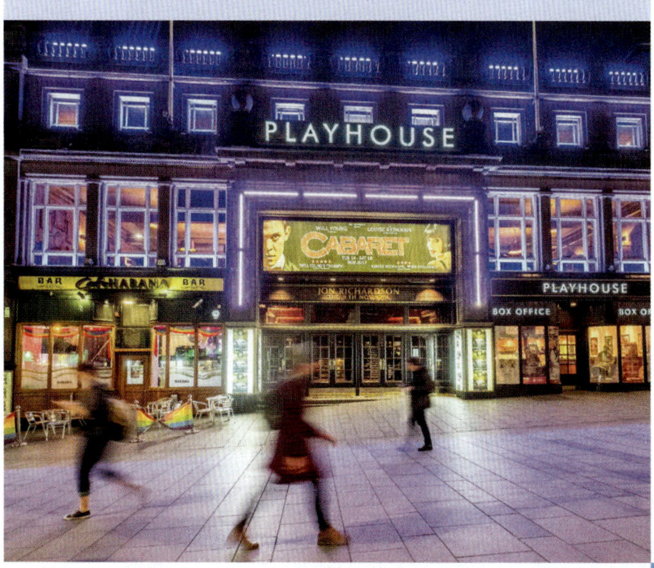
PLAYHOUSE
CABARET
JON RICHARDSON
PLAYHOUSE
BOX OFFICE

Festival Theatre
Edinburgh

The Festival Theatre, home to one of the UK's largest stages, also has its fair share of spooky goings-on. One of the strangest stories concerns Sigmund Neuberger, known as The Great Lafayette – one of the 20th century's most famous illusionists.

In 1911, he visited the Festival Theatre to perform his most ambitious production to date. As he was in action, a lamp toppled over – setting fire to the stage. Several people died, including the great man himself, who was later found beneath a trapdoor below the stage.

Even though he is long gone from this mortal coil, he often comes back to the theatre, continuing to mystify those who see him.

He isn't the only ghost, though. There is also a one-legged sailor, referred to rather unimaginatively as "Peg Leg". Long ago, off-duty sailors were hired to work in theatre fly lofts, because they knew about knots and how to raise and lower sails.

These narrow platforms, dimly lit during performances, can be daunting places – and on the narrow walkways high above the stage in the Festival Theatre there have been sightings of a limping figure, together with unsettling sounds of an artificial leg scraping on the floor...

The King's And Theatre Royal
Glasgow

One of Scotland's most historic theatres, The King's Theatre is home to the "Seat-tipper" – a naughty ghost who likes moving seats up and down. And a Grey Lady is said to waft along the top floor corridor.

Over at Theatre Royal Glasgow, its most famous phantom is poor Nora, who just wanted to be an actress. Either her acting was terrible or the selection panel were particularly difficult, because she was booed off stage after a disastrous audition and apparently took her own life.

She cocked a snook at the judges, though, as her continued presence ensures she'll last longer on stage than any of her contemporaries.

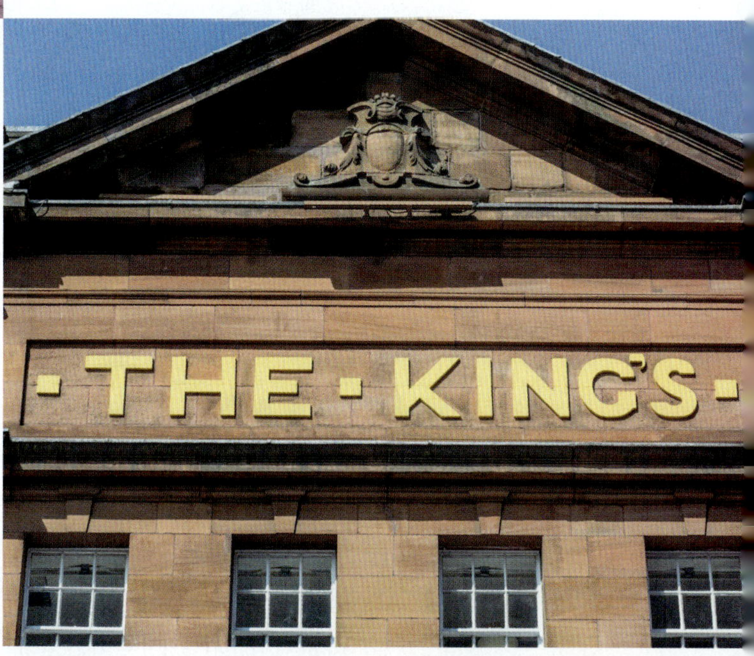
·THE·KING'S·

THE JOY OF GIN

AROUND THE WORLD IN 80 GINS

Refreshing The Soul
One Sip At A Time

£8.99 +p&p

- The ultimate guide to cool cocktails & top tonics
- Gin-spiring interiors for your perfect gin palace!
- Discover the most exciting gin joints & distillery tours

The Scandalous History Of Gin
A spirited trip through time

On Sale Now

ORDER ONLINE: www.dcthomsonshop.co.uk/joy
OR CALL: 0800 318 846 quoting GINMG
Lines open 8am - 6pm Mon-Fri
Postage Charge: £2.99. Also available in WHSmith stores and on Amazon

Scan me!

Fairies & Folklore

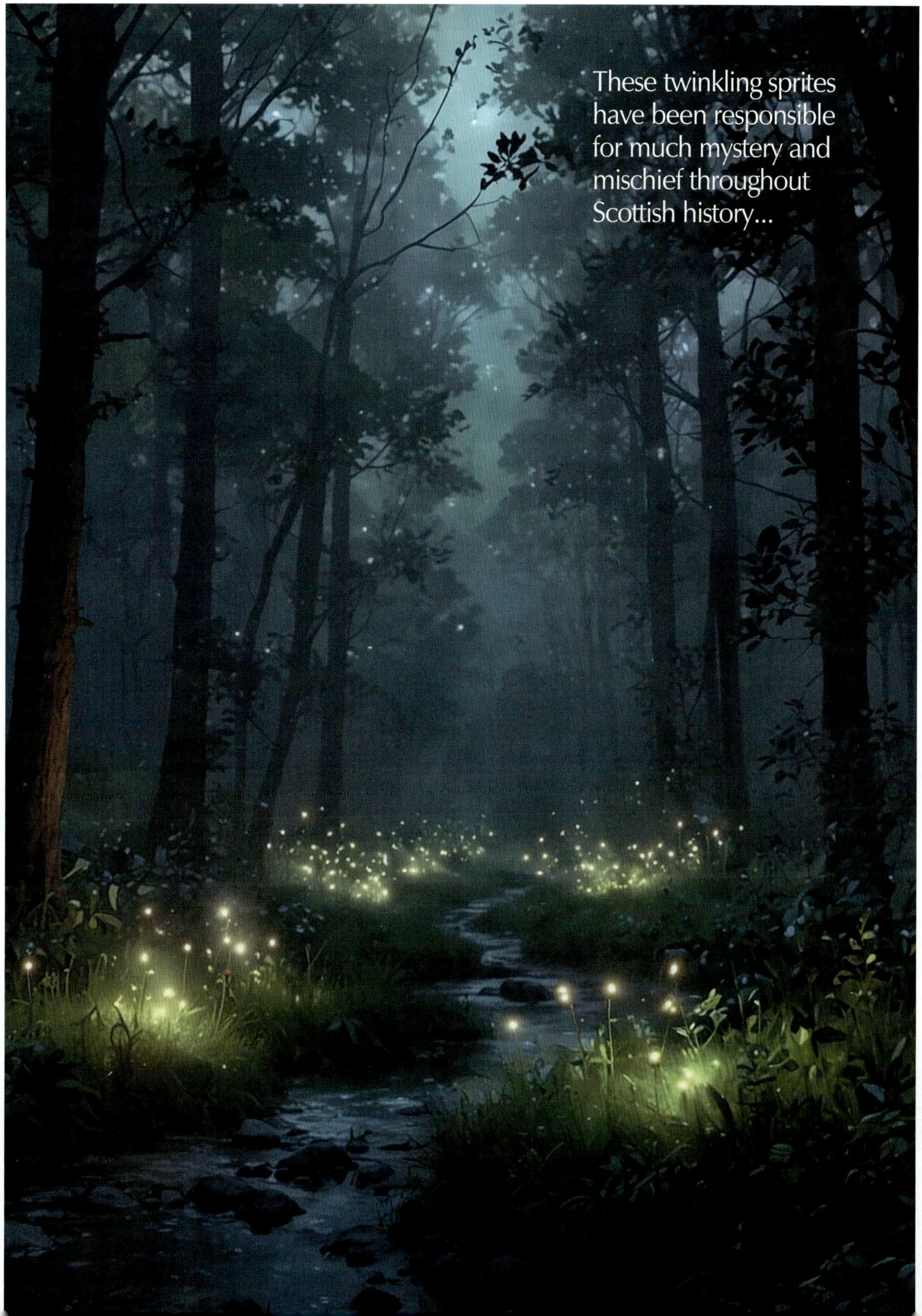

These twinkling sprites have been responsible for much mystery and mischief throughout Scottish history...

The Fairy Kingdom

Keep on the right side of these creatures to avoid their vengeance

A green path leads

FAIRIES – or faeries as they are often known – are an important part of Scottish folklore. These creatures are said to be able to change their shape and size, although many appear in tiny human form.

While most of us think of fairies as being joyful creatures, according to legend they can be rather devious and enjoy playing tricks on humans. The female of the species, although beautiful, is known to be particularly malevolent.

Fairies prefer to avoid humans if possible, choosing to dwell in remote hills, mountains and near water pools instead. When humans enter their territory, we should treat their domain with respect, and avoid wearing green – the colour of the fairies.

When discussing fairies, we should choose our words carefully – for even if we can't see them, it doesn't mean that they can't see us.

Highlanders would often refer to fairies as "good people", even when they believed they were up to no good. The terms, "the good neighbours", "the fairfolk" and "the

Fairies live in remote places such as the Fairy Pools on Skye

An illustration of Thomas Rhymer's ballad

James VI

people of the peace", were also common throughout Scotland.

In the 13th century, Scots poet and laird, Thomas of Erceldoune, became famous for his inability to lie, and for several prophecies which came true. When asked how he came by these gifts, Thomas wrote his famous ballad, *Thomas Rhymer And The Queen of Elfland*, which recounts his own encounter with a fairy.

In the song, Thomas speaks of meeting a fairy queen who was dressed in green and riding a horse with silver bells in its mane. In the poem, the fairy queen forbids Thomas from eating anything other than what she brings him – and he obeys. She then shows him three paths, one with thorns that leads to heaven, one fair and lovely that leads to hell, and lastly a green path that leads to fairyland.

She leads him down the green path and tells him, "ye maun hold your tongue, Whatever ye may hear or see, For, if you speak a word in Elflyn land, Ye'll neer get back to your ain countrie." The queen then takes him back to her fairy kingdom for seven years.

Once his seven years were up, he returned home with the gift of prophecy. Thomas went on to make several accurate prophecies – notably the death of Alexander III, and James VI inheriting the throne of England.

Skye Fairies

Over time, our fear of fairies may have lessened, but our fascination with these mysterious creatures has not waned.

If you fancy spotting one in the wild, you might want to take a trip to the Isle of Skye, which is rumoured to be a popular haunt of the "little people".

The Fairy Pools, are the perfect starting point. This bewitching beauty spot, at the foot of the Cuillin, has a magical feel to it. Featuring beautiful waterfalls and crystal clear water pools – this entrancing location is fit for a fairy queen.

The Fairy Glen, on the west side of Trotternish,

above the village of Uig, is another celebrated fairy hangout.

This spectacular place, which is filled with lochans, cliffs and grassy knolls, has an otherworldly feel about it.

In fact, it's so enchanting that it appeared on the silver screen in 2007, after being chosen as a filming location for the Hollywood fairy movie *Stardust*, starring Michelle Pfeiffer and Claire Danes.

Away With The Fairies

A magical whistlestop tour of some of Scotland's fairy hotspots and legends…

The Fairy Queen

Around 700 years ago, while roaming the Eildon Hills above Melrose, Thomas the Rhymer lay down and dozed off beneath the Eildon Tree. When he woke, he met the Fairy Queen. She led him away to Fairyland and when he returned, what had seemed like three days turned out to be seven years.

Before his return, the Queen gave Thomas the gift of speaking the truth and the ability to foresee events in Scotland's future; relating what he saw in rhyme.

"True Thomas" as he was also known, on account of the fact he couldn't tell a lie, is one of Scotland's best-known prophets. Should you ever be tempted to take a nap on this peaceful hillside perhaps it's worth remembering the Fairy Queen's parting words to Thomas… that one day she would return.

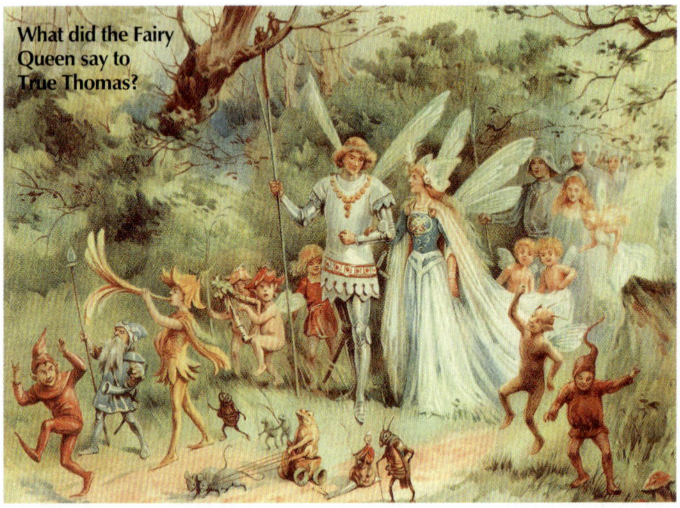

What did the Fairy Queen say to True Thomas?

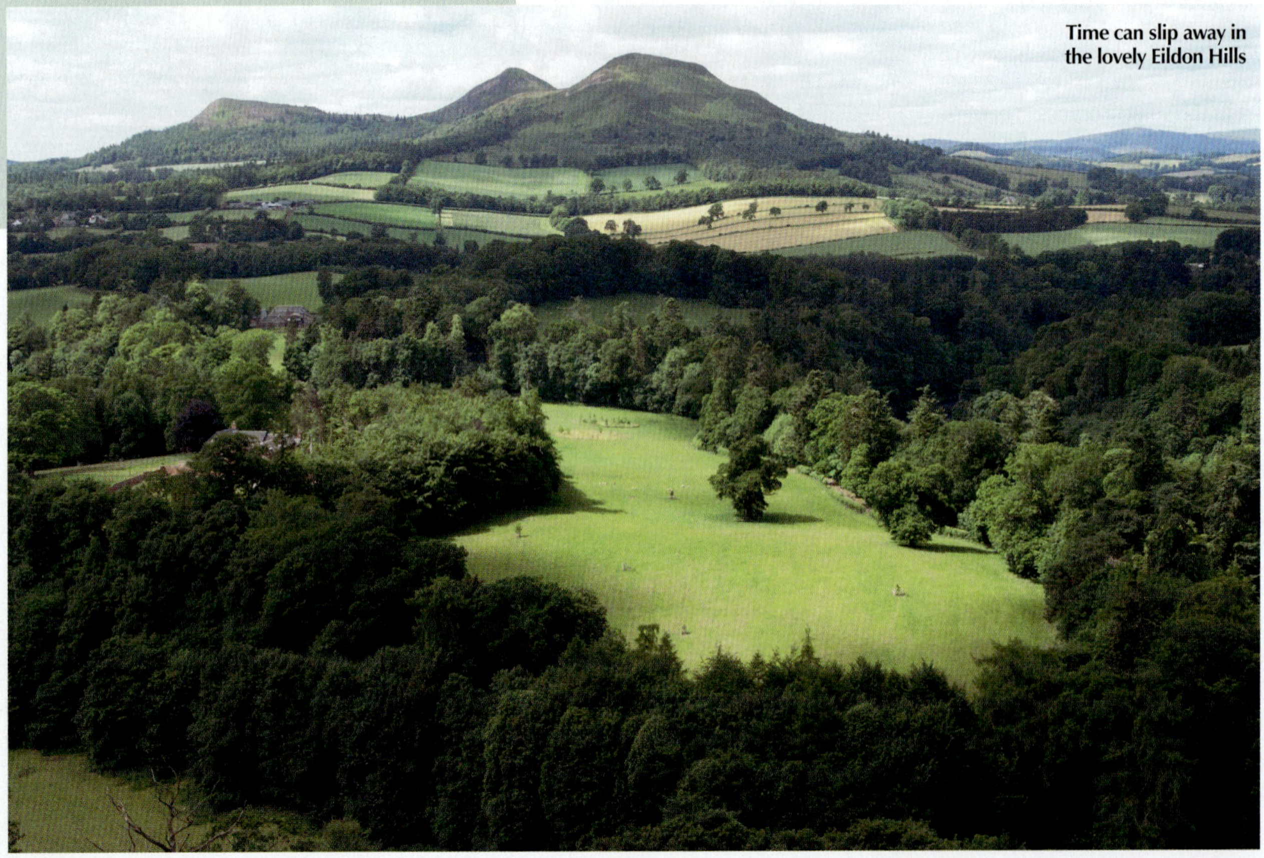

Time can slip away in the lovely Eildon Hills

Words: WILLIE SHAND Images: SHUTTERSTOCK, ALAMY

In The Glen Of The Fairies

Dun Sith, Spittal of Glenshee

The present kirk at the Spittal of Glenshee was built in 1831 to replace a much earlier chapel. However, when the glen folk decided to rebuild it in a more convenient location, they were to meet some serious objection.

Each day, they would return to discover all the previous day's work had been undone. From the Gaelic, sith, pronounced "shee", Glenshee gives us the Glen of the Fairies. Clearly, the fairies were making it known that there was only one place the kirk should be built. That was in the same place as its predecessor, immediately under the grassy knoll of Dun Sith – the hill of the fairies.

Gairloch, home of the Ghillie Dhu

The Ghillie Dhu

If you go down to the woods tonight you might get a big surprise especially if you meet the Ghillie Dhu.

Clad in green leaves and moss, this little dark-haired lad used to frequent birch woods around Gairloch. He hasn't been seen for a few hundred years since Sir Hector MacKenzie tried to catch him.

Some say the Ghillie Dhu means no harm and has a particular affection for children. Adults who trespass on his territory or damage the woods, however, may find themselves trapped in his arms as he squeezes tighter and tighter, until crushed into compost then recycled to improve the forest. »

The Baobhan-Sith

Only the very brave should wander alone on a moonlit night through the roofless ruins of Slains Castle, just north of Cruden Bay. This is the castle that provided Bram Stoker with inspiration for the creation of his character, Count Dracula.

Dracula, though, is not the only bloodthirsty character you might encounter in this clifftop castle.

Watch out for the Baobhan-sith; the blood-sucking fairies of Slains. These evil fairies tempt the unsuspecting to dance before sinking their razor-sharp fangs into their victims' necks. The only protection against them is to keep something made of iron close to hand – a knife, horseshoe, thimble… they could save your life. Iron, however, may not be quite so effective against Count Dracula!

Beware of the bloodsuckers

Supernatural Scotland

Fairy Hill Of The Caledonians

Walkers tackling Schiehallion in Perthshire, the "Fairy Hill of the Caledonians", should be extremely wary of entering any caves they may encounter – particularly the magical cave, Uamh Tom a' Mhor-fhir, on the hill's western shoulder.

This is a well-known haunt of the fairies and each year welcomes great numbers of them as they come together from all the surrounding glens.

Their great assembly is presided over by the Fairy Queen with her long golden-yellow hair and green silk robes.

If you are tempted to enter the cave, just be warned – inside, there are many gates to pass through and each will mysteriously close and lock behind you!

Stay out of the caves...

Dunvegan, guardian of Am Bratach Sith

> "*The Fairy Flag was a parting gift to a MacLeod chief*"

The Fairy Flag

In Skye's Dunvegan Castle hangs the frail, 1,000-year-old silk banner known as Am Bratach Sith, or the Fairy Flag. It was a parting gift to a MacLeod chief from his fairy wife.

"Unfurl it to the wind whenever crisis hits you. It will save you and yours twice – but woe on you all if you unfurl it the third time."

True enough, it has twice brought resounding victory to the MacLeods – once in 1490 and once in 1588.

In 1588, the MacLeods worshipping in Trumpan Church were unaware of MacDonald boats sailing into Ardmore Bay. They were seeking revenge for a recent massacre on Eigg.

The church door was barred with the MacLeods trapped inside, then the thatch set alight.

When the news was relayed to Dunvegan, the Fairy Flag was unfurled for the second time. Seeing it approach, the MacDonalds fled. However, the tide had turned and their boats were high and dry. The MacDonalds were slaughtered.

Afterwards, their bodies were propped against a dyke which was then tipped over them. This has ever since been known as The Battle Of The Spoiling Of The Dyke.

Fallen Angels

The selkie seal folk can walk on land and look human

SEALS or seal folk, have always played an important role in Scottish mythology, with the sea creatures often being viewed as fallen angels, too good to send to hell.

Originating from the folklore of Orkney and Shetland, a selkie or silkie, is a special species of seal which holds the ability to disguise itself in human form. This magical gift allows a selkie to remove their seal skins and walk among mortal beings, undiscovered.

Unfortunately, like most enchanting gifts, this transformation often comes at a cost – if a human male discovers a female selkie's seal skin, he can capture the creature. Without her seal coat, the selkie female cannot return to the water, so she is forced her to live on land as her abductor's wife.

Over the years, as these stories have been passed down from generation to generation, various versions of the tale have evolved.

In some versions of the legend, if a selkie wife is taken, she may buy back her seal skin and return to the sea to live with her fellow selkies, once she has produced human children for her husband.

In other versions, children which are born by a selkie are not truly human at all, but a mixture of the two beings, with human features and webbed hands and feet for swimming.

Like many mythological creatures, the male version gets off more lightly than the female of the species. While female selkies are often seized and kept against their will, selkie males are said to be flirtatious, often choosing to wed human women, although due to their unreliable personalities, those unions don't tend to last.

Causing a selkie physical harm, is said to have dire consequences. Legend has it that any person who kills a selkie and lets its blood drip into the sea, will trigger a fierce storm which will cause many a watery death.

In the northernmost of the Scottish islands, Orkney and Shetland, common seals are still referred to as selkies.

Main: Seals are still called selkies in Orkney and Shetland

Above: They can disguise themselves in human form

Supernatural Scotland 115

The Hidden World

The Reverend Robert Kirk was the leading authority on fairies – until the day he became trapped in their secret "seelie" land

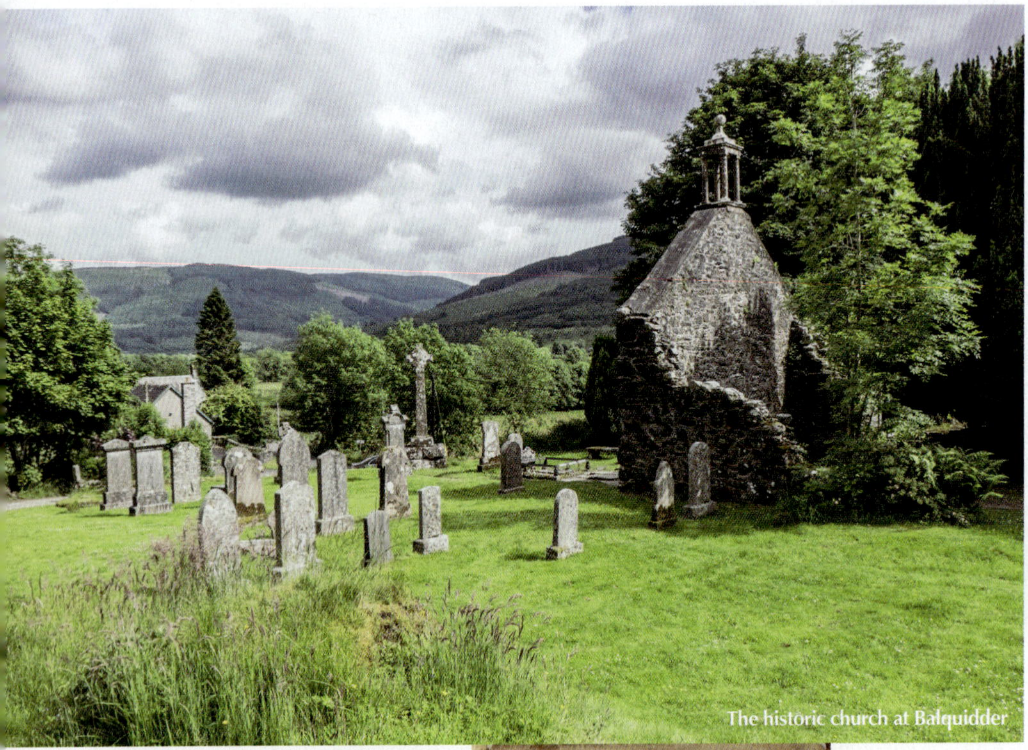

The historic church at Balquidder

IN his narrative poem *The Lady Of The Lake,* Sir Walter Scott described the landscape of the Trossachs, "So wondrous wild the whole might seem, The scenery of a Fairy Dream".

There's perhaps a hint of truth in it, too, with a map of the region revealing place names like Beinn an t-Sidhein, "the hill of the fairies" at Strathyre and, above Loch Katrine, Coire na Urisgean, "corrie of the goblins".

To the Reverend Robert Kirk, minister at Aberfoyle in the late 1600s, there was certainly no doubt in his mind as to the existence of fairies.

He was, after all, to become the world's authority on them. In 1690 he even wrote a book entitled *The Secret Commonwealth Of Elves, Fauns And Fairies.*

Robert, the seventh son of the Reverend James Kirk, was an extremely clever man having graduated as a Doctor of Divinity at just 20 years of age.

You'll find his grave beside the roofless ruins of Aberfoyle's Kirkton Church. He was well respected by his fellow clergy and by his parishioners at Aberfoyle, and his earlier church in Balquhidder.

At Aberfoyle, however, he changed and suddenly began behaving oddly. It wouldn't be the first time he was spotted in the middle of the night climbing the steep slopes of nearby Doon Hill – in his pyjamas! Observers might see him lying with his ear to the ground, listening… to the fairies, of course. As he revealed, they live in cavities just beneath the surface of the ground.

According to Robert, "Brownies" who have short stature, wrinkled faces and curly brown hair with a brown mantle or hood, will do anything to help folk. Friendly fairies are said to belong to the

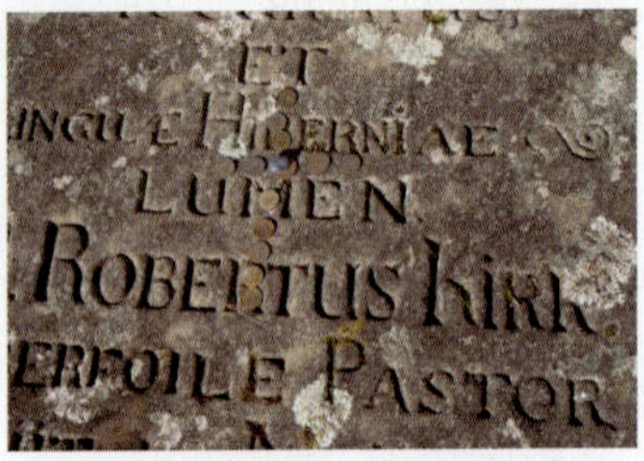

ET
LUMEN
ROBERTUS KIRK
PASTOR

Above: Does his gravestone truly mark Reverend Kirk's final resting place?

Right: Kirk's book of fairies

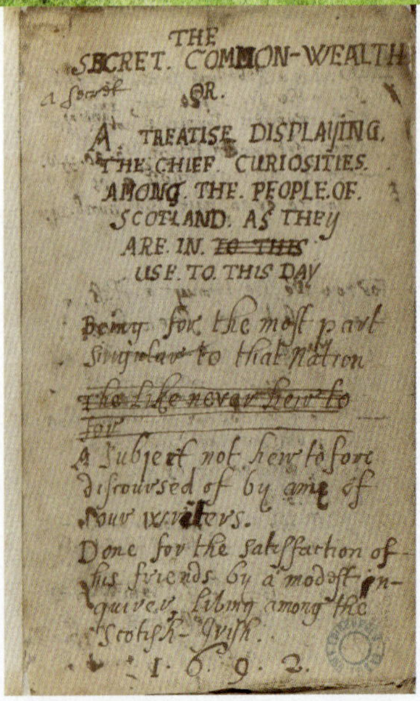

THE SECRET COMMON-WEALTH OR

A TREATISE DISPLAYING THE CHIEF CURIOSITIES AMONG THE PEOPLE OF SCOTLAND AS THEY ARE IN USE TO THIS DAY

A Subject not heretofore discoursed of by any of our writers.

Done for the satisfaction of his friends by a modest inquirer, living among the Scotish-Irish.

1692.

The magical Trossachs

The reverend's grave in Aberfoyle's Kirkton Church

"Seelie Court". There are, though, the less friendly sort, of the "Unseelie Court", that it's best not to cross paths with – the ones that steal babies leaving substitute changelings.

All the in-depth knowledge Robert gained of their secret world gave him plenty of material for his book.

Friendly or not, the elusive wee creatures were maybe less than happy at his exposing all their secrets, and it wasn't long after publishing his book that on one of his night visits to the hill he collapsed and died.

Robert Kirk's grave may well be at Kirkton Church but, as the legend goes, that's not where he rests. And we know this on the authority of the minister himself.

Just after his funeral, his ghost is said to have appeared before one of his relatives, when Robert tried to explain to him that he wasn't really dead but just trapped in the fairy world. To allow him to return to life, all his relative had to do was, at the baptism of the man's child, to throw a knife over his head.

Who knows, it may have worked but when the ghost of Robert reappeared at the child's baptism, the father was so shocked at the sight that he completely forgot to throw the knife.

As a result, to this day, Robert Kirk remains in fairyland, his spirit believed to be trapped within the large Scots pine – "The Minister's Pine" – that crowns the summit of Doon Hill.

Climb the hill to visit him if you dare, but be careful; like Robert, you too could end up away with the fairies…

Supernatural Scotland 117

The Queen Of Winter

The Cailleach bathes in a whirlpool and dictates the season

THE elemental power of Scotland's old Celtic gods is embodied by the Cailleach – pronounced kah-lee-ack.

She has many names – the Veiled One and Beira, the Queen of Winter among them – and according to Gaelic lore it was she who raised the mountains of the Highlands, guards the creatures of the glens, and heralds the coming of the deathly frosts of winter.

Known in legends and folktales across Scotland, Ireland and the Isle of Man, the Cailleach is at once mother, guardian, tyrant, and creator, whose whims are as unpredictable as the land itself.

She is a goddess, yet unlike monotheistic gods who inhabit a distinct plane from mortals, she is as much a part of our world as the winds and waters that define life in Scotland. She carries a hammer for shaping the hills and valleys, and is said to be the mother of all the goddesses and gods in Celtic mythology.

Worshipped and feared wherever the Gaels made their homes, she lives in the high places among stone and sky.

At Samhain, October 31, she descends to the Corryvreckan whirlpool off the Isle of Jura to wash her great plaid in the maelstrom.

The Corryvreckan is the third largest whirlpool in the world. Flood tides and inflow from the Firth of Lorne to the west can drive the waters of Corryvreckan to waves of more than 9.1m (30ft), and the roar

The Corryvreckan

"At Beltane the Gaels must rebel against her icy rule"

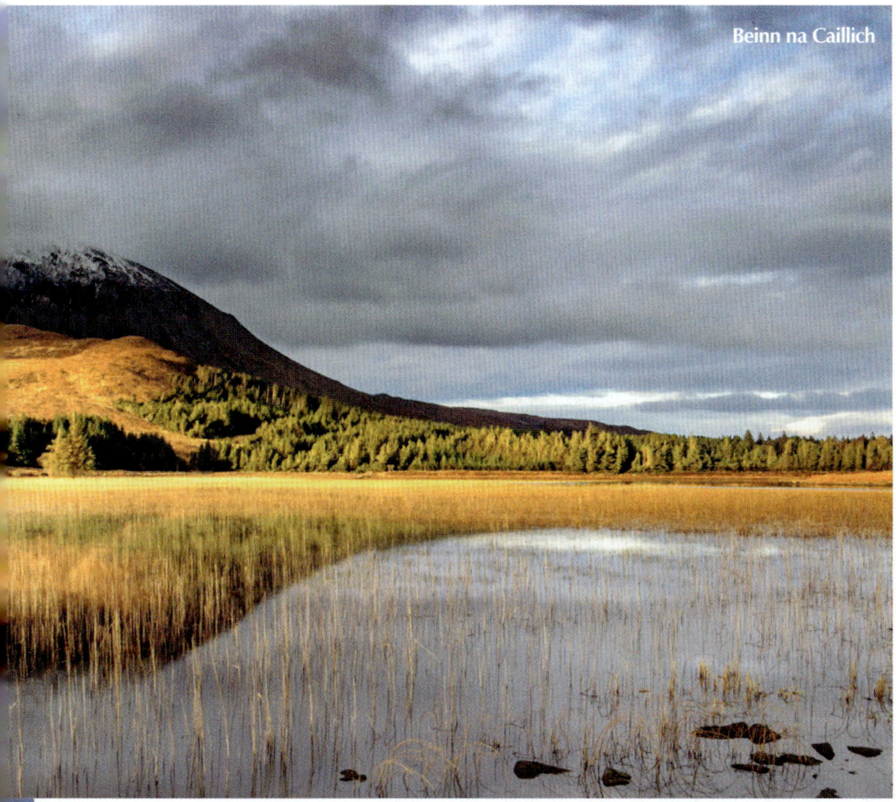
Beinn na Caillich

of the resulting maelstrom can be heard 16km (10 miles) away – it is said that this maelstrom is at its worst when the Cailleach washes her plaid.

Once she is finished the laundry, she hangs her great plaid up to dry. Ice crystals drift from it to cover the land in cold, bringing on the winter season.

Là Fhèill Brìghde, or Bride's Day is the first day of spring in the Gaelic calendar on February 1. This is the day that the Cailleach gathers her firewood for the rest of the winter. Legend has it that if she intends to make the winter last much longer, she will make the weather bright and sunny on February 1, so she can gather plenty of firewood to keep herself warm during the coming months. As a result, if Là Fhèill Brìghde is a day of foul weather it means the Cailleach is asleep, and will soon run out of firewood, meaning winter is almost over.

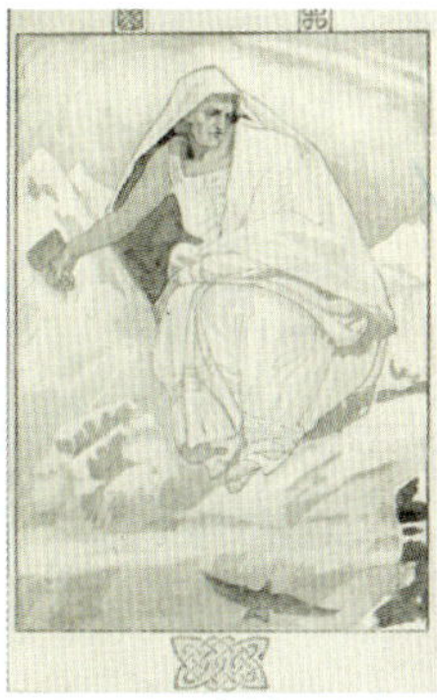

At Beltane on May 1, the Gaels must rebel against her icy rule with bonfires to make way for Angus and Bride, the King and Queen of Summer.

Forced to retreat she awaits the inevitable return of Samhain from her stronghold, the location of which varies depending on who you're speaking to. Popular locations include Ben Cruachan, Glen Nevis, and Beinn na Caillich on Skye.

Cailleach's Shelter

In Gleann Cailliche at Glen Lyon in Perthshire there is a stream named Allt Cailliche which runs into Loch Lyon. It is home to the oldest continuous Celtic ritual in the UK. In the glen there's a tiny shieling, known as known as Tigh nan Cailleach – Scottish Gaelic for "house of the old women".

The shieling shelters a group of small tapered stones representing the Cailleach, her husband the Bodach, and her family. Local legend claims that the Cailleach and the Bodach were once given shelter by locals, and while they stayed there raising their children the glen was prosperous.

When they left, they gave the locals the stones, with the promise that as long as the stones were taken outside to keep watch over the glen during the summer, and kept safe indoors over winter, the glen would continue to be fertile.

For thousands of years they have been brought in and out from their holdfast at Samhain and Beltane respectively. The last named custodian of the Cailleach was shepherd Bob Bissett as recorded in the 1970s, and though he has since passed away the ceremony is upheld by hands unknown to this very day.

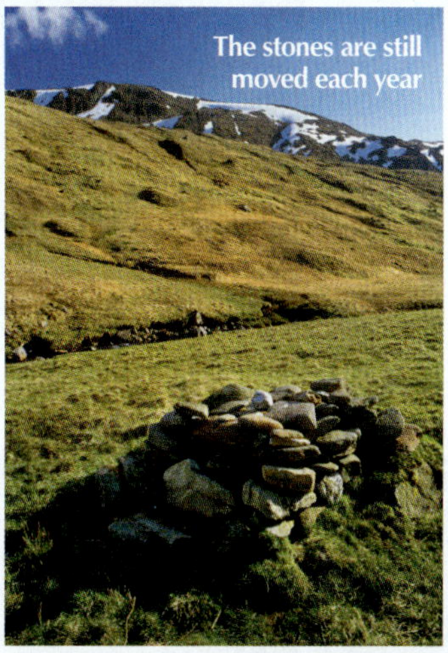
The stones are still moved each year

Compelling **NEW STORIES** from your favourite writers

£8.99 +P&P

The People's Friend

Feel-good Fiction

44 WONDERFUL STORIES

ROMANCE | COSY CRIME | NOSTALGIA | SUMMER ADVENTURES

SCAN HERE

ON SALE NOW!

ORDER ONLINE: www.dcthomsonshop.co.uk/44stories

OR CALL: **0800 318 846** quoting **PFFIC**

Lines open 8am - 6pm Mon-Fri
Postage Charge: £2.99
Also available in WHSmith stores and on Amazon

Horrible Hallowe'en

Light up the pumpkins, place the dooking apples in the bucket and ready yourself for guisers as October 31 is a time of tradition, fun – and frights!

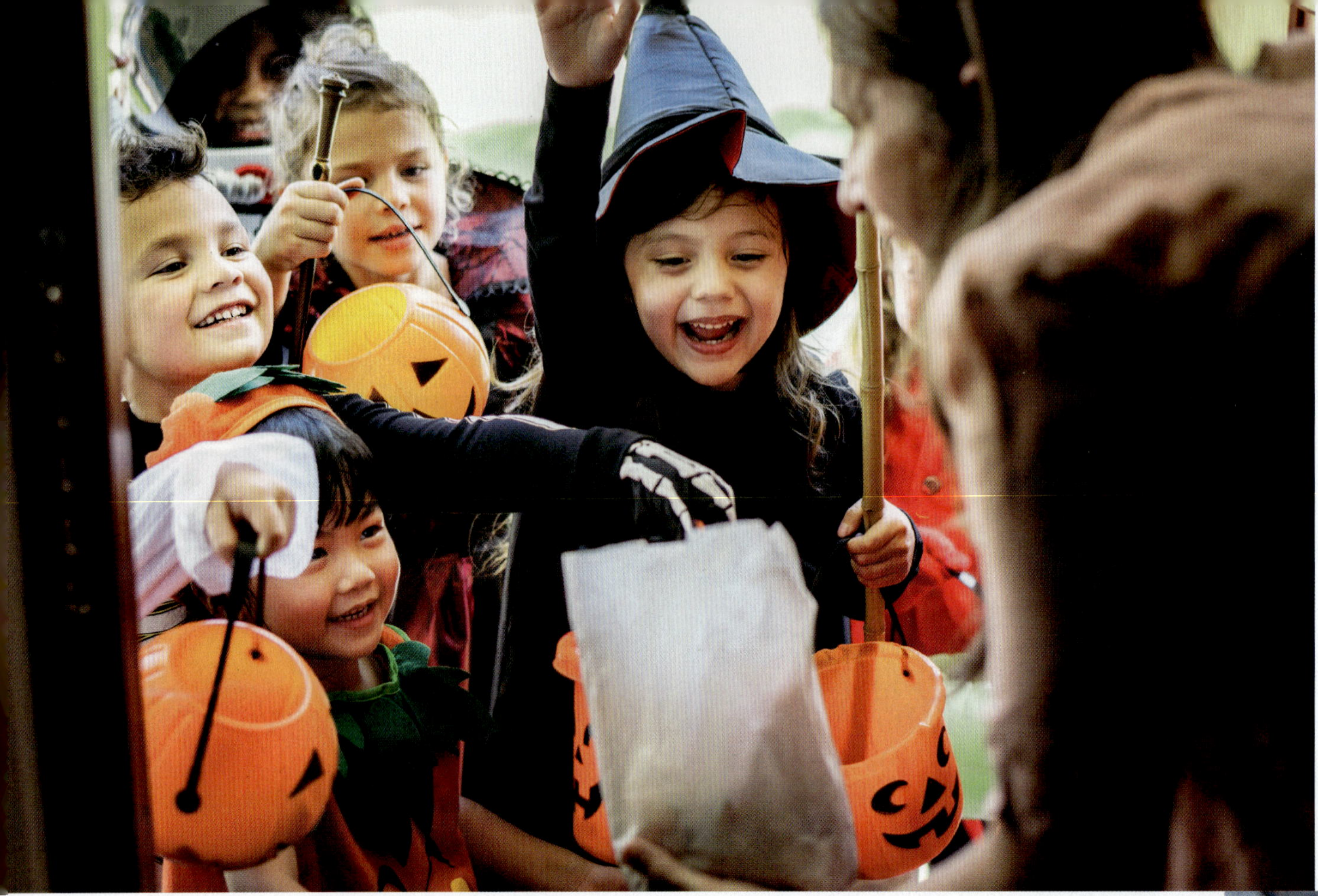

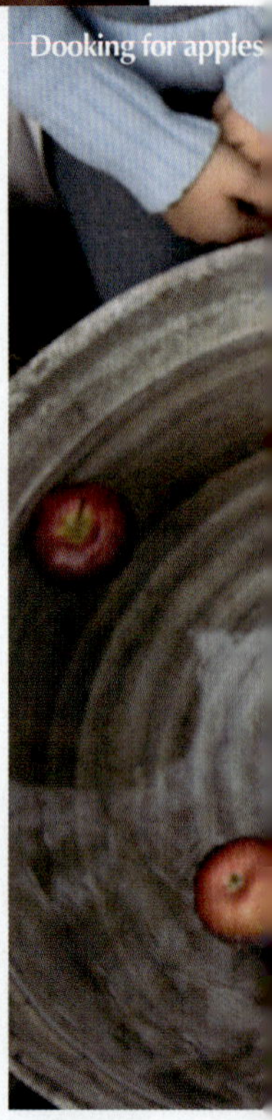
Dooking for apples

Bewitching Tales

How Scots Hallowe'en festivities were confused with something darker

Words: DAWN GEDDES Images: ALAMY, REX/SHUTTERSTOCK

THE way that we celebrate Hallowe'en has changed dramatically – many of us embrace Americanised customs like carving pumpkins and trick or treating, but some traditions originate much closer to home.

Hallowe'en, or All Hallows' Eve, is observed on October 31 – the day before the Christian celebration of All Saints' Day. The holiday originates from the Celtic festival of Samhain, which marks the end of summer.

It was believed that during this time of year the veil between the living and dead was at its thinnest. To ensure that no evil spirits came through, a series of rituals were performed – including setting bonfires alight on hilltops and donning masks to disguise yourself from any lurking ghosts. This is where the Scots tradition of "guising" or "disguising" comes from.

Over time, these traditions grew in popularity and, by the 16th century, us Scots were quite enchanted by the romance of this ghostly event.

This can be seen in the Scottish ballad Tam Lin, which describes rescuing someone from fairies on Hallowe'en night. It is the earliest poem to feature Hallowe'en. Robert Burns also documents the event in his 1785 poem *Hallowe'en*, describing how "merry, friendly, country-folks" in Scotland got together to "haud their Hallowe'en", marking the occasion by eating "butter'd so'ns" and telling people's fortunes.

Lisa Morton, author of *Trick Or Treat: A History Of Hallowe'en*, says that Scots added their own slant to the festival.

"While the Irish added traditions such as prank-playing, Scotland added more to the holiday's macabre side by playing spooky fortune-telling games and telling creepy stories at gatherings."

Lisa says our tradition of dooking for apples is inspired by the time of the year that Hallowe'en falls in.

"Apples are seasonal and tie into the harvest aspect of Hallowe'en. Bobbing for apples or 'dooking' is a game we know has been played during autumn for centuries – there's a drawing of it in the medieval Luttrell Psalter manuscript, which dates back to the 14th century."

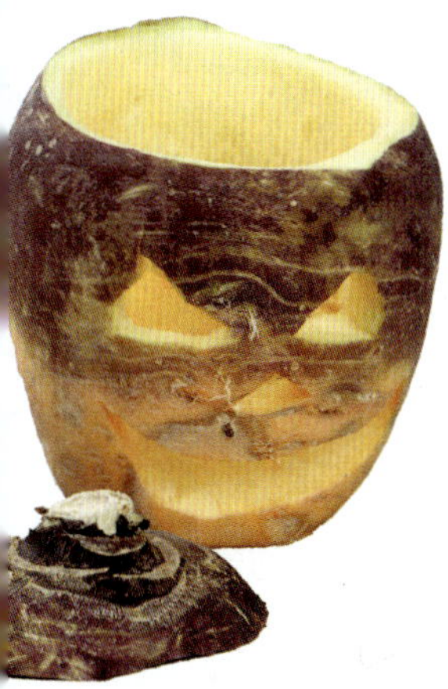

Hallowe'en expert Lisa says the meaning behind the holiday eventually became confused with something darker.

"British surveyor Charles Vallancey published the third book in his six-volume work *Collectanea De Rebus Hibernicis* in 1786. Vallancey had been sent over to survey Ireland in the late 1700s and became obsessed with Celtic history. He collected hundreds of thousands of words of his studies into numerous books.

"There was just one problem – Vallancey chose to simply disregard facts in favour of his elaborate theories. He decided, for example, that Samhain – the Celtic celebration which translates to 'summer's end' – was the name of a lord of death worshipped by the Celts.

"It didn't matter that Vallancey's work was dismissed by every other historian – his books made their way into libraries all over the world and started the notion that Hallowe'en is based on the worship of a lord of death."

Above: A turnip lantern

Right: *Godey's Lady's Book*

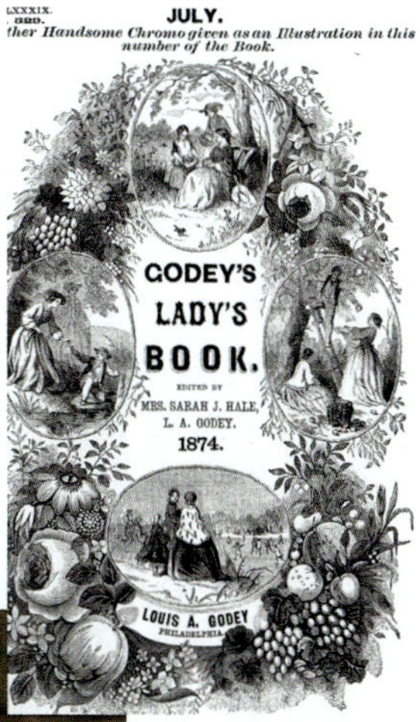
JULY.
GODEY'S
LADY'S
BOOK.
EDITED BY
MRS. SARAH J. HALE,
L. A. GODEY.
1874.
LOUIS A. GODEY
PHILADELPHIA

These darker connotations can be seen in the tradition of creating jack o' lanterns. The folklore legend of Jack, a blacksmith who outsmarts the devil, dates back to the end of the 19th century and was widespread across Europe and the US.

The story usually concludes with Jack forced to walk the earth for eternity, his path lit by an ember in a carved-out turnip.

In Scotland and Ireland, people began making their own turnip lanterns to ward off Jack's spirit.

When our Hallowe'en traditions caught on in the US, they opted for pumpkins instead. Carving faces into pumpkins wasn't new to Americans – it had been popular in the US for decades.

What was it about these Celtic traditions that caught the imagination of Americans?

Lisa says, "It started in the mid-19th century, and in a way people might not expect – magazines. Printing technologies made magazines very popular in the 1800s, especially among America's middle class.

"Magazines like *Godey's Lady's Book* put out stories about this quaint Irish celebration – American housewives loved these tales and started recreating Hallowe'en.

"As to its enduring popularity, it addresses some of our deepest fears as the days become shorter and nights longer. It encourages us to playfully explore our fears – something that's appealing on a profound level."

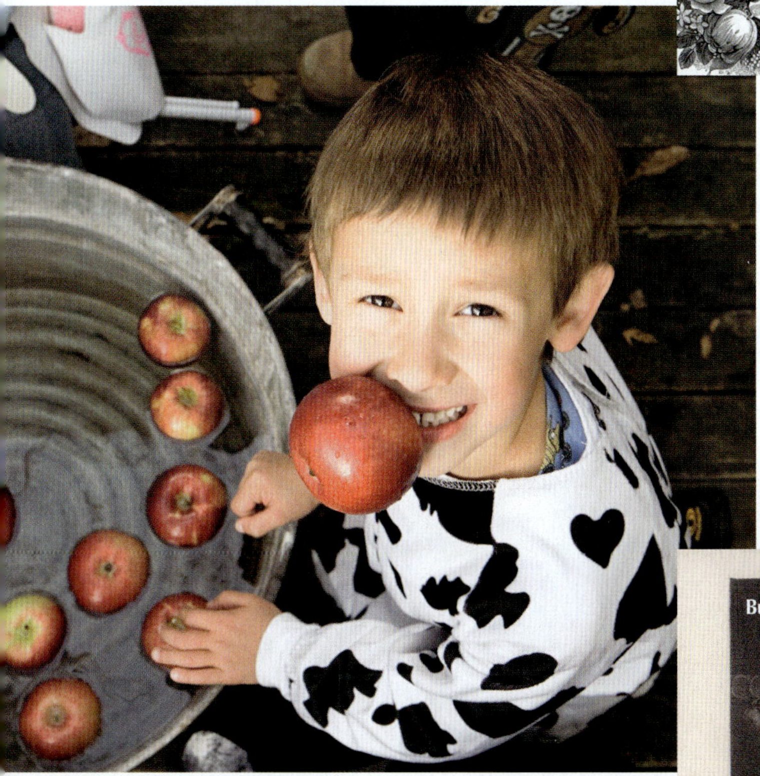

"To ensure no evil spirits came through, a series of rituals were performed"

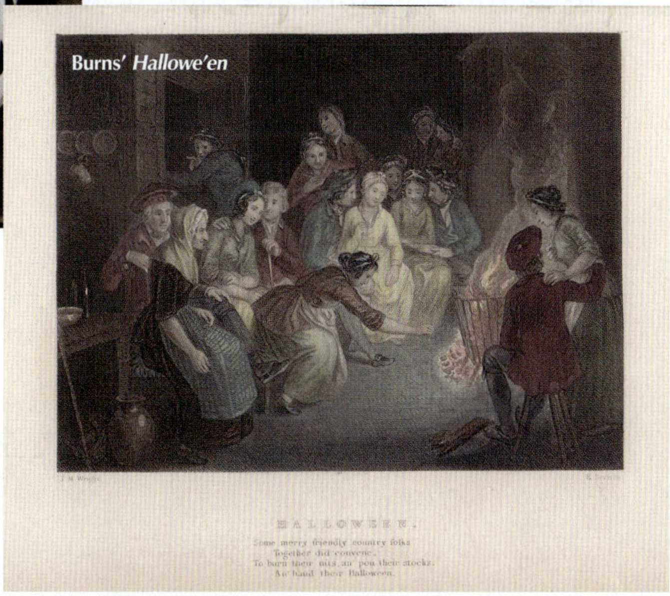

Burns' *Hallowe'en*

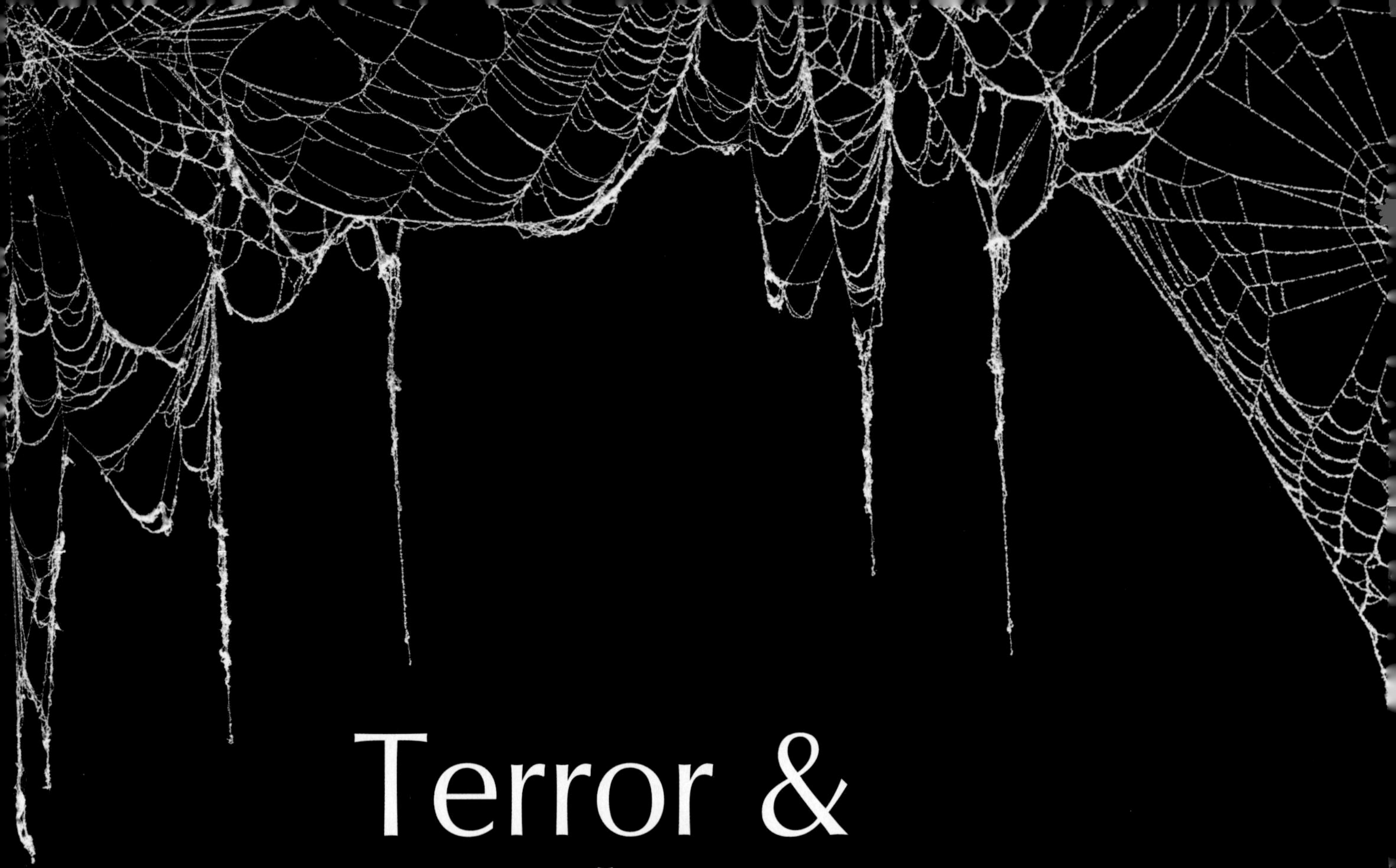

Terror & Tradition

A look at our finest Scottish Hallowe'en traditions featuring ghouls, guisers – and some sticky situations

Words: CHAE STRATHIE Images: SHUTTERSTOCK, ALAMY, EMILY FRAME ON COOKPAD

DESPITE what Americans might think, Hallowe'en is as Scottish as haggis, Irn Bru and grumbling about midges. It has its roots in the Celtic festival of Samhain and the name itself is a Scottish shortening of All Hallows' Eve, so if you're looking to throw a Hallowe'en hoolie, these Scots traditions are a must.

Neep Lanterns

Sledgehammer? Check. Industrial blowtorch? Check. Pneumatic drill? Check. OK – you're ready to create a neep lantern. This tradition was a rite of passage for Scottish children in the days before the Great Pumpkin Invasion and the cause of deep trauma for parents. The idea was that scary faces carved into neeps, along with the light from the candle within, would scare off ghouls. However, the most terrifying thing about it was the discovery that turnips appear to be made from solid concrete. Want a neep lantern? Best start drilling sometime around the end of April.

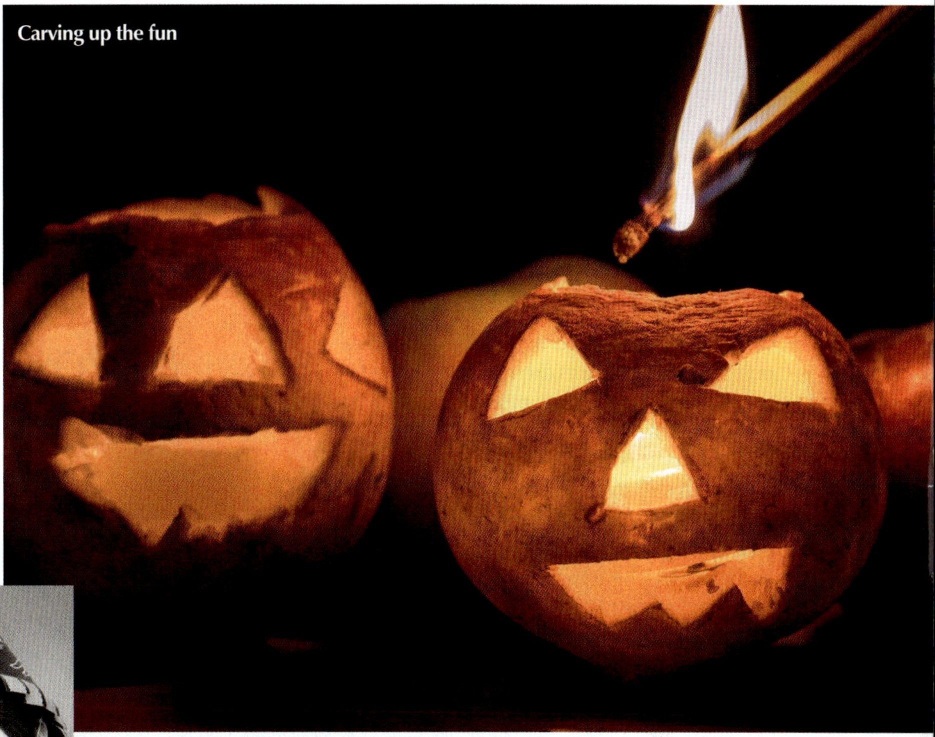

Carving up the fun

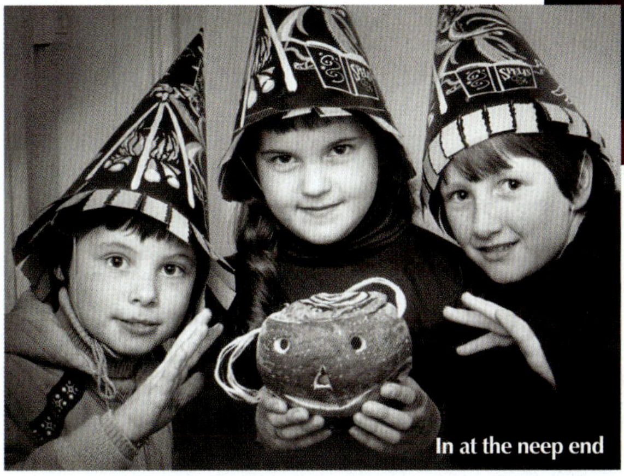

In at the neep end

"Want a neep lantern? Best start drilling around the end of April"

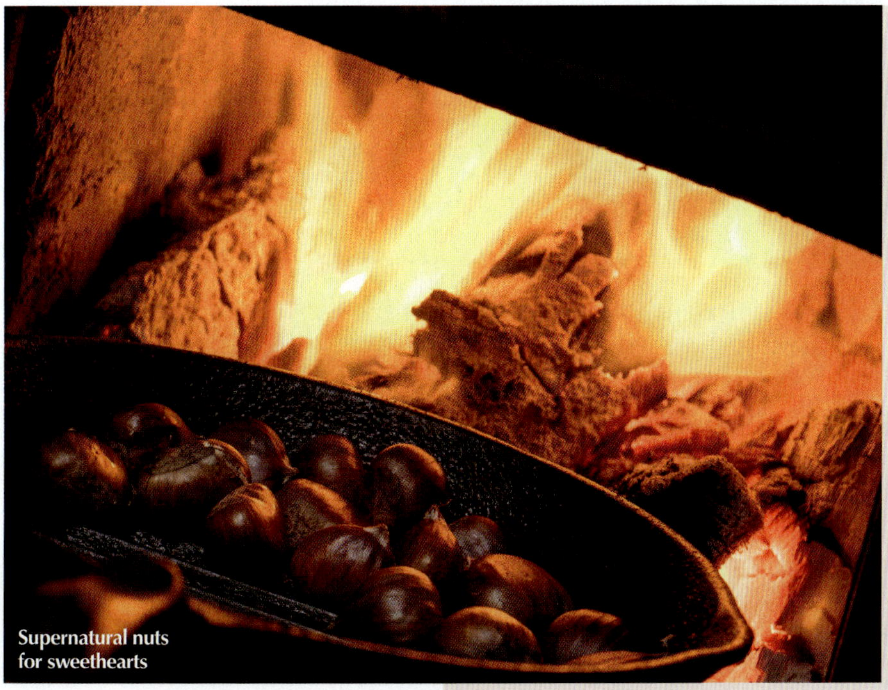

Supernatural nuts for sweethearts

Nut Burning

This is one of the less-popular Hallowe'en traditions these days, mainly due to the inclusion of a blazing fire and extremely hot nuts (Right! Who tittered at the back?). This once-common pastime was a way to find out if you and your other half would live happily ever after. A nut – often a hazelnut – was put in a fire and if it burned quietly and turned to ash all would be tickety-boo for the sweethearts going forward. But if the nut hissed and crackled? Well, let's just say a golden wedding anniversary gift would be a waste of money. »

Guising

Hallowe'en wouldn't be Hallowe'en without legions of costumed Scottish children traipsing round the doors self-consciously performing giggle-filled songs or upsetting the occupants with jokes of questionable appropriateness. The aim, obviously, is to be bestowed with piles of sweets or cash in return for going away as quickly as possible. Monkey nuts are not acceptable, and any form of fruit is a potentially arrestable offence. In the distant past, food was collected for the Samhain feast, known as the "Feast of the Dead", which is a slightly less common theme at kids' parties these days, it must be said. It was believed that by disguising themselves as ghosts, monsters and witches, children would blend in with spirits and remain safe. Spiderman, the Gruffalo and random celebs are the order of the day now.

> "The aim is to be bestowed with piles of sweets or cash"

The "guise" have it!

126 Supernatural Scotland

Dookin' with dignity

Apple Dookin'

When it comes to Hallowe'en, apples are the dook daddy. It's nothing new – it's an ancient Celtic tradition from a time when apples were deemed sacred – and involves players grabbing apples from a basin of water using only their teeth. The possibility of drowning adds a certain edge to the fun. A variation on the theme involves attempting to spear a floating apple with a fork dropped from between the teeth. But whatever method you choose to capture your prey, remember: dookin' is for life, not just for Hallowe'en. »

Treacle Scones

This one is based on the ancient Scottish tradition of making children look like idiots as revenge for all the pain, hassle and cost of being a parent. And it's guaranteed to work. The premise is simple: cover scones in thick, gooey, black treacle, suspend from strings and laugh as your sprogs attempt to take bites without using their hands. If they don't come out of it looking like they're halfway through the process of being tarred and feathered, you've failed. Tasty yet character-building. Modern doughnut-based versions are not nearly as funny.

Trick or treacle?

" *Based on the ancient Scottish tradition of making children look like idiots as revenge for all the pain, hassle and cost of being a parent* **"**

Supernatural Scotland **127**

Cabbages and pumpkins – the perfect pairing!

Cabbage Stalks

In this jolly whizz, cabbage stalks were cut, hollowed out and turned into a sort of pipe. Then boys and young men would pack the pipes with kindling and go door-to-door blowing smoke into homes to purify them. For several reasons, this is unlikely to make an unexpected comeback to become the Number One Hallowe'en party game any time soon. Blowing smoke through people's letterboxes is likely to get you arrested, while giving kids pipes tends to be frowned upon these days. It's health and safety gone mad!

> "For several reasons, this is unlikely to make an unexpected comeback"

Kale Pulling

Another tradition that has all but died out and, just like nut burning, kale pulling combines terrifying spirits and ghouls with romance. Surely an admin error back in the day. As referenced in a Rabbie Burns's poem called *Hallowe'en*, after dark people would close their eyes and pull stalks of kale from the ground. The amount of soil attached to the roots showed how wealthy your future lover would be, while the length and shape of the stalk was said to represent their height and figure. Just to be clear, if your true love is the same size and shape as a bit of kale, you might want to rethink your romantic standards.

"Combines terrifying spirits with romance"

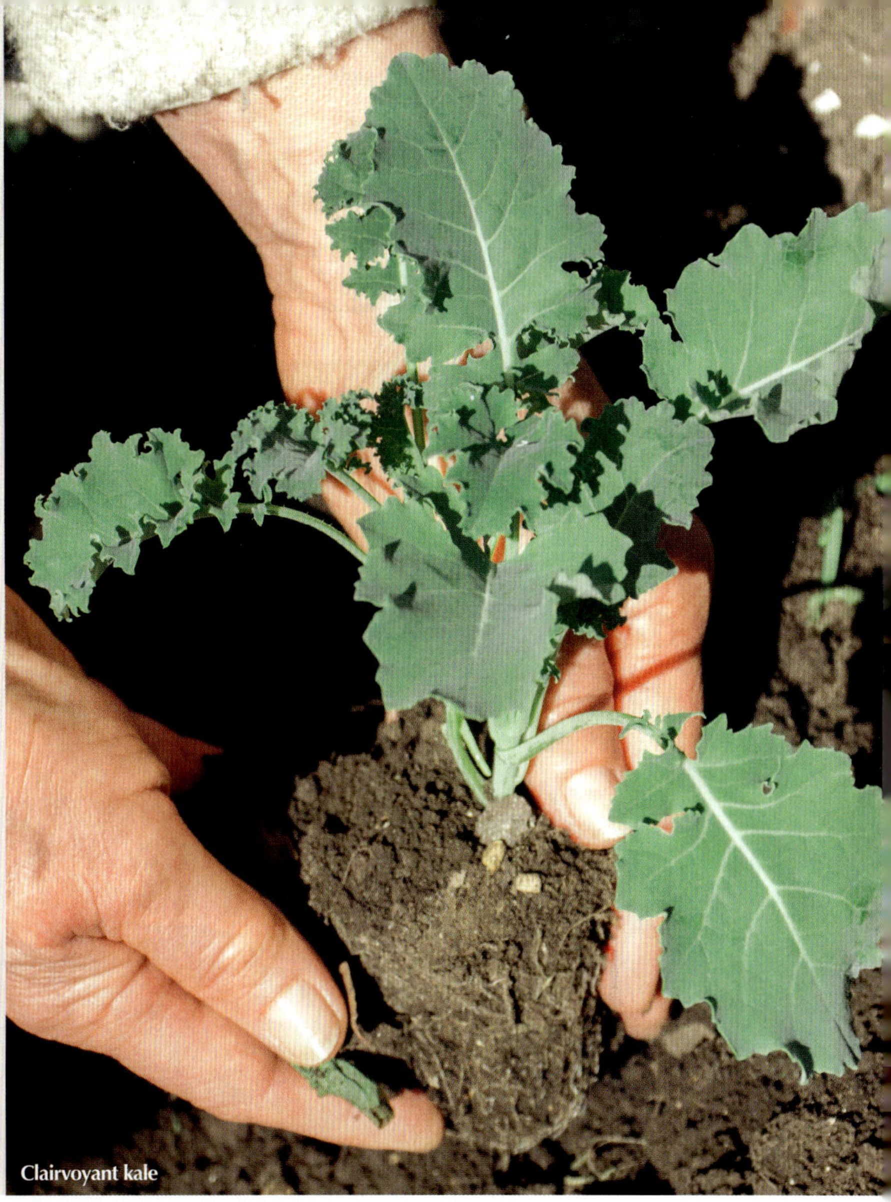

Clairvoyant kale

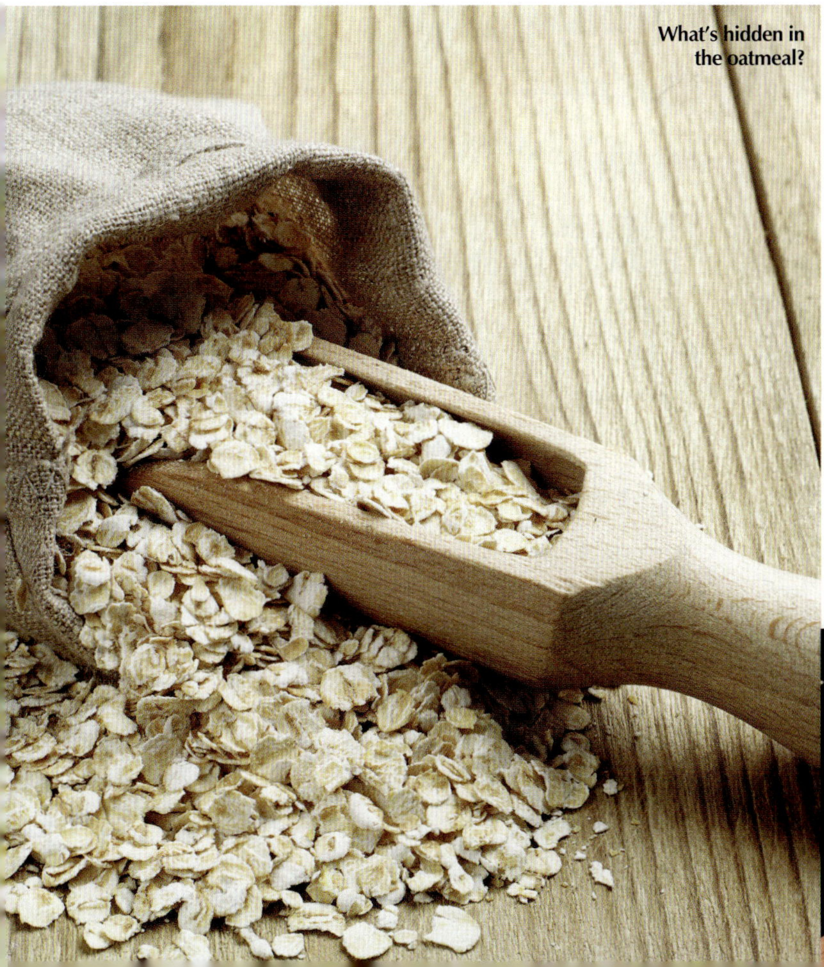

What's hidden in the oatmeal?

Fuarag

If messy games like treacle scone biting and apple dookin' are your bag, why not give fuarag a try? No, it's not a Gaelic swear word, it's a Hallowe'en tradition from the Western Isles that involves certain objects being hidden in a bowl of raw oatmeal, cream and sugar with blindfolded party guests scooping up spoonfuls to eat. The items you discover determine what fortune has in store. Find a ring? You're next to marry. A coin means great wealth beckons, while a button or thimble suggests life as a singleton lies ahead. Accidentally biting into any of these means that a visit to the dentist to replace a broken crown is in your future.

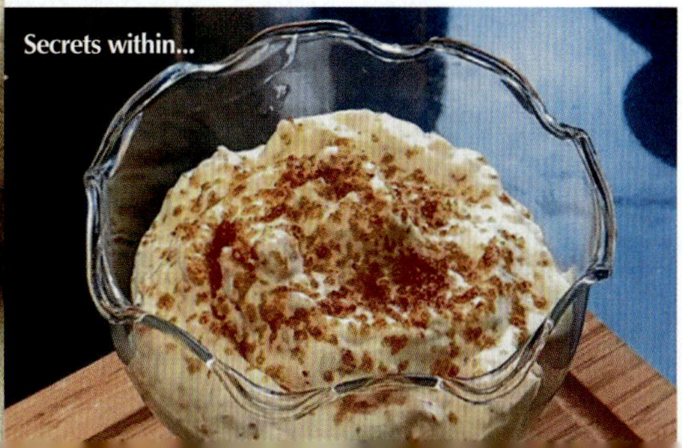

Secrets within...

SCOTLAND'S STORIES, PEOPLE AND PLACES

ARE YOU PASSIONATE ABOUT THE SCOTTISH LANDSCAPE, HISTORY, FOLKLORE, AND THE OUTDOORS?

The Scots Magazine offers an expert month-by-month update on Scotland including the latest events, cultural news, must-read features, breathtaking photography and 'The Big Interview', recently featuring celebrities such as 'Outlander' stars Graham McTavish and Sam Heughan!

Subscribe to The Scots Magazine today to enjoy entertaining and informative features exploring Scotland's people, places, and culture.

WHY SUBSCRIBE…

- Over 130 pages of entertaining and informative features
- Culture, history and travel articles from around the country
- Save on the shop price
- Delivery direct to your door

SAVE 33% when you subscribe by Direct Debit

OVERSEAS PRICES AVAILABLE

Only £10 for the first three issues*

Online: dcthomsonshop.co.uk/trails

Freephone: 0800 318 846 (UK)

Lines open Monday – Friday, 9am – 5pm.

The Scots Magazine is a monthly title publishing 12 issues per year. Prices shown are correct at time of going to print. Offers subject to change. *Saving of 33% based on the newsstand price of £4.99 per issue. Direct Debit offer for new customers only. £10 for the first three issues, then £13 every three issues thereafter. UK delivery only.

SCAN ME